AFRICAN LITERATURE TODAY

11 Myth & History

A review
Edited by ELDRED DUROSIMI JONES

HEINEMANN
LONDON · IBADAN · NAIROBI

AFRICANA PUBLISHING COMPANY
NEW YORK

Heinemann Educational Books
22 Bedford Square, London WC1B 3HH
PMB 5205 Ibadan PO Box 45314 Nairobi
PO Box 3966 Lusaka
EDINBURGH MELBOURNE AUCKLAND TORONTO
HONG KONG KUALA LUMPUR SINGAPORE NEW DELHI
JOHANNESBURG KINGSTON TRINIDAD

820. 996 JON

© Heinemann Educational Books 1980
First published 1980

Published in the United States of America 1980
by Africana Publishing Company
a Division of Holmes & Meier Publishers Inc
101 Fifth Avenue
New York NY 10003
Library of Congress Card No 72–75254
ISBN 0–8419–0577–0 (cased)
ISBN 0–8419–0652–1 (paper)

BRITISH LIBRARY CATALOGUING IN PUBLICATION DATA

African literature today.
    No. 11: Myth and history
    1. African literature (English) – History
    and criticism
    2. African literature (French) – History
    and criticism
    I. Jones, Eldred Durosimi
    820′.9′96   PR9340

ISBN 0–435–91651–3
ISBN 0–435–91652–1 Pbk

Set in 10 pt VIP Melior
Set, printed and bound in Great Britain by
Fakenham Press Limited, Fakenham, Norfolk

AFRICAN LITERATURE TODAY
Edited by Eldred Durosimi Jones

In the same series

Contents

Editorial

The contemporary writer in Africa is primarily concerned with the African present; but in getting to grips with it, he — like every other social being around him — is heavily dependent on his past. Chinua Achebe felt the need first to clear the ground with his historical novel *Things Fall Apart* before embarking on his examination of the near-contemporary scene in *No Longer at Ease*. His *Arrow of God*, another historical work, next preceded his examination of the post-independence scene in *A Man of the People*. This is consistent with his persistent counsel that we must find out when the rain first began to beat us.

The truth of the past (when we can discover or reconstruct it) is history, while the penumbra cast by an extraordinary event or personality — after it has been blurred by fallible memory, modified by corporate convenience, and heightened by imagination and poetry — constitutes the weighty metaphor that is myth. The process by which history becomes myth is continuous, subtle, almost intangible, though a skilled or otherwise influential treatment may make a distinguishable contribution to the growing myth, or give it new life or application.

Any event is thus capable of generating its own myth, though only those accounts or beliefs deriving from specially dramatic or momentous events are likely to be abiding. There are therefore hierarchies of myth, every group or subgroup of the larger society developing its own mythology. Soyinka's lorry-drivers and their touts in *The Road*, taking their cue from real life, created (quite apart from the more hallowed myth of Ogun) their own mythology of their departed predecessors now enlarged in stature by their translation through death on the road:

> Where is Zorro-who never returned from the North without a basket of guinea-fowl eggs? Where is Akanni the Lizard? I have never seen any other tout who could stand on the lorry's roof and play the samba at sixty miles an hour. Where is Sigidi Ope? Where is Sapele Joe who took on six policemen at the crossing and knocked them all into the river?

Have you known any other driver take an oil-tanker non-stop from Port Harcourt to Kaduna since Muftau died? Where is Sergeant Burma who treated his tanker like a child's toy?

Talk of this kind is the raw material of myth.

Momentous events and characters breed almost instant myths; the Nigerian Civil War, its passions barely cooling, is already breeding its own mythology of heroes and villains who in the centuries to come may become elevated (or demoted) into archetypes of good or evil and acquire a rhythmical coexistence with the seasons. Both in its ephemeral and in its abiding forms, myth has a potential social influence; the more recent the myth, the greater its potential for tendentiousness. The writer and his reader are in greatest danger when the source of the myth – the historical event – is closest to them in time or in personal involvement, a closeness which can reduce them to the level of prosecutor or defendant in an action; but as partisan accounts or narrow interpretations blur, special pleading fades into myth.

Mythology can be mediatory, even therapeutic, by enabling man to suffer the intolerable, gaze on the terrible, and sing of the ineffable; his great achievements as well as his remarkable disasters – sometimes self-inflicted, sometimes the will of 'fate' – pass into the poetry of myth, and become a compatible element of his ordinary existence. Thus Sopona (the killer smallpox) is deified and the self-destroyed Alafin of Oyo becomes the god Sango. In our own times, faced with the gap between his alienated state and the spiritual home from which he had wandered, Christopher Okigbo invoked from the collective memory 'Mother Idoto', a water goddess he had long forgotten or had ignored as an influence in his personal life:

> Before you, mother Idoto,
>   naked I stand,
> before your watery presence,
>   a prodigal,
>
> leaning on an oilbean;
> lost in your legend ...
>
> Under your power wait I on barefoot,
> Watchman for the watchword at
>   HEAVENSGATE;
>
> out of the depths my cry
> give ear and hearken.

To what extent was this just a poetic utterance; a literary expression of a spiritual yearning; a mere metaphor? To what extent was Mother Idoto real to Okigbo? What is real? Whatever the personal answers that Okigbo might have given to these questions, Mother Idoto has the reality of a myth which mediates intellectually between man and the imponderables that he confronts. Mother Idoto came to the rescue of a lost soul in the twentieth century when all else seemed ineffectual, and to that extent was real, real to Okigbo and real to his readers. This would be true even if Okigbo never at any time stood physically naked at the shrine of Mother Idoto.

African writers no less than the ancient Europeans are both users (beneficiaries) and creators of myth, and at least one of them, Christopher Okigbo, seems destined himself to become an abiding myth figure. The intensity of his poetic imagination, the passion of his practice, the almost knight-errant idealism which compelled his enlistment in the Biafran Army, together with the manner of his death – without a known grave – have all the ingredients out of which an abiding myth figure is born. Perhaps Ali Mazrui's (for him) therapeutic sublimation of his grief at the death of Christopher Okigbo in a fictional inquiry into the dead poet's act of self-sacrifice (*The Trial of Christopher Okigbo*), in the legendary setting of 'After-Africa', may be the start of the myth of the god Chris.

The Next Three Numbers

Number 12 will concentrate on new writers or writers whose works have not received sufficient critical notice.

Number 13 will focus once again on the novel. Articles are invited which will show trends and developments in technique, preoccupation, attitudes etc., of African novelists in general or of particular writers. Regional developments particularly in new or less frequently treated areas will be especially welcome. The deadline for the submission of actual articles will be December 1980.

Number 14 will be *Africans and Non-Africans Looking at Africa.* The deadline for the submission of articles will be September 1981.

Proposals for articles should be sent with a brief summary to the Editor, Professor Eldred Durosimi Jones
Principal's Office
Fourah Bay College
University of Sierra Leone
P.O. Box 87
Freetown
Sierra Leone
All articles should be well typed preferably on A4 paper and double-spaced. References to books should include the author or editor, place, publisher, date and the relevant pages. It is regretted that unsolicited manuscripts cannot be returned unless the authors provide return postage.

Rethinking Myth

Isidore Okpewho

No other concept in the entire field of the humanities has attracted as much debate as 'myth'. However, it may be well to note for a start that whatever definition has been advanced to date is only a variation of the classic delimitation which Jacob Grimm gave, in his *Deutsche Mythologie* (1835), to the genre of the oral narrative:

> The fairy tale [*marchen*] is with good reason distinguished from the legend, though by turns they play into one another. Looser, less fettered than legend, the fairy tale lacks that local habitation, which hampers legend, but makes it more home-like. The fairy tale flies, the legend walks, knocks at your door; the one can draw freely out of the fullness of poetry, the other has almost the authority of history. As the fairy tale stands related to legend, so does legend to history, and (we may add) so does history to real life. In real existence all the outlines are sharp, clear and certain, which on history's canvas are gradually shaded off and toned down. The ancient mythus, however, combines to some extent the qualities of fairy tale and legend; untrammelled in its flight, it can yet settle down in a local home.[1]

A discussion of the numerous theories which have succeeded the above statement would constitute a full-length dissertation, so we shall simply narrow them down to the two basic strands or approaches. The first approach may be considered formalistic in the broadest sense of the term. In this category belong all those scholars who conceive of the oral narrative in terms of units of ideas which the artist has derived from various traditional sources – traceable or otherwise – and grouped together into a convenient pattern of narration or performance. The most representative thinkers in this category are (a) the *diffusionists*, foremost of whom are the Finnish scholar Antti Aarne and the American Stitt Thompson, who, by compiling an index of 'types' of tales and the 'motifs' which they employ, have hoped to trace the worldwide distribution of various tales and possibly the origin of each of them; and (b) the *formalists*, mostly Russians, with Vladimir Propp as their doyen, who, from their observation of numerous folk tales or fairy tales, have established a set of motifs or 'functions' which this sub-genre invariably employs (irrespective of the characters involved) and the pattern of progression which the tale follows.[2]

The formalistic approach has engendered considerable scholarly activity throughout the world. On the African narrative tradition, perhaps the most representative efforts are (a) a 1966 University of California (Berkeley) doctoral thesis by a Nigerian, E. Ojo Arewa, involving a 'type' index of folk tales from north-eastern Africa, and (b) Denise Paulme's recent book, *La mère dévorante: essai sur la morphologie des contes Africains*, Paris, 1976. But the shortcomings of these methods are all too clear. Stitt Thompson has long issued a sad retraction:

> But the origin of all folk tales and myths must remain a mystery, just as the origin of language is a mystery. There is of course nothing mystical about it: it is merely impossible to recapture the needed facts. And in the absence of the facts, I would wish to leave the ultimate origin of any tale or myth with a large question mark rather than with a dubious answer.[3]

A comparison of the scheme of 'functions' which Propp has identified with the 'fairy tale' and the pattern which, in his *Heroic Song and Heroic Legend*, London, 1963, Jan de Vries has recognized in the life of the 'legendary' hero reveals no radical differences: so how do we separate the two sub-genres?

Perhaps the epitome of formalism, and the best manifestation of its weaknesses, can be seen in André Jolles's *Einfache Formen*, Halle, 1930.[4] Jolles is of course familiar with the work of Jacob Grimm and acknowledges it (pp. 16 and *passim*), but he prefers to concentrate on language as the crucible of cultural thought and the template on which the various units of that thought are structured in any culture. These units, as they appear in the aesthetic expression of language which is literature, he has called the 'simple forms' of literature and given the following designations: legend, saga, myth, riddle, proverb, case, memoir, tale and joke.

The failure of Jolles's distinctions is revealed when we compare two of these forms. The legend he considers as a group response to a need which presses them under certain historical conditions: an example is the image of St George which was specifically fashioned by the Christians during their persecution under the Roman Empire (pp. 44 ff.). The memoir, on the other hand, represents the *individual* urge to record a striking or unique event that may be said to represent its times: examples are Xenophon's portrait of Socrates in the *Memorabilia* and the portrait of Jesus in the various Gospels (p. 166). But it is hard to see how, in the case of the Synoptic Gospels, we can successfully draw a line between private memory and public ideology: for Christ did command a followership, and it is this followership which has orchestrated the convergence of four individual memories into one synoptic *vita*. The atomism of Jolles is thus just as inadequate as that of Thompson and Propp. Happily, towards the end of his life Jolles thought better of his system, and that system has failed to generate any radical developments in the study of the oral narrative.

The second approach to the study of the oral narrative may be called functionalistic: again, the term is used in a very broad sense, but we can safely trace its maturation through the evolutionism of Tylor and Frazer to the ethnography of Bronislaw Malinowski. In a number of publications, notably in *Myth in Primitive Psychology*, New York, 1926, Malinowski has stressed the belief that whatever analytical distinctions we make to the types of the oral narrative they must be rooted in the systems and usages of the people who practise these types. Most folklorists of the anthropological line are all too loyal to this approach. Perhaps the most outstanding articulation of the Malinowskian view, and a classic of the functionalistic delineation of the oral narrative, is William Bascom's paper, 'The forms of folklore: prose narratives'.[5]

The paper is a classic failure in many respects. The first mistake that Bascom makes is a formal one. Accepting Grimm's division of the oral narrative into myth, legend and folk tale, he proceeds to state that these forms 'are related to each other in that they are narratives in prose, and this fact distinguishes them from proverbs, riddles, ballads, poems, tongue-twisters, and other forms of verbal art on the basis of strictly formal characteristics' (p. 3). This is a strange statement. For one thing, are 'ballads' and 'poems' seen as distinct units, and what is it in 'proverbs' that makes them any less 'prose' than the forms which Bascom has so designated? For another thing, and more seriously, the distinction here between prose and non-prose is all too pedestrian, and more recent observations on the oral narrative have established the fallacy, for this genre, of the fashionable barrier erected between 'prose' on the one hand and 'poetry' or 'verse' on the other. I have myself argued against this barrier,[6] and so have others like Dennis Tedlock who has stressed that '"prose" (as we now understand it) has no

existence outside the written page'.[7] Together these various observations establish one incontrovertible fact: the context and the
resources of performance of the oral narrative – the dialogue of
moods between narrator and audience, the tidal play of emotions
within the man, the instrumental accompaniment to his act, the
histrionic punctuations to the text of it – make any differentiation
between 'prose' and 'verse' indefensible.

There are various other errors of judgement in Bascom's chart of
criteria (p. 6), some of which may simply be put down to lack of
information. If the fact that a tale has a 'conventional opening'
brings it under the category of prose narrative, obviously the well-
advertised 'verse' character of the oral epics of the Homeric tradition must be reconsidered:[8] for Pindar tells us clearly that the
Homeridae observed the convention of opening their performances
with a prelude to Zeus (Nemean Odes, 2.1). Next, it is hard to
see what the criterion 'told after dark' is meant to prove. In the
rural African society tales of all kinds are told after dark because
this is the regular time of leisure, after farmwork and dinner. But
under the urban patronage of radio and television any kind of tale
may be told during the day: Nigerian listeners may recall the
morning-time radio tales from the NBC regularly introduced by the
formula Alo o! Alo! (in Bascom's chart the alo is a 'folktale' told
after dark).

The last two major flaws in Bascom's system must be attributed
to the shortcomings of the anthropological tradition to which he
belongs. It may be recalled that Malinowski shared with the generations of Frazer and Boas the habit of calling the unlettered citizens
of non-European communities 'savages'.[9] But what seems paradoxical is that the same Malinowski saw fit to predicate his own
'civilized', scientific criteria on the classificatory systems which
these people used. It might be baseless to charge prejudice on
Bascom's thought, but he seems to me no less guilty of the field
explorer's missionary zeal than Malinowski was.

Experience has shown that, when the anthropologist identifies
the attitude behind a cultural artefact or mentefact as 'sacred'
instead of 'secular', it often means he does not understand it and
would rather abandon it to the mercies of its illogicality (or prelogi-
cality?). But what particularly makes nonsense of the distinction
between 'sacred' and 'secular' is that these scholars have constantly
ignored the basic play interest of a great deal of oral narratives,
even when they are located in an ostensibly ritual or religious
environment. The story of how Orunmila wived Iyewa and got her

with child[10] is a case in point. Anyone who prefers to read that story in terms of the virtues of childbirth, as Wande Abimbola has done, is welcome to his fancies. But if we can only reflect that the stories about Orunmila (who enjoys the same euhemeristic derivation in Yoruba oral traditions as Ogun, Sango and the other divinities) attained a religious character only because Orunmila (again like the others) achieved a cult, but that this fact has hardly altered the original affective interest of the stories, surely we will be better placed to appreciate the juicy details of the midnight act of the roguish Orunmila and the all too willing Iyewa in this story; that might help us to think better of our cavalier distinctions between sacred and secular. Bascom should know: he himself has done some work on the Ifa tradition.

The criterion of 'belief' is less defensible and far more capricious. It was variously adduced by Grimm and Malinowski, and Bascom of course upholds the ethnographer's canon: 'the distinction between fact and fiction refers *only* to the beliefs of those who tell and hear these tales, and *not* to our beliefs, to historical or scientific laws, or to any ultimate judgement of truth or falsehood' (p. 7). At least Malinowski was honest enough to observe that the details of a myth are generally subject to the peculiar interests of those who tell it, even between segments of the same little group (*Myth in Primitive Psychology*, p. 58). If, therefore, it is possible to recognize a plethora of 'beliefs' within one single tale tradition, what would be the use of a scientific system of the kind that Bascom recommends?

The trouble with the concept 'belief' is that we have to be sure what kind of belief we are dealing with: superstitious piety, or practical conviction. Superstitious piety is the mark of political or ideological interest, which is invariably a veneer for poverty of demonstrable fact: examples are the creeds of religious denominations or a group's claims to territorial title, the latter of which are often supported by their version of a myth of origin – as Malinowski discovered among the Trobrianders and P. C. Lloyd among the Yoruba.[11]

Even the element of practical conviction can be subject to whimsical manipulation. We may recall that Carl Wilhelm von Sydow recognized two first stages in the formation of the legend: the 'memorate' and the 'fabulate'.[12] In the memorate, a man narrates an experience of which he is either the subject or an eye-witness; in the fabulate, someone else narrates the same experience, often with a bit of fictive fleshing, as a story which he heard somewhere and which is prior to his own time. Perhaps a discovery which I made during one of my field trips may help us test the validity of von Sydow's distinctions.

On Christmas Eve, 1977, in the village of Ibusa in the Bendel State of Nigeria, I spent a long evening taping stories by and discussing them with a famed narrator, Mr Christopher Ojiudu Akaeze – aged 50 and a retired steward to white men. During one of our interludes, I asked him the origin of the *opanda* (a box-harp) on which he accompanied his tales. (I had turned off the tape-recorder.) Though the instrument is known and used in various parts of southern Nigeria, Ojiudu claimed it was first invented by a friend of his (at Ndoni in the Delta region) and that he had been present at the creation. His friend, he told, had been intrigued by certain musical sounds he heard every night around his house; so one night he decided to seek out the source of this music which had an unnatural sweetness to it. He found the music came from a little hut nearby, so he hid behind a patch of trees to listen. He revisited this strange scene a few more times, until one night he was surprised by one of the spirits who played the music. The spirit asked the human what he wanted; the latter replied he couldn't resist the music, it was so enchanting. Well, said the spirit, now you've heard it you'll have to play it and pass it on. But what, asked the human, am I going to play it with? The spirit produced the *opanda* and handed it to the man as a gift, enjoining him to play it thereafter to the delight of his fellows. Ojiudu said he saw the very instrument, from which he proceeded to make his own; he was the first to bring the instrument and the art of playing it to his own village.

After the interval of drinks and free chatting, I taped one more tale from him, and we got to talking again, still on tape. I thought the *opanda* story would make an interesting record, so I urged him to repeat it. This time the same story was told but with radical alterations: the man from Ndoni was no longer Ojiudu's friend, nor did Ojiudu see the actual *opanda* offered by the spirit; our friend was simply the first to introduce this kind of instrument to his community, and the encounter with the spirit was only a story he had heard from the Ndoni. There are other minor variations, but the significant change remains the loss of the element of 'personal experience' (von Sydow's phrase) from the fabric of the second version.

We may advance any number of reasons for this change. My own simple guess is this: when I turned on that tape-recorder, Ojiudu suddenly realized he was on record and chose not to be held accountable for anything that sophisticated people — for he had known the white man — might condemn as inelegant nonsense.

The validity of a line between the memorate and the fabulate has of course been questioned by other scholars.[13] What it all boils down to is that we must be very careful what use we make of the claims of our informants. Their generic values are not exactly interchangeable with the kind of analytical systems we are trying to build; the one is based on personal or partisan interest, the other on more or less objective criteria. The value of the ethnocentric faith which scholars like Bascom — and, more recently, Dan Ben-Amos[14] — have urged must therefore be seriously qualified if not altogether condemned. With the fall of this last and principal bastion, we may pronounce the functionalistic approach just as inadequate for our definitions of the oral narrative as the formalistic.

We therefore need a new approach, and I suggest a *qualitative* one, perhaps in a more precise sense than the other two approaches. By this I mean that we have to qualify every tale — whether it is in prose or verse, whatever the distinction means; whether it is set in a sacred or secular environment; in whatever manner of belief it is held in its indigenous setting — on the basis of our own scientific recognition of the relative weights of *fact* and *fiction* in it. This emphasis on the interplay of fact and fiction means, in effect, that we shall still be guided by the fluidity which Grimm recognized between 'history' and 'poetry' in his classic definition.

Heda Jason has made our task easier by suggesting that tales be arranged along a linear

> continuum of degrees of 'realness', shading to extremes at either end. The texts will be distributed along the continuum, and, with each retelling of a tale-plot, the tale may shift its place on the line ... The relationship may be expressed approximately as follows: the nearer, better-known, and more everyday the historical and geographical setting of the tale, and the nearer its actors to the narrator's personal experience, the more 'real' the happening of the tale will appear to the narrator.[15] I will now attempt a more positive grading of this continuum.

The closest that we can get to true history or real life is the legend, which for all practical purposes I take to mean a story that *strains* back at a real event but in which the historical details cannot — thanks to the oral mode of transmission — avoid the taint of fictive colouring. Like Grimm, I accept the combination of fact and fiction in the legend. But a decision about the level of historicity will depend on the text we are looking at; this means, theoretically at least, that if we have two texts of the same tale from two different communities – or two texts from two different narrators within the same community – they may happen to occupy two different points on the continuum. The one with a greater *tendency* toward fact we would call a 'historical legend', while the other with a greater tendency toward fiction we could call a 'romantic legend'.

The difference between these two kinds of legend is adequately illustrated by two recent volumes of West African martial tales edited by Gordon Innes: *Sunjata: Three Mandinka Versions,* London, 1974, and *Kaabu and Fuladu: Historical Narratives of the Gambian Mandinka,* London, 1976. In each collection, we have several versions of roughly the same subjects or historical moments. The events in *Sunjata* are much further back in time than those of the other book; Sunjata was reputedly a thirteenth-century emperor of Mali, while the figures in *Kaabu and Fuladu* were rulers of nineteenth-century kingdoms west of Mali. We are fortunate in having the bard Bamba Suso feature in both volumes; for the details of his performance of materials from two distinct periods help us to illustrate the essential difference between our two kinds of legend. What Innes says, in his introduction to *Kaabu and Faladu,* about the tales in the two books is most illuminating. After pointing to the affective and 'heroic' elements in *Sunjata,* he tells us (p. 29):

> The texts relating to nineteenth century characters, by contrast, have a much more factual, down-to-earth tone. They seem more concerned to give an account of events whereas in *Sunjata* the interest is more on the heroic qualities of Sunjata and his generals. One has the impression that the account of actual events is much less important in *Sunjata,* and audiences will accept versions which differ considerably from each other in their account of events. Such diversity of accounts in *Sunjata* is unimportant and does not disturb the listeners at all; what is important is that Sunjata is depicted as a great heroic figure. The actual incidents of his career are of relatively little consequence ... The nineteenth century figures, by contrast, are fairly ordinary human beings, not of Sunjata's colossal heroic stature, and their careers are recounted in a matter of fact way. They inhabit the everyday world which the rest of us inhabit, whereas Sunjata belongs to a remote, heroic age when men were cast in a different mould to the men of today The world of Sunjata is remote from our world, and in his world all kinds of wonders were possible. Sunjata, for example, while still a child, uprooted a baobab tree and carried it to his mother's hut, but it is hardly conceivable that an

audience would accept an account in which Musa Molo or Fode Kaba performed any such feat. They are bound by ordinary human limitations, but Sunjata is not. Indeed, the supernatural is much more prominent in *Sunjata* than in the texts here.

Time, therefore, would appear to be a principal factor in the overall character of the text. The Sunjata story comes from a far more remote past, so the audience can afford to give its outlook the benefit of its antiquity. But the nineteenth-century figures (some of whom died in this century) are of too recent memory; the facts about them are known both in the oral tradition and in some citable written records, and the bards dare not be too romantic in their accounts. The historic legend, unlike the romantic, is rather bashful about its flights of fancy, mainly because the events are too recent and may be all too easily contradicted by objective information.

This brings us to another consideration besides time. The antithesis to the objective is the affective and unreal, and here we can see the value of Grimm's emphasis on the 'poetic' or fanciful element in the oral narrative. We may recall the distinction which Thucydides made between his history and that of the likes of Herodotus. In defending his research methods against the romantic approach of the earlier school, he apologizes nevertheless that 'the absence of the mythic element [*to mē mythōdes*] in my account would seem to detract somewhat from its interest to the audience' (I.21–2). Thucydides is perhaps our earliest authority for the equation of the mythic with the romantic, and we seem justified thereby in revising our categorizations of the legend: there is still the 'historic' legend, but instead of the 'romantic' we may now safely speak of the 'mythic' legend.

Besides time, therefore, the creative or poetic temperament of the narrator is of paramount importance. This fact is brought out clearly when we compare tales from the same historical period: take the tales of *Kaabu and Fuladu* as Innes has described them and the Kambili story as edited by Charles Bird in *Songs of Seydou Camara, Volume I: Kambili*, Bloomington, Indiana, 1974, from the same broad Mandingo culture though from two different communities. One of the principal subjects of the latter tale is Samory Touré, leader of the Segu Tukulor Empire which fell to French colonial might at the turn of the century. Yet in that tale there is practically nothing historical in Samory's image: he is simply swamped by the fantastic world of magic and romance in which the bard has placed him. So, though Samory is as 'real' and 'everyday' (to quote both Jason and Innes) as the rulers in Kaabu and Fuladu, the Kambili story would qualify as a mythic legend while the tales in *Kaabu and Fuladu* would be called historic.

Whether a tale is a historic or a mythic legend, the essential thing is that the narrator has his creative consciousness set in a recognized historical period and around some acknowledged historical figure as actor. The outlines may be vague, as these traditionalists hardly think in terms of specific dates. But when a bard is singing about Sunjata or Chaka or Samory and his circle, his mind endeavours to hark back to some period of time dominated and defined by the figure of that hero. The legend can therefore be said to belong in 'historical time'; also the principal actors are necessarily human or anthropomorphic (even if reputed to be of superhuman origins), though they may sometimes be shown — especially in the mythic legend — as operating with or against non-human figures and forces.

But perhaps the vast majority of tales, especially in Africa, do not make any pretence to specific time-schemes. They are set in the most undetermined periods, and are often introduced by phrases like 'Once upon a time' or 'In the olden days'. Such a time-scheme we may call 'mythical time', in the sense that the creative imagination of the narrator does not have any constraints or obligations whatever to a time-bound image. The tales in this category can be divided roughly into two: aetiological tales and fables. Aetiological tales set out primarily to explain the roots of a society's traditions, customs or natural phenomena. Fables are told with a mainly entertainment or moralistic bias to them. The figures in mythical time can be either wholly human or wholly non-human, or else combined in varying degrees.

Of course, there is considerable potential for an overlap between these categories, as Grimm himself rightly observed. It may happen, for instance, that a clearly aetiological tale is set within historical time and around historical figures. In that case, it will have to convert automatically to some form of legend, most likely the mythic. I will demonstrate this potential with a story I collected on Christmas Day itself, 1977, again at Ibusa but this time from a retired elementary school teacher of mine, Mr S. O. Aniemeka.

This tale is told partly to explain the origin of the multiple chieftaincy and of certain taboos in the village. Ibusa was part of the old Benin Empire, and the Oba of Benin was faced with the problem of appointing a king for it. Two candidates had gone over to the imperial palace at Benin for the final decision. While they were seated in the antechamber, the Oba sent kola-nuts as refreshments for them through one of his guards. The nuts were a little rotten, and the offer was deliberate: the Oba had hidden behind a little aperture in the walls to observe the reactions of his guests to the defective entertainment. One of the candidates bit his nut, and spat it away with rude remarks. The other did not like his nut any better, but simply eliminated the rot and chewed the good part cheerfully. The Oba emerged shortly after and appointed the latter candidate King of Ibusa.

But the new king was plagued by an ungovernable wife. Whenever the king held council she would – contrary to tradition – make her presence felt and dominate the proceedings. One day, in a general assembly called by the king, she tried her usual style, but one of the elders of the village desecrated her with obscene words. The king rose and left in shame; the crowd broke up in disarray, and every section of the village claimed a chieftaincy for itself. When the news reached the Oba of Benin, he was angry that his own choice as king had been so violated. So he sent a portion of the imperial army on a punitive expedition against Ibusa. The people got wind of it, and hid in the forest. When the army got to one end of the village, they found nothing but the paw-prints of bush-rats. So they decided there could be no human beings around there; to this day that portion of Ibusa does not eat bush-rats. The army moved to another end of the village and found nothing but the hoof-marks of antelopes; they likewise abandoned that part, which to this day taboos the eating of antelopes. And so on, until the punitive expedition departed the village without firing a single shot.

The tale has finished off in an aetiological strain; but it is set well within a recognized historical moment and has an acknowledged historical image (if not exactly named) as a principal actor. It is first a nationalistic proof by the citizens of Ibusa that the famed might of Benin never really touched them; secondly, a socio-historical portrait of the sovereignty of Benin, whose Oba could dispose kingships by his will and wisdom and visit his might on any community that flouted his word; and only thirdly an explanation of certain traditions. Even though much of the tale is built on some universal narrative motifs,[16] it sets out primarily to recreate a proud moment in a people's history when republican temper got the better of imperial high-handedness. A tale like this is clearly a legend, of the mythic variety.

There are stories, however, which set out solely to trace the origins of a people's customs and habits and are totally uncomplicated by specific personalities and moments. A good example is the Congolese story recounted by Jan Knappert, 'How the Ngbandi learned to travel on water'.[17] Briefly, the people had observed how the *sia* mouse transported her young ones on a large leaf floating on water, and how the *ndoko* water-bird, perching on a floating stick, alternately dipped and surfaced in the water; they learnt to model their boats thereby. Other aetiological tales may of course sound somewhat less serious than this one, but they belong in this category none the less. For instance, a student in one of my folklore classes has reported an Igbo (eastern Nigeria) tale on why the mosquito forever haunts the ear. There was, long ago, a beauty contest in which many creatures vied for the hand of Ear in marriage. Mosquito was rejected right from the start on account of his exiguous size. The little creature has never ceased to harass Ear as a way of proving to her that, though small, he is a force to be reckoned with. A tale like this may sound trivial; but, like tales about the contest of Sun and Moon, or about man's loss of immortality, or about the origin of night, the Mosquito-Ear tale is simply another intellectual effort by man to understand the phenomena with which he continually lives in a system of naturalistic − as against scientific − rationalism.[18]

Our final category of oral narratives is the fable. Here, the creative imagination can afford to be liberated of the constraints of time, tradition, even rationalization. The spirit of the fable is largely *play*; of course lessons may be drawn from it, but it appeals to our sense of configuration in a slightly less rigid way than the aetiological tale does. Because the fancy is freer, and the setting arbitrary, the images of the tale move closer to the abstraction of *symbol* than to the fact-bound realms of *reason*. The experiences of the tortoise do not record what we *have* done at any particular historical moment, especially because he operates in a world different from ours; rather they tell us what we *should* or should not do under the kind of circumstances that his mythic situation suggests or symbolizes. The setting is timeless, the message larger than one isolated historical experience can convey: we can thus appreciate Max Luthi's point that 'the *Marchen* plainly invites symbolic interpretation'.[19]

Our discussion has consistently borne out that mobility of forms which Jacob Grimm noted in his definition, but we must be careful not to let our qualifications get out of hand. For instance, our line between historical time and mythical time may be challenged on the grounds that the most unimaginable or else most banal events are sometimes set in the age of an acknowledged historical figure. One could perhaps argue in defence that, for all its fantasy or banality, such a tale is little more than a mythic sketch of the qualities or atmosphere by which the historical figure or period is reputed to be characterized. But this logic is so speculative as indeed to force the tale back into the sphere of the mythic from which it seems to be nursing historical ambitions. A good example is again provided by Benin. Its influence is so pervasive in the oral traditions of mid-western Nigeria – all of which was part of the old Benin Empire – that even tales in which animals are the sole actors could be set by the narrator in the empire. A tale will begin with the stock formula, 'In the ancient land of Benin'; but this means no more than 'Once upon a time', and as the tale proceeds we see a massive wrench between the facts of it and its presumed historical setting. For so long as the tale lacks the active participation of an acknowledged historical figure, its claims to historicity are a fanciful joke such as only a fable indulges in.

It may well be that, in a putative original format, the tale did reflect historical events in the old empire with specific human actors who have simply dropped out of the tradition in the wear of time; these historical figures have then been replaced by animals and a pattern of behaviour which bears no marks of the serious socio-political purpose of the original tale. But these are real losses, and we should not be stampeded into according the tale a place in historical time simply because a recognized historical period has been imposed upon the pattern of it.

We may now construct a model of relations which will take account of our findings. We have started from the historic legend, which is as far as we can come to a real-life event; but we have seen how steadily the element of fiction invades the territory of fact, until we get to the fable which has no need whatever of historical fact nor uses – as the aetiological tale does – a present reality as the basis of its excursion into the past. We need a model to represent this continuum. But our model must be able to account for the kind of mobility of types and element which we have continually stressed; a mobility which encourages the manipulation of the personal element in the so-called memorate and fabulate, and which enables the multiple chieftaincy story from Ibusa to straddle the territories of both mythic legend and aetiological tale. Perhaps the following model would best represent that 'continuum of degrees' which Heda Jason has suggested:

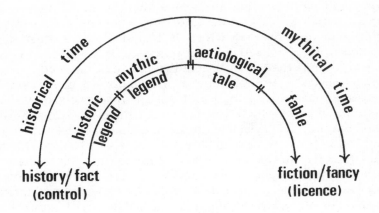

The arrows at both ends of the arc indicate that a tale has every chance of moving either way. Here we can see the value of our qualitative approach to this subject. For though we have allowed time a consideration, movement in the arc depends more on the creative whim of the narrator, and the movement can indeed amount to an extensive leap. Take the animal fable set in the Benin Empire. It does not even need to recover that serious socio-political purpose or cast of historical figures which we may assume it once had; all the narrator need do is avail himself of the ready-made pattern of motifs and attitudes in the story in his glorification – or denigration, as the case may be – of a chosen society in a chosen place and time, and the tale will make a goodly leap over the aetiological category and be transformed quickly into a mythic legend. The story-teller can use his liberties any way he wants, especially when there is a handsome patronage in the bargain. The creative or 'poetic' genius of the narrator is what makes the most difference to the fortunes of the tale in its movement within the generic continuum.

The above scale particularly helps us to locate each tale both within its appropriate class and in its relation to other tales in the class. Historical accounts will naturally tend towards the arrow on the left end of the arc, but we can still draw a line between one historic legend and another. We hear, for instance, of professional chroniclers among the Rwanda of central Africa who discourage any applause from their listeners as a distraction to their rigid faith to the facts of their accounts;[20] obviously, if the flights of fancy are restrained there is a poor chance of fact being overtaken by fiction. But we do not learn of such a discouragement in the tradition of historical narratives that Innes has observed among the Gambian Mandinka, so there is a greater danger here that, under the impetus of audiential approbation, the tale in this tradition will abdicate some of its real-historical qualities in favour of the affective appeal of the mythic. The Rwanda tale may thus be assigned a position prior to the Gambian at that left end of the arc. Or compare the Congolese tale of 'How the Ngbandi learned to travel on water' with the Mosquito-Ear tale from the Igbo of Nigeria. We may have good and obvious reasons to decide that the Congolese tale showed greater 'sobriety' than the Nigerian, thus awarding to the latter a position closer to the right end of the arc as having a higher quality of fanciful *play*.

This assessment of the relationship of history/fact on the one hand and 'poetry' or fiction/fancy on the other helps us to determine the true sense of the mythic element. The closer a tale gets to historical reality, the less capable it is of being an illustration or vehicle of larger, timeless, abstract ideals. But the other end of our arc is occupied by tales whose intellectual content is much stronger than in tales with a time-bound scheme: the aetiological tale, which rationalizes age-old customs and natural phenomena; and the fable, which in many cases points to a moral and thus re-creates, through the power/play of symbol and mimesis, that canon of ideals which have guided man since the undetermined origins of organized society. If such a scheme is accepted, then clearly the more 'poetic' or mythic a tale is, the stronger is its content of intellectual or symbolistic play.

We are therefore in a better position to define the concept 'myth'. Myth is not really a particular type of tale, as so many scholars (including Grimm) have pointed out in their generic definitions; nor is it the spoken counterpart of enacted sequences in ritual, as scholars like Jane Harrison[21] would have it. It is simply that quality of fancy which informs the creative or configurative power of the human mind in varying degrees of intensity; in that sense we are free to call any narrative of the oral tradition – so long as it lays emphasis on fanciful play – a myth. Such an understanding enables us to account for several generations of the concept of myth, first as oral narrative and now as fanciful idea. One major shortcoming of Bascom's paper is that it chooses to underestimate the contemporary usage of the term as 'popular' and 'objectionable' (p. 7). The value of our qualitative definition is that it recognizes 'that literary

terms cast their shadows diachronically'[22] and seeks a safe synchronic base for the progressive growth in meaning of the concept
of myth.

We may as well tackle a few more problems of definition raised
by the earlier approaches to the study of the oral narrative. André
Jolles gives the 'joke' the last position in his scale of 'simple forms',
an underestimation which seems to me quite arbitrary. The joke
can be located at various points in our continuum, but it will
depend what kind of a joke we are dealing with. The well-known
story of the American general in the Second World War, whose
company was surrounded by a ring of Japanese soldiers and who
replied 'Nuts!' to the enemy's warning to surrender, is no doubt
borne out by the records. But the movement of the story within
'historical time' will depend very much on the amount of 'poetic'
flavour that the narrator brings to it. The story remains a joke, a
matter for fun; but it enhances the heroic conduct of the general,
rather than trivializing the heroic ethic as Jolles would have had it
(Formes Simples, pp. 197 ff.). There are of course jokes that trivial-
ize. An obscene joke about the duke, which is obviously a lie, is still
a mythic legend; if the duke was not a notable personality he would
not attract legendary attention, even an uncharitable one. What
counts is that his historical personality has been treated to a fictive
fancy which nevertheless succeeds in affecting an audience. Other
jokes, however, have no acknowledged historical subjects; they are
simply a product of outright fabrication, designed solely to impress
us by their aesthetic and configurative charm. Such jokes belong
clearly in the fable category.

We may also dispose of the formal confusion that bedevils Bascom's categories. The distinction between 'prose' and anything
else that is thought to be unlike it is ultimately meaningless in our
scheme. Epics, sagas and ballads – in whatever forms they are
transcribed – are obviously mythic legends, in as much as they
re-create historical figures and moments with a relatively high
proportion of the 'poetic' or fictional element. In this category
belong the epics of Sunjata among the Mandinka, of Lianja among
the Nkundo of Zaire, of Ozidi among the Ijaw of Nigeria, of Da
Monzon among the Bambara, of Mehmed the Osmanli Turk in the
guslar tradition of Yugoslavia, the American legends of Daniel
Boone of the frontier and Stacker Lee of the black underworld, as
well as the Iliad and Odyssey of Homer, the Anglo-Saxon Beowulf,
the poems of the Icelandic Edda, the ballads of the Child collection,
the Slavic Tale of Igor among the Russians, and countless others

that we have formed the habit of separating by clearly inadequate criteria.

The need for the qualitative approach to the study of the oral narrative was long overdue. The formalistic approach served the purposes of cultural historians who sought for units of ideas – in their simplest or least reducible forms – that could be matched, like dominoes, until a convenient mosaic was achieved that would represent the primordial outlook of man. The functionalistic approach laid undue emphasis on the modes of thought, belief and usage of individual societies. But the atomism of these scholars soon proved inadequate, and their systems began to lose their credibility and their usefulness the moment they recognized that what was 'myth' in one community could be 'legend' or 'folk tale' in another.[23] However, since few of these theorists on myth have failed to acknowledge the fundamental *creative* quality of it, what was needed was a method which would explore the tidal interplay of fact and fiction with an emphasis on the fortunes of the latter. It was thus inevitable that the discussion on myth should be lodged in the premises of those who saw it principally as literature and were best qualified to assess the various levels of that fictive or symbolistic character which marks any kind of narrative, be it oral or written.[24]

NOTES

1. B. Feldman and R. D. Richardson, *The Rise of Modern Mythology*, Bloomington, Indiana University Press, 1972, pp. 412–13.
2. A. Aarne and S. Thompson, *The Types of the Folktale*, Helsinki, 1964, and S. Thompson, *Motif-index of Folk Literature*, 6 vols, Bloomington, Indiana University Press, 1955–8; V. Propp, *Morphology of the Folktale*, Austin, Texas, 1968. A structuralist like Claude Lévi-Strauss is not particularly interested in these generic divisions of the oral narrative, but his methods have a striking kinship with those of Propp: see C. Lévi-Strauss, *Structural Anthropology*, Vol. 2, London, 1977, pp. 115–45.
3. S. Thompson, 'Myth and folktales', in *Myth: A Symposium*, ed. T. Sebeok, Bloomington, Indiana University Press, 1958, pp. 176 f.
4. This work has been published in French as *Formes Simples*, tr. A. M. Buguet, Paris, 1972. My page references are to this French edition.

5. In *Journal of American Folklore*, 78, 1965, pp. 3–20. Further references to this publication are by page.

6. I. Okpewho, 'Does the epic exist in Africa? Some formal considerations', *Research in African Literatures*, 8, 1977, pp. 171–200; *The Epic in Africa: Toward a Poetics of the Oral Performance*, New York, 1979.

7. D. Tedlock, 'Toward an oral poetics', *New Literary History*, 8, 1977, 507–19; cf. his 'On the translation of style in oral narrative', *Journal of American Folklore*, 84, 1971, pp. 114–33.

8. The 'metrical criteria' by which classics like the Homeric tales have conventionally been read have been questioned by M. N. Nagler in his *Spontaneity and Tradition: A Study in the Oral Art of Homer*, Berkeley and Los Angeles, University of California Press, 1974, pp. 8 f.

9. In his *Argonauts of the Western Pacific*, London, Routledge and Kegan Paul, 1922, Malinowski declares that 'the native is not the natural companion for a white man' (p. 7). On p. 21 he turns the joke on savagery to his own Slavic origins!

10. W. Abimbola, *Sixteen Great Poems of Ifa*, Paris and Zaria, 1975, pp. 134–55.

11. P. C. Lloyd, 'Yoruba myths: a sociologist's interpretation', *Odu: Journal of Yoruba and Related Studies*, no. 2, 1955, pp. 20–8.

12. See C. W. von Sydow, *Selected Papers on Folklore*, ed. L. Bodker, Copenhagen, Rosenkilde and Bagger, 1948, pp. 60–88, for a detailed discussion of the 'legend'.

13. See in particular L. Degh and A. Vazsonyi, 'The memorate and the proto-memorate', *Journal of American Folklore*, 87, 1974, p. 239.

14. D. Ben-Amos, 'Analytical categories and ethnic genres', in *Folklore Genres*, ed. D. Ben-Amos, Austin, Texas, 1976, p. 224, and his 'Introduction: folklore in African society', in *Forms of Folklore in Africa*, ed. B. Lindfors, Austin, Texas, 1977, pp. 2–8.

15. H. Jason, 'Concerning the "historical" and the "local" legend and their relatives', *Journal of American Folklore*, 84, 1971, p. 134.

16. Stitt Thompson's Motifs B437.1 ('Helpful Rat') and B443.2 ('Helpful Antelope').

17. J. Knappert, *Myths and Legends of the Congo*, London, Heinemann, 1971, p. 169.

18. An evolutionist view of culture would naturally judge the naturalistic prior and inferior to the scientific rationalism: see J. G. Frazer, *Apollodorus: The Library*, London, Heinemann, 1921, p. xxvii. The structuralist (i.e. synchronic) view sees no qualitative difference between them: cf. C. Lévi-Strauss, *The Savage Mind*, London, Weidenfeld and Nicolson, 1972, p. 222, and *Tristes Tropiques*, Harmondsworth, 1976, p. 47.

19. M. Luthi, 'Aspects of the *Marchen* and the legend,' in *Folklore Genres*, op. cit., p. 23.

20. A. Coupez and Th. Kamanzi, *Littérature de cour au Rwanda*, Oxford, 1970, p. 77.

21. J. Harrison, *Themis*, Cambridge, Merlin Press, 1912, p. 328.

22. K. K. Ruthven, *Myth*, London, Methuen, 1976, p. 82.

23. Franz Boas was possibly the first to observe this: see his *General Anthropology*, Boston, Mass., 1938, p. 609, where, incidentally, he also says: 'The reference to religious ideas and rituals does not constitute a useful criterion either, for these may enter into myths as well as into folktales relating to recent occurrences.'

24. Of those myth studies in which one may identify a qualitative interest, Richard Chase, *Quest for Myth*, Baton Rouge, Greenwood Press, 1949, deserves special mention. G. S. Kirk, *Myth: Its Meaning and Functions*, Cambridge, Cambridge University Press, 1970, is a useful contribution. He considers 'fantasy or the use of ingenuity' a 'more rewarding' criterion than time in the study of oral narratives (p. 40 n.). But he is hopelessly confused on the concept of 'historical time' and his entire generic discussion (pp. 31–41) is only a slight variation of Bascom's.

The African Historical Novel and the Way Forward

Hugh Webb

F ew would doubt that the relationship between literature and society is a close and meaningful one. Equally it is apparent that literary forms are never solely *literary* forms. As Georg Lukács has pointed out:

> The genuine categories of literary forms are not simply literary in essence. They are *forms of life* especially adapted to the articulation of great alternatives in a practical and effective manner and to the ex-position of the maximal inner potentialities of forces and counter-forces.[1]

Each work of art arises out of the particular alternatives of its time. In the modern African historical novel the attempted dynamic rendering of these alternatives (by giving a total picture of a society in motion) is an important motivating formal principle. It is clear that African novelists proceed from this principle to create literary works that, in their shaping and ordering, give significant insights into the potentialities of a fictional treatment of historical material. In the African historical novel, the articulation of socio-political alternatives is well under way.

S. O. Mezu's work *Behind the Rising Sun*,[2] first published in 1971 (the year following the end of the Nigerian Civil War), is clearly a historical novel in the sense that it deals with a particular period that can be identified as *closed*. The war has ended; the novelist looks back. Mezu projects certain fictional figures through a carefully patterned historical framework. He shows the personal destinies of these characters and, by so doing, attempts to portray the kind of individual paths that can directly express (through their typicality) the problems and contradictions of this particular period of modern African history. By contrasting the nature of these various individual paths, Mezu posits (within the work) a search for authentic values as part of a consideration of the way forward out of the nightmare of fratricidal conflict.[3]

Mezu emphasizes the essential relationship between the personal and the national, the particular and the typical, the time-conditioned and the timeless, in the title of his novel. For the rising-sun motif possesses plurisignificance of the sort that can unify and hold together such potentially disparate elements of historical experience. A symbolic representation of the rising sun made up the official shoulder-patch on the uniform of the Biafran armed forces. It was the emblem of secessionist Biafra. Carried by the individual protagonists, it also represented the larger national ideal. The rising sun is, of course, also a natural and timeless phenomenon. By the use of this artistic device, Mezu pulls his strands of moral alternatives together. The multiple implications carried by this combination of references can be shown working effectively in lines such as these (p. 228):

> For the people, the war was no more. The past was a receding nightmare. The rising sun was a dream; its zenith, a dark noon. Behind, lay the ruins of youth and the remains of age.

Mezu's novel is totally concerned with an investigation of what happened behind that rising run. In the final section of the work one finds explicit statements by two of Mezu's 'truth-tellers', Tudor and Yvette. Tudor is shown to be thinking of an historical novel that would be, as he puts it, 'faithful to fact and figures and the real characters of the various participants in the struggle, the struggle they had been through' (p. 240). Yvette, projected as being one of the new breed of African women, speaks of 'a mixture of joy and sorrow, of goodness and evil, of moments of heroic sacrifice and mean cowardice' that went into the making, and destruction, of the Biafran state. A strong moral purpose is evident in the remark by Yvette that stands as the concluding line of the novel: 'We owe it as a duty to tell our children nothing but the truth, the entire truth' (p. 241). To the extent that *Behind the Rising Sun* is clearly a response to these demands, while encompassing them within the text itself, one can ask: how does Mezu intend to tell the 'truth' in his historical novel in terms of Yvette's grand alternatives? An indication of his approach is provided by his choice of a passage from René

Maran's preface to *Batouala*[4] that becomes a frontispiece quotation for *Behind the Rising Sun*. It reads, in part:

> Ce roman est donc tout objectif. Il ne tâche même pas à expliquer: il constate. Il ne s'indigne pas: il enregistre. Il ne pouvait en être autrement.[5]

The pursuit of objectivity is a hazardous task in literature. The really interesting question, in relation to Mezu's novel, is not whether he succeeds but the influence that such an approach has on his planned presentational 'witness' of historical events.

The historical events that provide the framework for this novel are, as one would expect, all closely connected with the Civil War and with the Biafran war effort in Europe. References to the contemporaneous student riots in Paris and disturbances in Senegal, combined with the presentation of complete telex messages marked TOP PRIORITY (p. 24) and reportage of actual dates and events of the war period, help to create the necessary aura of verisimilitude and fix the historical locale. The reader is told of black-market deals for arms and planes, of financial dealings of all sorts (legitimate and otherwise), and of the activities of the Biafra Historical Research Centre. One reads of emergency night-airlifts, of the BEL (Behind Enemy Lines) squad, and of the inexorable movement towards disaster – the end of Biafra. Yet all this material is no mere background padding. For Mezu, through an authorial ordering of details, gives to his work the necessary spatial and temporal features that make possible a fully rounded 'witness' to the actions of certain figures who move through his novel. In his handling of these figures – the central group is divided roughly into those who are seen to be corrupt and ultimately destructive (such as Professor Chancellor Obelenwata and Chief Tobias Iweka) and those who are honest and creative (Freddy Onuoha, the girl Titi, and Tudor Opara, the soldier) – he is attempting an examination of the moral values that informed the Biafran conflict. Onuoha, the pivotal figure of the work, moves between both groups as he is seen to be gaining a total grasp of the situation. A real commitment to humanistic ideals, as opposed to corrupt self-seeking, is the positive around which Mezu organizes the world-view of such figures as Onuoha. This young man moves, gradually, into a position of hardened maturity. At the end of the conflict, for example, Onuoha has no strong opinion about Tudor's projected historical work. He is shown as being 'only interested in a fair account that would expose the strength as well as the weaknesses of the noble revolution' (p. 241). This is a view that the whole thrust of the narrative reinforces and sustains.

S. O. Mezu appears to be working from the thesis that, within the determining context of a historical crisis, there exist certain personal crises that coincide with the more general events.[6] From a portrayal of the various crises of conscience in the individual figures, he proceeds logically to an examination of larger, national issues that arise from the historical conflict as a whole. In this regard, the created characters' ability to generalize about their predicament is of great importance as a unifying formal feature of the work. Chief Iweka, for instance, holds the opinion that people 'at home' do not understand the amount of exertion of those working for the cause abroad. He promises that, after the war, 'he would get everything straight'. Those who worked abroad, he says, 'deserved real credit for winning the war' (p. 25). The war, however, is never won. In terms of the moral, perceptual guidelines that Mezu sets up, these are seen as hollow words from a hollow man. Facing such hypocrisy, the younger Biafrans begin to realize their unique position in the middle of contemporary events. As one of them remarks: 'These old cronies . . . now realize in the moment of great catastrophe that they need the intelligence of the young generation to survive, that they need you and me' (p. 41). Mezu allows the realization that the Biafran leaders (at home or abroad) are no heroic knights in shining armour to slowly dawn on his youthful protagonists. It is a movement from innocence to understanding that is presented here. Carried along with this movement is the whole dialectic that resides in the moral and political dilemma raised by civil warfare. Is it enough to fight, regardless of motives and values? That question underlies Mezu's interpretative approach to the historical reality. Having observed the common paradox that there 'was something admirable and brutish about man's behaviour', the narrator of the novel concludes that there are basically two types of people (p. 142): 'Some build and others destroy in this world of individuals, with their cowardice and their bravery, their callousness and their generosity.' Thoughts such as these appear to provide the basis for Mezu's artistic world-view. After an ironic treatment of the Nigerian national anthem, for example, Onuoha is shown thinking that the country appears to have lost its sovereignty to a new form of colonialism where the nation is separated into tribal cliques that divide and slaughter. 'It was difficult to see in such a land a fatherland. It was more of a murderland' (p. 192). Because of the projected typicality of

Onuoha's position, his thoughts take on a general significance within the historical sweep of the novel.

In an interesting extension of his interpretative approach, Mezu attempts to project a possible postwar direction, a socio-political alternative for the future. Throughout those sections of the novel that present scenes of actual warfare, one finds certain hints regarding the continuing imperturbability of the Nigerian landscape. Here is a strong link with a safer time in the past (p. 160):

> The vegetation was dense, very dense and rich with lusty undergrowth. But it was not too difficult to follow the ancient paths once trodden by ancestral feet. They had survived the war better than the modern roads.

It is from a basis suggested by these 'ancient paths once trodden by ancestral feet' that Mezu projects his socio-political alternative. Onuoha and his friends set up a communalist village centred on a life close to the soil and on the collective values that this life is seen to sustain. They call the new community Umuoha, meaning 'the communal children' (p. 229). Umuoha is to be a commune of rebirth directed towards the future (comparable, in some ways, to Wole Soyinka's Aiyéró in Season of Anomy).[7] Yet, in Mezu's work, such a utopian alternative to disorder appears as an appendix to the novel rather than a formally integrated element in the general narrative design. The creation of the Umuoha concept can be seen as part of Mezu's attempted handling of a paradox of art – that it can resolve imaginatively issues which cannot (for the present) be effectively resolved in action.[8] It does not succeed. It is apparent that the rather simplistic views regarding moral standards (straight against crooked, creators or destroyers) that are projected by the authorial design leave the communalist-village idea insufficiently grounded within a comprehensive search for practical alternatives. Behind the Rising Sun, nevertheless, is totally engaged with a search for a way forward. It is aimed at the rebirth of a whole generation in the enduring light of the rising sun. Mezu's work is formed to serve that purpose.

Ali Mazrui's novel The Trial of Christopher Okigbo[9] is a radical experiment in the historical novel form. At the time when the novel was written, the author was Professor of Political Science at Makerere University (Uganda). His professional concerns, as a political scientist, are reflected in this novel of ideas. The compositional principles that lie behind a work such as this, determining the total shape of the novel, appear to coincide with an aesthetic and political investigation of events in the near past. Consequently, *The Trial of Christopher Okigbo* can be seen as an attempt to represent (by artistic projection) the *meaning* of the Nigerian Civil War period in particular, and of contemporary African events in general. In other words, it is a fictional attempt to represent the specific qualities of the period, historically. Large socio-political trends and historical forces are symbolically localized by means of an imagined trial. People are on trial and values are on trial, in the service of a clarification of the problems of modern African societies. While Mazrui writes in his preface of fictionalizing his anguish at the death of a friend (Giraffe) and of Christopher Okigbo,[10] the central formal thrust of this work is away from personal anguish and towards a general investigation of wider moral and political values.

Christopher Okigbo, the Nigerian poet and Biafran officer killed in the Civil War, is the focal point of Mazrui's novelistic investigation. Mazrui makes use of factual details from Okigbo's life and work – his university studies, his poetry, his views on the function of art, his gathering involvement with the Biafran cause, and his death on the war-front – as the basis for this trial of African values. By means of a highly innovative arrangement of parallel presented worlds, the Herebefore and the Hereafter (existing in the temporal sense, both separately and simultaneously), Mazrui opens up vast potential areas of action and comment. The Herebefore is presented on the same plot-level as the traditional historical novel milieu. The African Hereafter, on the other hand, is an imaginative creation of a state where those countless millions of the after-life (normally treated as merely deceased) congregate in a vast panoply of interacting experience, beyond the usual confines of human activity. It is in this literary creation of parallel worlds that the radical nature of Mazrui's formal experiment lies.

The after-world is peopled by all those Africans who have approached the ultimate rites of passage. Yet, by the device of summoning the voices of those still living as 'evidence' for the trial, Mazrui achieves a novelistic overview of past events within a framework of judgement that can provide the verdict of past, present and (prophetically) future ages. *The Trial of Christopher Okigbo* is full of quotations from, and references to, a whole range of African leaders and writers. In the Hereafter one finds, for example, Nkrumah, Tom Mboya, Lumumba, Tafawa Balewa, Olympio, Okigbo (as a disembodied voice) and even Chaka the Zulu. As witnesses from the Herebefore come Julius Nyerere,

Obote, Senghor, Gowon and Ojukwu, Chinua Achebe, Soyinka, Robert Serumaga, Mazrui himself (as political scientist)[11] and many others. Even Lord Byron, as another poet who died for a cause, makes an appearance as a witness for the defence, on sub-poena.[12] Mazrui's central figure Hamisi Salim (himself on trial for the 'sin' of miscalculation) is selected, by the elders, to defend Christopher Okigbo. A Ghanaian, Apolo-Gyamfi, appears for the prosecution. The novelist, then, carefully sets out the limits of his Hereafter world and, having selected the narrative situation and its specific guise, he achieves a definite consistency of illusion. More important, he allows himself a wide freedom of reference. With a 'cast' of millions, he ranges across the whole field of contemporary African values.

Any trial must centre on the charges and Mazrui's trial of Christopher Okigbo, as an inquiry of ideas, works on a network of charges. They are all directed towards an examination of the role of the artist, the value of art and the function of art as a truth-telling exercise. A consideration of the nature of the charges serves to clarify the novel's concerns. The reader is informed that the prosecution is going to suggest that (p. 41):

> Okigbo had no right to consider himself an Ibo patriot first, and an African artist only second. That was to subordinate the interests of generations of Africans to the needs of a collection of Ibos at an isolated moment in historical time.

It is made clear that this is a 'high' charge of more than individual significance. Apolo-Gyamfi, for the prosecution, states that Okigbo 'was to dilute art with the blood of tribalism' (p. 70). This man, he says, 'who had once recognised the grand panorama of human experience, dwindled into a petty negotiator for the merchandise of violence' (p. 71). Okigbo is thus presented, by the prosecution, as a man who has squandered a unique gift in a sacrificial act of escapism. As Apolo-Gyamfi puts it (p. 72):

> If the great artist has to sacrifice himself for anything, he should only sacrifice himself for the universal. To die for the truth is martyrdom. To die for knowledge is martyrdom. To die for art is martyrdom. But when a great thinker or a great artist dies for his nation, that is an indulgence.

It is clear, from this line of attack, that Mazrui is concerned with investigating large questions, not only of the validity of Biafran secession (Okigbo, by extension, is held to represent the nation) but of the role of art in life and of the position of the artist as a unique human being. The novelist attempts to link the two elements – the creation of art and the creation of a nation – into an aesthetic unity and by so doing, to make the implications of his work reflect on both spheres of activity. Hamisi Salim defends Okigbo on both counts, as activist and as poet. Significantly, his defence rests on the contention (shared by Wole Soyinka, amongst others)[13] that these two activities are, or should be, indivisible (p. 80):

> Art is a heritage from the past, honoured and augmented by the present, and then transmitted to the future. But the transmission is not unilinear, and the continuity is a social continuity. In Africa it is society which gives meaning to art. How then could Christopher Okigbo be deemed guilty for giving his life in the cause of his immediate society?

By levelling and answering these charges, within a dialectic of prosecution and defence, Mazrui allows the treatment of his ideological concerns to proceed within a structured *debate* situation. The presentation of conflicting ideas (alternatives) is thus incorporated in a novel of historical concern.

There are certain formal features in Mazrui's work, particularly on the level of presented ideas, that lead to an artistic disharmony. Despite the author's attempts to establish, through the network of charges, a unified artistic-sociological-political treatment of ideas, the impression remains that there is a substantial difference between the creation of art and the creation of a nation. While he does attempt a description of such factors as the competition of rival elite groups in Nigeria (on the level of human tragedy), Mazrui does not succeed in establishing a connection that is central to the realization of his narrative strategy – that of Okigbo, poet and soldier, to the Ojukwus and Gowons of the socio-political struggle. The result is that these two strands tend to work as mutually competing areas of interest within the novel. The frequent quotations from Okigbo's poetry, such as (p. 7):

> The stars have departed,
> the sky in monocle
> surveys the worldunder.
>
> The stars have departed,
> and I – where am I?

do little to consolidate the necessary connection. Okigbo's poetry (personal and metaphysical in approach, imagistic in technique) tends to emphasize the universal, rather than the particular, and works as a disruptive element in the general treatment of political events. Similarly, by extending the charges to cover Biafra, attention is distracted from Mazrui's handling of questions concerning artistic creation. Even if one sees Okigbo as a committed writer, in the broader sense of an artist who attempts an internal orientation of awareness, Mazrui's presentation of the man as one of a poetic, truth-telling social vanguard is hardly enough to preserve the necessary formal unity upon which the work depends. Mazrui, with the evident concern of a political scientist (as novelist), presents various verdicts on the charges in an aesthetic attempt to close a discussion that is essentially open-ended. Consequently, the verdicts of NOT PROVEN on Okigbo and Biafra create a distinct sense of anticlimax rather than a unified concluding design. The author writes, in his preface, of his ambivalent feelings about the Civil War: 'My moral support was for the Federal side; my sympathies were with the Ibo' (p. x). It can be seen that The Trial of Christopher Okigbo attempts an imaginative resolution of this conflict. It is, however, a striking example of a novel where internal discrepancies in artistic form result from what Lukács has called 'unresolved (and therefore especially compelling) social contradictions'.[14] Despite the fact that Mazrui does not succeed in 'Making harmony among the branches' (p. 145), his historical novel clarifies, at least, the possibilities that are created by formal experimentation.

Ayi Kwei Armah's historical novel Two Thousand Seasons[15] stands as the most achieved work (in the sense of total unified form) within the present corpus of Anglophone African literature. It represents a significant instance of the harmony of literary form that can be created by an artistic design uniting structure and meaning, ideology and performance. Two Thousand Seasons is clearly a work that is adapted to the articulation of great alternatives. The novel appears, in its origins, to stem from the sort of comment made by Modin, in Armah's earlier work Why Are We So Blest? that 'war against the invader' should be an educational process for creating 'new anti-European, anti-elitist values'.[16] Two Thousand Seasons represents Armah's literary 'warfare', directed (as it is) to the articulation of values that will enable the African peoples to move forward, collectively and fruitfully. In the scope and scale and profound human importance of its subject, it is epic in sweep. In the explicit handling of great alternatives of conduct (constantly balanced one against the other), it is dialectical in nature. The total epic-dialectic form is aimed towards what Wole

Soyinka and Dennis Brutus have called for, in their Declaration of African Writers (1975), 'the full retrieval of the African past in the quest for a contemporary self-apprehension and design for the future'.[17] The work proceeds from a very clear awareness that culture is not neutral politically (to use Meredith Tax's phrase)[18] and that it is impossible for it to be so. Such an awareness carries with it the realization that men and women can fully comprehend their own existence only when it is seen as something historically conditioned. Armah, by portraying changes of viewpoint and relationships, changes of possible and actual resolutions (as forms of literary organization),[19] attempts a cultural synthesis of the highest order.

The novel's title is based on an imagined prophecy of the female visionary Anoa, who has spoken of a thousand seasons and another thousand seasons: '*a thousand seasons wasted wandering amazed along alien roads, another thousand spent finding paths to the living way* (p. xv; italics in original). A passage from Armah's prologue (a forceful, poetic and visionary description of the modern African moral inferno) makes it clear that the work is aimed at a reshaping of the meanings of historical experience, a reshaping that will help to rescue the integrity of Africans alienated from 'the way' by centuries of Arab and European destruction. The seer-narrator of the prologue speaks of the 'remade' who are 'pointers to the way, the way of remembrance, the way knowing purpose' (p. xv). That the way of purpose rests on a racial imperative is also clear. Those who have been destroyed are spoken of as having known 'Whiteness' but 'of our own blackness they have yet to learn' (p. xvii). It becomes apparent that the novel incorporates a specific, collective pan-African vision of the essential oneness of the black peoples, suffering from a common oppression and with a common need for future directions. One also notes the narrator's projected role not only as visionary truth-teller but as a racial healer. The larger aim is 'to find ... our healing self, we the black people' (p. 13). The proud, positive statement that ends the prologue makes it very clear that *Two Thousand Seasons* is not to be seen as a manifesto of disillusionment (p. xviii; italics in original):

> *Leave the killers' spokesmen, the predators' spokesmen, leave the destroyers' spokesmen to cast contemptuous despair abroad. That is not our vocation. That will not be our utterance.*

The most significant formal aspect of Armah's work (in the sense that it defines and shapes the whole narrative) is the fact that this tale of two thousand seasons is told in the collective voice. This device allows Armah to shape his novel to suit the collective, racial response at which it is aimed. As the thrust of ideas within the work is directed towards a communal, rather than an individual, interpretation of historical events, the use of a narrator who can be seen to be 'speaking' in terms of the whole African experience is of obvious artistic advantage. Not only does the collective voice reflect the collective solution, but (by its nature) it enforces a view of the presented details of Armah's story that amounts to a striking reassessment of African history itself. It also, of course, moves the narrative viewpoint away from the individualistic focus of a figure such as Freddy Onuoha (in *Behind the Rising Sun*) and into the traditional realm of African oral narrative: the Speaker, the wise one, and his communal audience sharing the group experience. Here again one notices narrative technique that reflects, and reinforces, the ideological thrust of the novel. In *Two Thousand Seasons* there is a strong sense of a gathering, shared tale. It is indicated by the constant use of rhetorical questions: 'What need then had any cripple for dreams of vengeance?' and 'Why after that should the cripple acquiesce in silent suffering?' (p. 44). Such questions call for an imaginative response from the reader/listener and work to involve this response with intellectual awakening. 'Hear this for the sound of it' (p. 54), says the collective voice, and the concept of 'sound' clearly includes that of *meaning*. With a faceless narrator such as this, Armah also achieves another important formal task: to divorce the temporal locus of the action from the western concept of time. It is vital to the success of his work that Africans should see that (p. 1):

> We are not a people of yesterday. Do they ask how many single seasons we have flowed from our beginnings till now? We shall point them to the proper beginning of their counting.

The use of an all-seeing narrator allows Armah to range over centuries of experience and to locate the modern colonial period as a relatively temporary phenomenon, no matter how destructive it has been to 'the way'.

The comments and questions of Armah's narrator are embedded within an exciting, parabolic story that traces various representative African groups as they move from a period of natural egalitarianism (origins) into successive stages of oppression (by the Arab predators and European destroyers – both, significantly, seen as 'white') and then, out of slavery, into a condition of awakened revolt. The white threat that leads to alienation is defined in these terms (p. 3):

> Killers who from the desert brought us in the aftermath of Anoa's prophecy a choice of deaths: death of our spirit, the clogging destruction of our mind with their senseless religion of slavery ... Killers who from the sea came holding death of the body in their right, the mind's annihilation in their left, shrieking fables of a white god and a son unconceived, exemplar of their proffered senseless suffering.

The Africans are shown, by the use of particularly located episodes, in the process of resisting the threat and of being subdued by the invaders and their minions, the self-appointed African 'kings'. Armah employs the description of representative situations (such as the killing of Arabs at the height of a sexual orgy, or the selling of an initiation-group of young people into slavery) as definite parables for the experience of the whole race. Always, within the historical-record stream of the narrative, there are hints of the positive alternatives available. Speaking of the askari-zombis, the voice states that 'The new-found end of their lives was how to keep from doing anything different from the hollow cycle of shitting, smoking, fucking, drinking, eating, playing' (p. 47). Immediately afterwards, the reader is told of those who were trying ways to end this humiliation, finding ways to destroy the destroyers. The narrative voice also provides a commentary on the presented events. Regarding the African puppet-kings, for example, it tells us that the 'quietest king, the gentlest leader of the mystified, is criminal beyond the exercise of any comparison' (p. 100). By such means, Armah succeeds in embedding a subtle dialectic of values within the framework of narrated situations while preserving the strong authorial control that is always guiding and stressing the implications inherent in the thousand seasons spent travelling the alien road.

Forming a substantial part of the narrative is the account of an elite group of young people – eleven girls and nine boys – who are sold into slavery, revolt, and then return to meet their aged teacher (Isanusi) and to organize armed resistance against the destroyers. In the process, they set free other groups, some of whom (an enlightened minority) join the struggle. The small group is made up of those who are committed to a return to 'the way'. They are surrounded by violence and apathy. Clearly, here, Armah sets up a microcosm of the total situation along Fanonist lines. His select group is formed from those who are (as Fanon puts it) 'engaged in the struggle ... freed from colonialism and forewarned of all attempts at mystification...'.[20] In *Two Thousand Seasons*, their success is shown to depend upon the use of violence, committed by the people, organized and educated by those who see that 'between the creation of life and the destruction of the destroyers there is no difference but a necessary, indispensable connection' (p. 319). The extent to which Armah incorporates the militant ideas of Frantz Fanon within his novel is an indication of his projected solution to the problems of the neo-colonialist period. The use of 'rightful' violence is shown as necessary for a return to the straight path ahead.

As the positive pole of moral values, the concept of *the way* (and the search for it); plays an essential part in the formal structure of *Two Thousand Seasons*. The way is never exactly defined, except by its negative alternatives. The way is not that of a people who have lost sight of origins and are deaf to purposes. It is seen as the forgotten *and* the future way. It is the way of reciprocity, the way of beauty, and the way of collective endeavour. The way is 'not a random path' (p. 61). It is the path of wholeness, creativity and hospitality. It is 'an energy in us, strongest in our working, breathing, thinking together as one people; weakest when we are scattered, confused, broken into individual, unconnected fragments (p. 151). The way is shown not to be a blind groping backward along a nostalgic road. Yet its closest meaning is said to be 'the search for paths to that necessary beginning' (p. 233). The way is a companionship of the mind and the spirit: 'There is no beauty but in relationships. Nothing cut off by itself is beautiful' (p. 321). Weapons and violence are not beautiful in themselves.[21] Only if they are used 'for creation's life', for the finding of the way, are they seen as positive things. For death is not the way. The way is life. The search for the way, of which Armah is careful to avoid a close definition, becomes the central formal thread that unites this novel. The process of reading the work is the process of growing understanding of *the way*. One sees, then, that the forward-reading dimension corresponds (in an exact sense) with an awareness of the meaning and importance of the ideas that lie beneath the narrative surface.

In formal design and direction *Two Thousand Seasons* is essentially a forward-looking work. As the narrative voice points out: 'What are we if we see nothing beyond the present, hear nothing from the ages of our flowing, and in all our existence can utter no necessary preparation of the future way?' (p. 317). Whether or not

Ayi Kwei Armah's racial vision is accepted and subsumed, this novel (by the example of its formal coherence) will be seen as a necessary preparation of the way ahead for much of modern African literature.

NOTES

1. Georg Lukács, *Writer And Critic and other essays*, ed. and trans. A. Kahn, London, Merlin Press, 1970, p. 21. The emphasis is mine.
2. S. O. Mezu, *Behind the Rising Sun*, London, Heinemann, 1971.
3. *Behind the Rising Sun* carries a dedication 'To all the innocent victims of the Biafran War'.
4. René Maran, *Batouala*, 1921, repr. Washington, DC, Black Orpheus Press, 1972, and London, Heinemann, 1973.
5. 'Therefore this novel is entirely objective. It does not even attempt explanation: it is a witness. It does not criticize, it registers. I could not do otherwise.'
6. A feature that Georg Lukács notes as being part of the 'classical form' of Scott's historical novels. See Lukács, *The Historical Novel*, trans. H. and S. Mitchell, 1937, repr. Harmondsworth, Penguin, 1969, p. 42.
7. Wole Soyinka, *Season of Anomy*, London, Rex Collings, 1973.
8. A paradox that has been noted by Arnold Kettle in 'The progressive tradition in bourgeois culture', in *Radical Perspectives in the Arts*, ed. Lee Baxandall, Harmondsworth, Penguin, 1972, pp. 166–7.
9. Ali A. Mazrui, *The Trial of Christopher Okigbo*, London, Heinemann, 1971.
10. Mazrui writes in his preface: 'Why not write a novel? Why not write a novel set in the Hereafter, with dead men living again, and live issues debated by the dead? Why not put Christopher Okigbo and Giraffe on a platform of destiny beyond the grave? In short, dear Ali Mazrui, why not fictionalize your anguish?' ibid., p. x.
11. Ali A. Mazrui, as anonymous political scientist, appears through a 'voice from the clouds'. ibid., pp. 137–8.
12. Lord Byron arrives from 'After-Europe'. Mazrui clearly recognizes the audacity of the 'subpoena' device. See the narrator's remark: 'if Counsel for Salvation could unearth a connecting theme between Byron and Biafra, he might be on his way towards making legal meta-history'. ibid., p. 109.
13. Wole Soyinka's 'voice of vision' statement is, in fact, incorporated in the text of Mazrui's novel. It reads, in part: 'The artist has always functioned in his society as the record of mores and experience of his

38   *The African Historical Novel and the Way Forward*

society and as the voice of vision in his own time. It is time for him to respond to this essence of himself.' ibid., p. 90.

14. Lukács, *Writer And Critic*, p. 9.
15. Ayi Kwei Armah, *Two Thousand Seasons*, Nairobi, East African Publishing House, 1973. Subsequent pagination references are to this edition. And London, Heinemann 1979.
16. Armah, *Why Are We So Blest?*, New York, Doubleday, 1972, p. 222. And London, Heinemann 1974.
17. Soyinka and Brutus, 'Declaration of African Writers', *Issue*, vol. IV, no. 4, 1974, p. 8. Armah's work also has affinities with another part of this Declaration: 'To refurbish and render accessible the reality of an African civilization through works of literature.'
18. Meredith Tax, 'Culture is not neutral, whom does it serve?', in *Radical Perspectives in the Arts*, p. 15.
19. A process outlined (on the theoretical level) by Raymond Williams. See Williams, 'Literature and sociology: in memory of Lucien Goldmann', *New Left Review*, no. 67, May–June 1971, p. 15.
20. Frantz Fanon, *The Wretched of the Earth*, trans. C. Farrington, 1961, repr. Harmondsworth, Penguin, 1971, pp. 117–18.
21. 'We do not utter praise of arms. The praise of arms is the praise of things, and what shall we call the soul crawling so low, soul so hollow it finds fulfilment in the praising of mere things.' *Two Thousand Seasons*, p. 320.

Myth, History and the Poetry of Kofi Awoonor

Thomas R. Knipp

As Africans struggle with the enormous political, social and economic problems that beset their continent, they are also in the process of creating the intellectual milieu within which they confront these problems and define their world and themselves. There are a number of useful phrases that come to mind for anyone studying attentively the creation of this African reality – phrases like 'climate of opinion' and 'usable past'. Of course, there are different climates in Africa, and different opinions, but the process goes on in somewhat similar ways over much of the continent. And the process is mythopoeic.

In Africa, as in perhaps no other part of the world, creative writers and intellectuals have a strong voice in shaping national and continental realities. They are, after all, parts of the ruling elites; sometimes policy-shapers of Cabinet rank, sometimes voices of opposition. Their voices are heard, and behind their words lie the important African realities. Because of his extraordinary poetic talent and because of the force and passion of his criticism and other prose statements, Kofi Awoonor's is an important African voice, and a clear one. In this paper I propose to listen to that voice; to analyse some of Awoonor's verse and prose as parts of the mythopoeic process and product. Further, I want to consider Awoonor's contribution to an African historical mythology and his ambivalent attitude and ironic relationship to the African past and present.

One of Carl Jung's famous aphorisms is: 'Every psychology – my own included – has the character of a subjective confession.' In remembering, every individual creates his own past; in perceiving, he limits and defines his world. This is as true of the collective as it is of the individual, the two being intertwined in reciprocity, and this 'subjective confession' dimension of the collective mind under every aspect – political, social, religious, economic, scientific – is myth.

In casting about for a working definition of myth that would explain the mythopoeic energy of West African literature and the mythopoeic function of a sophisticated, conscious – even self-conscious – artist like Kofi Awoonor, I came across the following in Henry Nash Smith's *Virgin Land*:

> I use the words [myth and symbol] to designate larger or smaller units of the same kind of thing, namely an *intellectual construction* that fuses concept and emotion into image. The myths and symbols with which I deal have the further characteristic of being collective representations rather than the work of a single mind.[1]

Myth, the larger construction that fuses concept and emotion, is usually narrative: a story or a gathering of stories. When these stories are, or purport to be, a chronological and interpretive arrangement of actual events causally explained or connected, they are called history. One of the most useful definitions of history (and historiograpy) thus defined is my own: History is myth; it is the reorganization of the past according to the needs of the present.

The African historical myth within which Awoonor functions and to which he contributes is, in an important sense, a counter-myth; a response not only to experience but to an unacceptable pre-existing mythic interpretation of African experience and the African past, which can be called the white or European myth of Africa. There is an extensive scholarly and polemic literature that deals with this subject. A partial list of authors includes Philip Curtin, Frantz Fanon, G. D. Killam, O. Mannoni and Ezekiel Mphahlele.[2] The following quotation from Dorothy Hammond and Alta Jablow's *The Africa That Never Was* illuminates the process and partly defines the character of this white myth:

> Four centuries of writing about Africa have produced a literature which describes not Africa but the British response to it. The literature persistently recounts the fantasy of the Englishman in confrontation with Africa. As in a morality play, the British and the Africans are the exemplars of civilization and savagery respectively ... The image of Africa remains the negative reflection, the shadow, of the British self image.[3]

This is a myth of conceptual polarities. On the one hand exist those *values* which are white, civilized, rational, progressive (even millennial), creative and European; on the other are the black, savage, instinctual, regressive (even atavistic), destructive and African. Within the context of these perceived values, the history of the relationship between Europeans and Africans emerges as the history of the imposition of European values on benighted Africans for *mutual* benefit.

As it appears in European and American literature, this myth can be and has been, analysed, even categorized. Virtually all the major European writers who concern themselves seriously with Africa function within, and respond to, this myth, including Gide, Gary, Cary, Waugh, Hemingway, Greene and Bellow. White Africans such as Paton, Van der Post, Lessing and Elspeth Huxley are also confined within the boundaries of this myth. Whether the writer functions within the Rider Haggard tradition of heroic struggle against a brutal continent or the Conradian tradition of the search for the unknowable self in the unknown continent, he draws on and activates these mythic values. As an example, Graham Greene, a man of great human compassion and no great love for western technological culture, perceives Africa primarily as a myth and a value system, as the following quotations from *Journey Without Maps* illustrate:

> Africa has always seemed an important image, I suppose that is what I mean, that it has represented more than I can say.

> When one sees to what unhappiness, to what peril of extinction centuries of cerebration have brought us, one sometimes has a curiosity to discover, if one can from what we have come, to recall at which point we went astray.

> I thought for some reason even then of Africa, not a particular place, but a shape, a strangeness, a wanting to know. The unconscious mind is often sentimental; I have written 'a shape', and the shape, of course, is roughly that of the human heart.[4]

One of the most important facts about this myth, this European way of seeing and realizing Africa, is that it has been part of the education of the African elite, including the creative writers. An encounter with the white myth has been an integral part of the process of westernization. The myth has not only reached out to assault young Africans in the attitudes of white teachers and missionaries, it has lain in wait for them in texts, libraries and external examinations. For many creative artists the process of re-establishing a personal Africanness has been the process of seeing – and then seeing through – the white image and myth of Africa. This pattern of experience is most important in understanding the particular ironic tone in much African poetry. The poet has journeyed intellectually into the West. His poetry is a statement of and part of the process of returning from that journey to reconnect with his rooted past. In becoming westernized the poet has dissipated his African heritage and even destroyed it; in returning he seeks to rebuild and reunite. Thus the westernized African is seen as a prodigal. In many poets, including Awoonor, this mythic definition of the self interacts with the longer mythic explication of Africa's past, especially its historical encounter with the West.

Without belabouring the point with excessive analysis and documentation, one can make the following assertion. An historical myth of a primitive and violent continent inhabited by a savage and volatile people penetrated altruistically by a benign and enlightening Europe is more than useless to the Africans encountering it; it is destructive, replete, as it is for them, with overtones of self-hatred and cultural suicide. It is not, in other words, a usable past.

With varying degrees of self-awareness and self-confession, African writers have set out to set this record straight, to create a usable past, to relate and interpret their culture and its past to their own (Jung, again) 'subjective confession', and to define their own relationship to it. Those writers who write about their writing show a high degree of awareness of this process of the counter-myth and of their own conscious involvement in it. Achebe's confession that *Things Fall Apart* was a response to Joyce Cary's *Mr Johnson* is, perhaps, the most famous example. Africans certainly do not all agree on the component parts of the counter-myth (thus there are, if not many myths, at least many mythic variations). The dispute in conference after literary conference between the negritudinists and their opponents is well known. But African intellectuals and artists are united at this deep level of myth-making. Senghor speaks for many when he says that 'Negritude is myth ... true myth', and he exemplifies and vivifies the process by defining negritude and describing its characteristics as follows:

> Negritude is the sum total of the values of the civilization of the African world ... Negritude then was intuitive reason, reason which is embrace not reason which is eye. More precisely, it was the communal warmth, the image-symbol and the cosmic rhythm which instead of dividing and sterilizing, unified and made fertile.[5]

The positive, generative, humanistic quality of this mythic Africa is a very clear direct refutation of Gide's Africa of tom-toms, for instance, and other European valuations of Africa's past and present. The process and content of this counter-myth have been studied extensively, but the best systematic overview of the subject is Claude Wauthier's *The Literature and Thought of Modern Africa*.[6]

In narrative and chronological form — that is, as history — this counter-myth of Africa can be construed as a paradigm, a conjugation of a process moving through time. It has, I suggest, five 'tenses':

(1) The rich black past — sometimes warm, sometimes glorious — in which a secure black identity was and can again be rooted. This rich past exists in a double sense: first as history, as the record of the past glories of Mali and Ghana, of Benin, and Ife; and, second, as the culture, more or less intact and accessible in the villages, of the people from which the poet was torn by the process of westernization (an ugly word).

(2) The cynical conquest of the continent and its culture by greedy and rapacious Europeans.

(3) The period of bondage during which whites exploited Africa and exported the enormous riches that were there and during which the black personality was further purified by redemptive suffering.

(4) The rebellion and triumph of resurgent blacks against often decadent, always exploitative white domination.

(5) The productive and creative future in which African glory returns and African leadership enriches the quality of life not only for Africans but for all the human family.

Implicit in this historical paradigm are a host of cultural characteristics, personality traits, aesthetic perceptions and metaphysical concepts. They are described and interpreted variously by the various advocates of negritude, Africanity, the African personality, and so on. What is important is the underlying unity of the pattern and the process.

Kofi Awoonor's poetic relationship to the counter-myth is both oblique and intricate. It is oblique because his poetry neither narrates nor dramatizes nor illustrates the historical process as made 'real' by the mythic paradigm. But his relationship to it is intricate because, in a sense, he *believes* the counter-myth. It provides him with a point of view, a basis for interpreting both events and literary works. It is the context, sketchily presented, within which he interprets the literature of Africa in *The Breast of the Earth*; and it provides not only the force but the meaning itself of the tropes and motifs of his verse. Finally, it is within the counter-myth that he establishes and maintains his own uneasy, *ironic* relationship to his poetry, his country and (not too far-fetched) perhaps his life itself. Within the counter-myth he defines and carries out his assigned role, the poet as prodigal.

I do not want to twist Awoonor's discursive and critical prose to fit my paradigm, but I think his various comments do reveal an awareness of and a concern for the mythic function and process. For instance, in a presentation at the University of Washington in 1973, Awoonor put forward a number of 'simple propositions' for the edification of critics of African literature. These are mythic; they comprise his own compressed statement of Africa's history and culture. Some key statements are as follows:

(1) Africa has never been a historical or cultural desert. Everything that happens there today comes out of a continuous process of human activity [a clear assertive refutation of the white myth of African darkness and European influence].
(2) There do indeed exist original and expandable ontological systems that define man, his world, time, place, and events . . .
(3) Lastly, Africa continues to expand, change, adapt . . . It restates all his complex personality in terms of its authentic inevitable historical reality.[7]

A further key point of his presentation is not only that contemporary Africa *restates* its personality in terms of its own reality but also that it does this through its artists. Awoonor concludes his presentation with his own 'intuitive and observed awareness of the role of Africa's artists'. The artist, he says, 'celebrates a reassemblement of all things in the journey towards a harmonic order'. He could not be clearer, and the mythopoeic task of the artist could not be more unequivocally stated. Rooted in the continuity of an African ontological system and bearing an imperative to restate the continent's complex personality, the artist *reassembles* all things 'in the journey toward harmonic order'.

That is the aesthetic and critical view of the man who wrote *The Breast of the Earth*, which is a deeply personal book that grows out of the author's perception that 'cultural self-discovery has become an essential aspect of our new quest for self and race' (p. xiii).[8] Although the book is subtitled *A Survey*, it is neither comprehensive nor systematically consistent. Awoonor allows for this; he calls it both 'a personal testament' and a 'salutation'. Its most important omission is an aspect of its personalness. Although uniquely qualified to write it, Awoonor omits any in-depth study of Armah (of whom he does not approve) and also really ignores most of the Ghanaian literary scene. More important, he provides no deep analysis of the politics and economics that have alienated him from Armah, nor does he study closely those forces at work on the continent that have exiled Armah, Beti and Mazrui, that killed Okigbo, and that imprisoned Soyinka, Ngugi and Awoonor himself.

Yet *The Breast of the Earth* is an important book in two ways. This importance lies first in what the book tells us about the works of various African writers. The extended analyses of Tutuola and Achebe are excellent, and the comments on Okigbo are so insightful that one wishes they were much longer and more comprehensive. Secondly and more significantly, the book is important for what it shows us of Awoonor, and, through him, what it shows us of the dilemma of the modern, post-independence African writer. If he does not analyse modern African conditions extensively, he does acknowledge the disintegrative torment of contemporary African life. 'The recent succession of rapid military coups is only a visceral manifestation of a more deep-seated malaise – the inability of Africa to reconcile herself to herself and to search through the debris of her history for the pieces with which to build that true self in her own image' (p. 31). In a very important sense, this debris is where Awoonor finds himself; it controls his perspective and is the *vantage point* from which he writes both his poetry and his prose. It accounts for the irony, the anger and the sorrow in his poetry. And from this vantage point he examines the component 'tenses' of the historical paradigm. Awoonor, the poet-critic-scholar, is standing in the debris of modern Africa trying to piece together the past and the present – trying to make the counter-myth work.

A critical assertion I believe to be both true (or at least true enough) and useful in understanding this complex artist is that in *The Breast of the Earth* Awoonor develops his *version* of the mythic paradigm of African history and that his poetry can be read – partly, at least – as a symbolization of this black myth. Cathedrals of doom, sacred huts and drunken dogs acquire their force and meaning in his poetry from the myth – that is, from the reality Awoonor the African perceives in the continent's past. To extend this, although it is obviously possible for African poets including Awoonor to write poems about anything they want to from traffic in Lagos to pretty girls in San Francisco, they do write much about the African present and the African past. Thus, a working out of the complexities of the historical myth or counter-myth provides a basis for a hermeneutic for much African poetry.

The first short section of *The Breast of the Earth* is a compressed but evocative description of the past out of which contemporary African writers have emerged. Awoonor describes briefly the old Africa – holistic, integrative – which, for all its diversity, was united in a continuum of perception and belief and which had a real ontological centre.[9] This vital, viable continental life was then destroyed by the penetration and exploitation of the continent by Europeans. Awoonor's sharpest criticism in this section is directed at Christianity; the Christian churches, and their missionaries who 'subverted the solidarity and integrity of the African society' (p. 23). The result of this subversion in contemporary Africa has been the emergence of a westernized elite suffering from 'alienation, confusion, and uncertainty'. In a fine clear statement of the devastating consequences of the white myth, Awoonor insists that 'the new African intellectual was produced to deny the relevance of the African personality and culture to the new aggressively "progressive" world' (p. 31). The structure and intention of *The Breast of the Earth* is, I think, clear. Awoonor begins with his interpretive retelling of the African historical myth and then, having established it and having concluded at that point – that vantage point in the debris – in which the fifth 'tense' of the historical paradigm has foundered, he proceeds to analyse selected major African writers and works in the light of the mythic reality. The rest of the book is an account of the struggle of African writers to rediscover or to create in and from the debris their truth, their myth, their ontological centre.

Quite rightly, he recognizes Achebe's pre-eminent success in discovering this centre in Africa's traditions and in Africa's past. Further, while identifying *Arrow of God* as the better book, Awoonor sees *Things Fall Apart*, which, he recognizes, 'seems to have been inspired by a need to respond to Cary's sniggering laugh at Africa', as having the greater mythic impact (p. 262). Achebe's success in both books, however, is rooted 'in his use of African themes, *in the creation of an African past*' (p. 280; my emphasis). His whole valuation of Achebe is based on the mythopoeic force of his novels and on Awoonor's recognition of the myth/counter-myth antithesis.

Achebe is a novelist, not a poet; in spite of *Christmas in Biafra*, this is true. Thus, the focus of Awoonor's critical attention is Achebe's fiction. For insight into his own self-aware role as a poet of the counter-myth, we must study his comments on and selections from the work of Christopher Okigbo, a poet with whom it is clear that he identifies closely. In his critical discussion of Okigbo, 'the most eclectic African poet of our time' (p. 280), he describes him as taking on the functions of priest, guardian and diviner; the functions, in other words, of the keeper of the myth, which he himself accepts in *Night of My Blood* and *The Breast of the Earth.*

In his discussion of Okigbo, Awoonor quotes the entire short invocation to Idoto which stands at the beginning of *Heavensgate.* The key lines are the first four:

> Before you, mother Idoto,
>   naked I stand;
> before your watery presence,
>   a prodigal

Awoonor says that Okigbo's poetry is summed up in the words ordeal, agony, cleansing, and that he 'was a poet of the sacred journey, the pilgrimage'. But this journey or pilgrimage is the pilgrimage of the prodigal; the one who leaves the hearth, who wanders and dissipates his heritage and, only then, returns to be restored and to serve. It is quite clear in his own verse that this is a role that Awoonor also accepts and shares. This concept of the prodigal is the key to understanding the mood and tone of Awoonor's poetry and its relationship to the counter-myth. The prodigal, in the westernizing process, journeys out of the rooted self and then, broken but purged, back to the debris of both Africa's troubled and unstable present and the delayed dream of her bright future, there aesthetically to pick up the pieces of the past to make them the receptacle of the future.

In words he could have used autobiographically, Awoonor delineates the process clearly in his sympathetic summary remark on Okigbo (pp. 224–5):

> An apprentice poet whose path to poetry began with a fascination with the masters of English and American verse and with myths other than his own, he quickly became his own master, gaining power as a poet who returns in his ideas and technique to the oral sources, and combining the function of the poet and the priest, he grew into a clear-voiced diviner whose role as a poet in old Africa has always been taken for granted.

This is a rich description of the prodigal poet and of the vantage point from which he views his African subject and theme. It is from this perspective that he is able to treat the past with loving nostalgia and the future with hope while treating the present with irony.

There is irony in the concept of redemptive alienation (not unlike the doctrine of the fortunate fall and Awoonor is not above a bit of Byronism here and there) and irony in the other component parts of the vantage point itself. Certainly there is irony in the fact that everywhere the debris of the broken dream of post-independence Africa, so sadly different from the hopes of earlier poetic and political prophets, provides the mythic task of the prodigal poet and also in the fact that he is able to heal both self and society *only* after a fruitless journey in search of false (alien) gods. There is irony too in the relation of the African past to the African future. For Awoonor there is no *civilisation de l'universel* such as Senghor found in Teilhard, no collective of the world's workers such as Diop found in Marx; these and other sharp, linear, western concepts of the future are replaced by African and cyclical concepts which turn back upon the past. For Awoonor, as for Okigbo, the medium through which the future finds the past and the past becomes the future is the artist; the poet.

But if the future of which Okigbo and Awoonor write becomes less linear and western and more cyclical and African, it also becomes less clear and more opaque; less political and more poetic. This is perhaps the final irony of the prodigal poet in the debris — and the toughest — that he is not talking about the 'real' socio-political future of African people. He is creating and talking about myth itself. Awoonor comes to know what Plato and Dante and More and Milton came to know. The future tense of the mythic paradigm is not — nor will it be — a society or a government; it is a poem.

Still, in the final chapter of *The Breast of the Earth* Awoonor calls his fellow African writers to their mythic task (p. 355):

> In Africa where despair deepens in the practice of politics and in the lives of the ordinary people, the writer must represent the vanguard of the armies that will liberate the masses from ignorance and cultural stagnation and restore for them their earlier attachment to life.

To this end he instructs them 'to return to the traditional sources of inspiration'. In his poetry he answers his own call.

In narratives like *Things Fall Apart* a novelist can give the entire counter-myth a local habitation and a name. But poets work differently. With Awoonor, as with many poets, it is not the assertions that reveal most truly the attitudes and sensibility of the poet. These are revealed rather in the individual words, the images and motifs, the patterns; above all in the objects that come to the surface of the mind and work their way into the poems. It is these that carry the tone and mood and reveal the poet's valuation of experience – personal and historical – and his relationship to the world in which he lives.

Thus far in this paper I have argued for the following critical conclusions: (1) the existence of a myth/counter-myth dynamic (perhaps tension is a better word) in the perceptions of African 'reality' and in the literary response to Africa; (2) the existence of a workable paradigm of the myth of African history as a process and as the source of African values; (3) the self-conscious and deliberate participation of Awoonor and other African literary figures, like Achebe and Okigbo for example, in this mythopoeic activity; (4) that Awoonor approaches this material and his own mythopoeic task ironically as a prodigal returning from the experience of westernization to the debris of post-independence African life. From his particular vantage point in the debris, Awoonor seems to be working with a Platonic myth: an ideal Africa with an essence, a past and a future, against which the present harsh reality is to be measured. The counter-myth provides not only the standard against which the present is to be judged, but also the basis of hope for a future built on the rooted past; hence the tag words and phrases in Awoonor's critical prose: tags like 'traditional sources', 'earlier attachment to life', 'real cultural foundation' and 'the creation of an African past'. In this context, one demanding cyclical process in which the poet, like the continent itself, must go back in order to go forward, Awoonor's Ewe poetic forms and patterns are not just conveniently available aesthetic structures like the ode or the sonnet; they are a necessary cultural assertion. They speak of essence and identity. And it is in this context that the reader must see the meaning of the paternal instructions Awoonor acknowledges in the poem to his father which he recited at the University of Washington:

> You spoke, as always, of how I am
> the one who must resurrect
> ancient days, raise again those
> misty-glories of men and women
> who linger vaguely in the memorials of the tribe.

The Ewe forms and the instructions from his father are mythic – fused and charged with mythopoeic energy, but they are not talismanic. They do not protect the poet from the ravages of alienation resulting from the journey of the prodigal poet or from the realities of contemporary Ghana, which are the harsh realities of economic inflation, political instability and social disorientation. To the degree that Awoonor's poetry is about these specifics (and it frequently is) it is about the discrepancy between experience and observed reality on the one hand and the mythologized past and future on the other. It is in handling these tensions that Awoonor, like many modern poets, becomes an ironist. And it is important to assert that Awoonor, Ewe forms and rooted past included, is a sophisticated modern poet working with the juxtaposition of myth and reality and the intermixture of belief and anger. The most personal irony, of course, is the irony of the prodigal: of the poet as African and the African as poet. Like Peters's *Satellites*, Pepper Clark's *A Reed in the Tide* and Okigbo's *Heavensgate* (for instance), *Night of My Blood* reflects the prodigal's journey. In fact, the poet as prodigal and the poem as journey constitute the poet in the poem in modern Africa; yet Awoonor the poet says:

> If I had known, if only I had known
> I would have stayed at home
> I would not have gone to them.[10]

But not to have gone, not to have experienced the purging alienation of the journey out and the healing rediscovery of the journey home, would be to have failed to become a poet at all.

Night of My Blood is one of the finest and one of the most important volumes of poetry ever to come out of Anglophone Africa. In his introduction to it, Ezekiel Mphahlele calls it 'the truest poetry in Africa'. I believe that Mphahlele is right, not only because a number of individual poems are of extraordinary quality, but because the poems deal with the counter-myth from the vantage point I have tried to identify and explicate. But Mphahlele makes this claim at the end of his introduction only after having made a number of specific statements about the Africanness of the poems. He recognizes part of this Africanness as the *sorrow* of the continent and its people. 'Here is death,' he says, 'where so many lost children of Africa will be found.' And if there is the theme of sorrow, there is also a tone and a point of view of sorrow: 'his constant sense of loss and bewilderment' and 'the plaintive voice of those at the cross-roads'. But in this context of sorrow there are the voice and action of hope; Mphahlele cites Awoonor's 'plea for the feast of oneness' and his 'groping back, to connect with his father's gods'. If, then, this is the *truest* poetry, it is because the poet speaks at the strategic time when it is most appropriate – most African – to make new resolutions and to return to the old sacrificial ritual. 'It is time to restore the fences perforated by termites.'

Implicit in Mphahlele's introductory analysis and in the poems themselves are the assumptions that certain *values* inhere in the tradition and past of Africa, values that are lost by the alienated prodigal but that, paradoxically, can only be rediscovered and revived by the aesthetic effort of the returning prodigal. These values have a cleansing power. They can cleanse and restore those who 'wander away from the peace and wisdom of the traditional hearth', and they can protect those who remain, but these latter – paradoxically again – only through the efforts of the returning wanderers. The mythic implications of the norms *peace* and *wisdom* in this context are capable of almost limitless explication, but they are clearly the characteristics of the benign state toward which good men strive, and they inhere in the hearth which stands as metaphor for Africa. Those who wander from this hearth not only suffer loss but risk cultural and psychological death.

Mphahlele points out that 'Awoonor's poems supplement one another, and a continuity of theme is maintained'. This is an important point; a volume of poetry is more than a random gathering of poems. Its arrangement determines the movement and even the visibility of themes. A volume can and often does achieve a kind of cumulative theme and statement; it is a whole greater than the sum of its parts. This is true of *Night of My Blood*, which opens with 'My god of songs was ill', a poem which had appeared in his earlier collection *Rediscovery*, and which ends with 'They do not sound for me'. The similarity of statement in the two poems is significant, but the difference is perhaps more so. In the first the prodigal poet finds that he cannot sing:

> My god of songs was ill
> And I was taking him to be cured.

He finds that by returning to his traditions he can rediscover his voice. In the fetish hut he finds meaning and statement (p. 22):

> The cure god said I had violated my god
> 'Take him to your father's gods'
> But before they opened the hut
> My god burst into songs, new strong songs
> That I am still singing with him.

Here the force and meaning of the fetish, the hut and the cure god come from the values that the counter-myth attributes to the African past. Here also the cyclical process of the historical paradigm is indicated by the fact that the poet's 'new strong songs' are generated by a return to ancestral gods; to traditional Africa.

In the last poem of the collection, which begins with 'fetish drums sounding away', traditional African music stands as metaphor for the whole warm, living tradition of African life; but here the title, 'They do not sound for me', suggests alienation rather than reconciliation. The poet asks (p. 96):

> Where are they? Where did they pass
> with these songs
> and drums and gongs and dance?

The concluding paragraph of the poem suggests that, though the poet is not completely cut off from his past, he is still at a great cultural distance from it (loc. cit.):

> Gong and rattlers will sound for me
> O, children of my mother, they do not sound
> The wind and the smoke machines
> they sound in top voice hand beating
> over mouth
> revealing to me always
> The messages of far away.

Within the parenthesis of meaning provided by these two poems of 'loss' and 'reconnection', the other poems – the individual poems – can be read as contributions to the counter-myth, which, in turn, provides a basis for interpreting the statements, tropes, motifs and assumptions in the poems themselves. That is, the counter-myth provides a hermeneutic for the interpretation of the poems.

This can be demonstrated in individual lines and statements virtually everywhere in the collection. Consider the following lines from 'Exiles' (p. 23):

> Should they return home
> And face the fences the termites had eaten
> And see the dunghill that has mounted on their birthplace?

Here the positive image and meaning of Africa's tradition and past are carried by the norms of 'home', 'fences' and 'birthplace'.

'Fences' suggests order, control, organization, discipline, while the connotations of home and birthplace are ubiquitous in the language; however, here they define an Ewe village, not the pastoral countryside of the home counties. And the exiles' departure allows the termites of westernization to destroy the fences of African order and coherence. With the fences down, the birthplace is covered with dung. In 'Desire' the poet receives a cowrie from a villager. This shell, the ancient common currency of many African market places, representing the African past and tradition, also symbolizes the poet's own ontological centre in that tradition (p. 24):

> In the coloured cowrie you hear the sea
> And the throbbing vibrations of your own soul.

The cyclical process of African history and the values inherent in the experience of that history underlie 'The anvil and the hammer', in which Awoonor says (p. 29):

> The trappings of the past, tender and tenuous
> woven with the fiber of sisal and
> Washed in the blood of the goat in the fetish hut
> Are faced with the flimsy glories of paved streets . . .
>
> Sew the old days for us, our fathers,
> That we can wear them under our new garment.

Here, clearly, the old becomes the basis of the new; the old which is 'tender and tenuous and woven of perishable sisal'; the tradition, the past, which comes from the father-ancestor and which must be worn like an amulet or a medal under the garment of the new age. In this poem the interaction of statement and symbol exists only within the value context of the counter-myth. The tender and tenuous past is sanctified by the cleansing (sacramental) ritual of animal sacrifice in the fetish hut, conversely, the goat's blood and the fetish hut itself – savage and unacceptable objects in many 'European' contexts – derive a positive and valuable connotation from the role they play in transforming a rich African past into a hopeful African future.

Over and over again, in short poems and long, Awoonor tells the sad story of Africa's history, usually from the vantage point of the prodigal struggling to reconnect with this past. Myth and metaphor operating together occasionally achieve statements of great compression and resonance. All of Europe's insensitive and destructive

domination of Africa is conjured up in the nine lines of 'The
cathedral' (p. 25):

> On this dirty patch
> a tree once stood
> shedding incense on the infant corn:
> its boughs stretched across a heaven
> brightened by the last fires of a tribe.
> They sent surveyors and builders
> who cut that tree
> planting in its place
> a huge senseless cathedral of doom.

In 'The weaver bird' the rich past, the European desecration and the
elusive future are brought together in one image (p. 37):

> We look for new homes every day
> For new altars we strive to rebuild
> The old shrines defiled by the weaver's excrement.

One of the interesting characteristics of *Night of My Blood* is the
remarkable consistency of tone, perspective and vantage point. The
myth of the prodigal controls the movement of the collection
almost completely, as Mphahlele has suggested. Everywhere are
lines of alienation, loneliness and regret. The following are a random sample:

> Our tears cannot fall
>
> I stood at death's door
> and knocked throughout the night
>
> I am seeking; I am seeking
>
> The sea god has deserted the shore
> Uprooted the yams you planted

Everywhere the continuity of human intercourse in African time
(history) and place (society) is ruptured. Everywhere in the collection the African view of this historical experience is asserted, but
this dominant theme can best be demonstrated by a structural and
thematic analysis of the three major poems in the volume: 'I heard a
bird cry', 'Night of my blood' and 'Hymn to my dumb earth'.
   'I heard a bird cry' is a militant, angry poem (anger is never far
from the surface of Awoonor's poetry) and, in its message that the
future must be found in the structured past, a conservative one.

Although its statement is oblique and its progress difficult, it is clearly related to Awoonor's dominant themes and, therefore, to the African historical counter-myth. It begins with a reference to a tree 'dried in the desert'. Whether this is read as a symbol of African culture or not, the opening image is barren, parched and painful. The poem has many tears and much bitterness; specifically the bitterness of the prodigal who finds on returning home no fatted calf but only a ruined homestead (p. 42):

> I shall leave you
> So that I can go to perform the rites of my gods
> My father's gods I left behind
> Seven moons ago

Upon returning, in an image conjuring up Harold Macmillan and the empire, he portrays both Africa and himself as victims (p. 43):

> The winds of storm have blown
> destroying my hut

The past, to which he wants to return, is in ruins. A series of images projects this vision: 'The fallen walls of my father's house', 'the Smithy shop ... on fire', 'drunken dogs are/Trampling precious things underfoot'. The whole history of the West in Africa can be read in this last image.

The hope contained in the centre of the poem lies in the fact that he, the prodigal, can return to the shattered past and restore it. He can, and he does. Speaking to 'my people', he says (p. 45):

> I put down my white man's clothes
> And rolled a cloth
> To carry the ram's head
> And go into the thunder house.
> When you started the song
> I sang it with you
> My steps fell in
> With the movement of your feet to the drums
> I put my hand in the blood pot with you.

Here is the act of reconnection and reconciliation, to which he brings the sad knowledge of the prodigal (p. 49):

> If I had known
> If only I had known
> I would have stayed at home
> to clear the bush
> That crowded the sacred hut.

But this is the central irony of the African poet prodigal: had he stayed at home, he would not have had the experience and wisdom to make the reconciliation and to rebuild, making the new out of the old. Here too the images of Africa are reversed, refurbished, redeemed by the hermeneutic of the countermyth; peace and wisdom are found in Africa and are symbolized by tropes of drums, blood pots and sacred huts. The poem then concludes with the hope that the past gives to the future (p. 53):

> It was in the season of burning feet,
> And the feast is ready for us.

'Night of my blood' is a poem about a journey; in fact, it is a poem about two journeys. In describing the journey of Africa from the rooted past through the chaotic westernized present to the hopeful future, it also reflects on the migration of the Ewe centuries ago from their home on the upper Niger to their present home in southern Ghana. This is also a poem of hope, not only because it ends with the reassuring beat of the drums but also because the first journey – the survival and success of the migrating Ewe – functions as a counterpoint of hope to those caught in the struggle of the contemporary cultural journey. It is only in this context of historically sanctioned hope that the poet and the journeying people for whom he speaks can cope with the key words which work their way through the poem: the noun 'terror' and the verb 'stumble'.

The movement of the poem is the movement of this journey or these journeys. The people of whom the poet speaks begin in the rooted past (p. 85):

> We sat in the shadow of our ancient trees
> While the waters of the land washed
> Washed against our hearts
> Cleansing, Cleansing.

Can any image of tradition and the cultural past be more of an affirmation – more of an epiphany – than that? In 'I heard a bird cry', while considerable emphasis is placed on the ambivalent role of the prodigal, the guilt for cultural destructiveness is attributed to others – to the drunken dogs. Here in 'Night of my blood' the role of the others is largely ignored. Freely, it seems, the Africans left their past (loc. cit):

> We walked from the beginning
> towards the land of sunset.

Although they are accompanied by the purifier who carries the fly whisk of the ancestors, the journey is heavy with destructive consequences. 'The glories of a thousand shrines' are pulled down and the paths of the fathers are muddied. Thus, writing, as it were from mid-journey and bearing 'the terror of the burden of the journey', the poet cries out for the strength of a continuity that must survive shattered shrines and obliterated paths (p. 55):

> Gather us, gather us unto yourself our fathers
> that we may bear the terror of this journey.

The poem ends with the percussion of hope – the rhythm of the drums – an image hermeneutically defined within the counter-myth (p. 57):

> The drums beat that day and many days
> and still beat for the deliverance
> from the terror of the burden of that journey.

By a repetition of the verb with an alteration of tenses, the poem achieves the final clear interaction of the two journeys. The drums beat then and still beat; and having signalled deliverance once, they promise deliverance again.

It is clear from a careful reading of the poems in this collection and elsewhere (*Rediscovery, Messages*) that there is a distinctive Awoonor stamp to much of his poetry. His lines are compressed and spare with a surface simplicity. His images, references and allusions are to basic human conditions like hunger and thirst and basic human activities like being born and dying, talking and reaching, building and tearing down, defiling and defaecating and, above all, journeying. He deals with the ceremonial accoutrements of African life and culture – ram's heads, fetish huts, blood pots. He 'cries out' constantly to the fathers and the ancestors. These traits, plus the tone of voice of the guilt-laden prodigal, make it possible to identify characteristic Awoonor lines and poems. And, to restate a basic argument of this essay, these characteristic marks of his poetry derive their energy and meaning from a tradition, a myth and a hermeneutic in the development of which Awoonor is participating.

These characteristic Awoonor devices can be found here and there in the 'Hymn to my dumb earth', the longest poem in the volume; but they are not nearly so noticeable because this is an atypical poem in a rather wonderful way. It is a poem of excess; a

collage, rather than a pastiche, of literary allusions, political references, parodies, word play, lines from others of his own poems and
personal experiences. Where in other poems he distils experience
and thought into mythic tropes, here he immerses himself in the
momentary and the specific; here he speaks of Malcolm X, Bud
Powell and his cousin Dede.

   Reminders of other poets and other poems are everywhere – hints
of T. S. Eliot, Dylan Thomas, Joe de Graft and Lenrie Peters. The
overt attacks on the 'party' and on contemporary life and politics in
Ghana are especially like the satires in Peters's *Satellites*. As in
Peters, the topical and specific are handled with flashes of word-
play (p. 89):

> The African personality
> Long live the Party and the Leader
> The party is over ...

The party here clearly refers to Nkrumah's CPP, whose slogan
Awoonor uses in a satiric context. Elsewhere the word-play
parodies both the Bible and Christian hymns, as in the line 'O come
all ye faithless'. And the thematic direction of all this is pointed by
his use of lines from his other poems (p. 91):

> ... if only I had known
> I would have stayed at home

The poem is infused with rage at the facts of contemporary life in
Ghana. He speaks of cynical political leaders, limping beggars and
prisoners brutalized by the police. But the rage is encapsulated by
what might be called an ironic fatalism. Betrayal by the West, by the
elite, by the party and by Nkrumah is presented as inevitable. The
ironic refrain 'Everything comes from God' runs through the poem.
The line is Moslem in its fatalism, seeming to make the people
impotent in the face of their exploitation. Like famine and flood,
Osagyefo and the CPP come from God – parodies of Christ,
Mohammed, and all messiahs. The poem unfolds through nine
pages in this angry, jazzy way; but then, like a new melodic pattern
in the third movement of a symphony, the stately mythic language
and imagery emerge (loc. cit.):

> The love of motherland, oh motherland
> we pledge to thee the tenderness
> of ancestral shrines rebuilt with raffia
> cut by the banks of the Aka river.

Even here, however, the echoes of other poets are everywhere –
Marvell, Okigbo, Thomas – demonstrating as it were, the truth of
his line 'My soul is locked in alien songs'.

And so we have the prodigal groping his way back. But the hope
that seems to underlie 'Night of my blood' is missing. The poem
begins with a shocking image (p. 83):

> The affairs of this world are like the
> chameleon faeces
> into which I have stepped.

It ends as a dirge; a lament for a dead sister/cousin whose death
seems to be the death also of his hold on the old, true Africa:

> Then my mother's only daughter died ...
>
> Ao, my mother's only daughter
> An only child
> She alone, I alone
> Ao, Ao, Ao, Ao.
>
> The beads she had
> Were famished earthworms
> When the sun dries the earth;
> The yellow of ripening guava
> The green of the medicinal avia,
> The blue of the Lagosian dyer's palm
> The red, the flame of the prize cock's horn –
> All, all, all in the rainbow of our discontent.

The poem ends with emphasis on the words *alone* and *discontent* –
and with the final refrain 'Everything comes from God'.

'Hymn to my dumb earth' is an especially interesting Awoonor
poem because it is atypical and because no other poem of his uses
so many specific details of the debris which constitutes the vantage
point of the poet as prodigal. But like his other longer (major)
poems, it derives its force from the body of meaning that inheres in
the counter-myth of African history and experience. He is betrayed
by the party because the party is a product of the corruption of
westernization; he is alone not only because of a kinswoman's
death but because of what has happened to Africa. The implications of this poem are most terrible of all. His own 'African personality', which is found, not in the rhetoric of the CPP but in palm
mats, raffia shrines and his sister's coloured beads, may really be
lost to him for ever. This would be – for him and for all prodigals –

the tragic failure of the myth, the failure of the future rooted in the past, the failure of the fifth 'tense' of the historical paradigm. 'I heard a bird cry', 'Night of my blood' and 'Hymn to my dumb earth' are the most important of Awoonor's many fine poems because they explore the African counter-myth most fully. 'Hymn to my dumb earth' may be the most significant of these because, in confronting most uncompromisingly the pathos and pain of contemporary Ghanaian life, it passes beyond irony to expose the tragic implications of the myth; of the African reality itself.

NOTES

1. Henry Nash Smith, *The Virgin Land*, New York, Vintage Books, 1959, p. v.
2. For a sampling of commentary on the white attitude toward Africa see the following:
   Philip D. Curtin, *The Image of Africa*, Madison, Wisconsin, University of Wisconsin Press, 1954.
   Frantz Fanon, *The Wretched of the Earth*, New York, Grove Press, 1963.
   G. D. Killam, *Africa in English Fiction 1874–1939*, Ibadan, Nigeria, Ibadan University Press, 1968.
   O. Mannoni, *Prospero and Caliban*, New York, Praeger, 1956.
   Ezekiel Mphahlele, *The African Image* (rev. ed), New York, Praeger, 1974.
3. New York, Twayne Publishers, 1970, p. 197.
4. New York, The Viking Press, 1971, pp. 10, 11, 33.
5. Léopold Senghor, *Prose and Poetry*, edited by John Reed and Clive Wake, London, Oxford University Press, 1965 and London, Heinemann, 1976, p. 97.
6. New York, Praeger, 1967. Second English Language Edition, London, Heinemann, 1979. The counter-myth is also discussed or illuminated in a variety of other works including the following:
   Chinua Achebe, *Morning Yet on Creation Day*, Garden City, New York, Anchor Press/Doubleday and London, Heinemann, 1975.
   K. A. Busia, *The Challenge of Africa*, New York, Praeger, 1962.
   Philip D. Curtin (ed.), *Africa and the West*, Madison, Wisconsin, University of Wisconsin Press, 1972.
   Victor Ferkiss, *Africa's Search for Identity*, New York, World Publishing Company, 1967.
   Kenneth Kaunda, *A Humanist in Africa*, London, Longman, 1966.

Lilyan Kesteloot, *Intellectual Origins of the African Revolution*, Rockville, Maryland, New Perspectives, 1968.

Janheinz Jahn, *Muntu: The New African Culture*, New York, Grove Press, 1961.

Ezekiel Mphahlele, *The African Image* (revised edition), New York, Praeger, 1974.

Davidson Nicol, *Africa: A Subjective View*, London, Longman, 1964.

Wole Soyinka, *Myth, Literature and the African World*, Cambridge, Cambridge University Press, 1976.

7. Kofi Awoonor quoted in Karen Mosel, *In Person: Achebe, Awoonor, and Soyinka*, Seattle, Washington, University of Washington, 1975, p. 140.

8. Page number references in the text refer to Kofi Awoonor, *The Breast of the Earth*, Garden City, New York, Anchor Press/Doubleday, 1976.

9. One of the best scholarly assertions of the cultural continuity of Africa is Jacques Maquet, *Africanity: The Cultural Unity of Black Africa*, London, Oxford University Press, 1972.

10. All poetic quotations are indicated by pagination in Kofi Awoonor, *Night of My Blood*, Garden City, New York, Anchor Press/Doubleday, 1971.

The Middle Passage in African Literature: Wole Soyinka, Yambo Ouologuem, Ayi Kwei Armah

Lemuel A. Johnson

Introduction

The Middle Passage in literature is, at bottom, a metaphor for displacement and exile. Predictably, the historical trauma of the slave trade generates the metaphor's dramatic and often decisive points of departure or reference:

> To my mind it all started with the scarlet handkerchiefs ... It was the scarlet did for the Africans. ... When the kings saw that the whites – I think the Portuguese were the first – were taking out these scarlet handkerchiefs as if they were waving, they told the blacks, 'Go on then and get scarlet handkerchief.' ... And they were captured.
> (Esteban Montejo, Autobiography of a Runaway Slave)

> Aye, lad, I have seen these factories ...
>
> Have seen the nigger kings whose vanity
> and greed turned wild black hides of Fellatah,
> Mandingo, Ibo, Kru to gold for us.
>
> And there was one – King Anthracite we named him – ...
>
> He'd honour us with drum and feast and conjo
> and palm-oil-glistening wenches deft in love,

and for tin crowns that shone with paste,
red calico and German-silver trinkets ...

(Robert Hayden, 'Middle Passage')

In effect, whether it be in the elegantly studied ironies and memory of Hayden's poetry or in the casual precisions of the Cuban Esteban Montejo's recall, the Middle Passage has remained an enduring, even necessary, motif in the literature of the black diaspora. Until the politics of post-independence provoked contemporary African authors to outrage and to a near-fatalistic vision of history, the motif had been virtually absent from modern African literature. As may therefore be imagined, its use in the literature has been graphic and accusatory whenever the texts set out to examine the various implications of that context and those principles to which the selections from Hayden and Montejo introduce us. Of course, this intensity is not really surprising, given the literary, and satirical, perception of ancient and modern 'ships of state' in writers such as Wole Soyinka (*A Dance of the Forests*, 1960), Yambo Ouologuem (*Bound to Violence*, 1968), and Ayi Kwei Armah (*Two Thousand Seasons*). This 1973 novel of Armah's is treated here as a climactic dramatization of our theme as developed with slow intensity through his *The Beautyful Ones Are Not Yet Born* (1968), *Fragments* (1969) and *Why Are We So Blest?* (1972). The exacerbated and pointed reminiscence which marks the treatment of the Middle Passage motif in literature is, incidentally, present in other genres. Thus, for example, it is worth noting that the Goree flashback in Mahama Troare's film *Reou-Takh* (1971) is graphic and accusatory. The branding-of-the-slaves scene in Ousmane Sembène's latest film, *Ceddo* (1978), linked as it is to religious and political exploitation, is one of the film's most intensely rendered sequences.

Two Thousand Seasons provides us, accordingly, with a most comprehensive vision of the catastrophic reaches of slavery. We are as a consequence invited to contemplate a multi-form Middle Passage by the oracular *okyeame* voice with which Anoa opens the novel (pp. 26–7):

> Slavery – do you know what it is? Ah, you will know it. Two thousand seasons, a thousand going into it, a second thousand crawling maimed from it, will teach you everything about enslavement, the destruction of souls, the killing of bodies, the infusion of violence into every breath, every drop, every morsel of your sustaining air, your water, your food. Till you come again upon the way.

The Beautyful Ones Are Not Yet Born is rather more concentratedly bitter and plain-speaking. The novel representatively establishes a vision which eschews irony, casualness and the oracular when it parallels the thrust of the selections from Hayden and Montejo. The contemporary political and moral understanding of the issues involved is as a result unequivocally presented in the novel's unhappy sense of historical symmetry (pp. 130, 148):

> And yet these were the socialists of Africa, fat, perfumed, soft with the ancestral softness of chiefs who have sold their people and are celestially happy with the fruits of the trade.

> He could have asked if anything was supposed to have changed after all, from the days of chiefs selling their people for the trinkets of Europe.

We shall return to Armah in a later development of premise and theme.

The Ships of State

> When a trader wants slaves, he applies to a chief for them, and tempts him with his wares ... Accordingly, he falls on his neighbours and a desperate battle ensues. If he prevails and takes prisoners, he gratifies his avarice by selling them.

The above rendition of our Middle Passage context and principals is from *The Interesting Narrative of the Life of Olaudah Equiano, or Gustavus Vassa, the African* (1789). The nature of its focus here serves as a fine prelude to Wole Soyinka's treatment of the Middle Passage as ancient and modern political tragedy. In this Soyinka, of course, parallels Armah. Armah's formulation runs true to form, however: it is brutal in its enraged clarity. Soyinka's also runs true to his own rather distinctive style: though deadly, it seems flamboyantly posed. 'As a writer I have a special responsibility because I can smell the reactionary sperm years before the rape of the nation takes place' (1972, p. 8). The statement of the case does seem rather melodramatic; yet it is most useful, indispensable even, given the several categories in this analysis of the Middle Passage. The focus on conception, for example, anticipates the development later in this essay of two corollary Middle Passage themes: an *abiku* or *ogbanje* motif and the rites of passage implications of that motif. It is, however, the political thrust of Soyinka's concern which is of immediate consequence here.

The politics of the Middle Passage is, of necessity, a politics of villainy. This perception is further reinforced by a literature of contemporary and retrospective disenchantment. Political traumas associated with colonial seduction and autocratic self-indulgence result in a series of character portrayals which emphasize sycophancy and avarice. This is virtually always the case; it is only further intensified by Armah's focus on excremental pathology and by Soyinka's megalomaniac, and cannibal, powers-that-be. Soyinka, however, never quite attains Armah's hard-eyed rage. In this respect, though at diminished intensities, he is more in tune with the orgiastic black humour with which Ouologuem launches his past and present ships of state. Thus, Soyinka's deadliness, early and late, echoes the comic melodrama of autocratic self-indulgence and sado-masochism which distinguishes the 'armpit' scene in *The Lion and the Jewel* (1963). Therefrom comes a portrait of the ruler and, by extension, a comment on the 'stubborn continuity' of a certain political genealogy (*CP 2*, p. 25):

> *(Baroka in bed, naked except for baggy trousers, calf-length. It is a rich bedroom covered in animal skins and rugs. Weapons round the wall. Also a strange machine, a most peculiar contraption with a long lever. Kneeling beside the bed is Baroka's current Favourite, engaged in plucking the hairs from his armpit. She does this by first massaging the spot around the selected hair very gently with her forefinger. Then, with hardly a break, she pulls out the hair between her finger and thumb with a sudden sharp movement. Baroka twitches slightly with each pull. Then an aspirated 'A-ah', and a look of complete beatitude spreads all over his face.)*

The portrait is of one of powers-that-be who 'love to have [their] hairs ruffled well below the navel', as Soyinka puts it four years later in *Kongi's Harvest* (*CP 2*, p. 64). In the early Soyinka of *The Lion and the Jewel*, the fate which yokes victims ('outpullers of sweat-bathed hairs') to predator is benignly contained. When the play ends, the abuse of power and complicity in such abuse are all tempered and diffused in a comically ambiguous fertility dance. The later *Kongi's Harvest* is, of course, unwilling to surrender to such optimism. There, the climactic dance is pathological and is choreographed into a near-literal representation of the cannibalistic implications of political rapacity (*CP 2*, pp. 131–2).

We are thus introduced to what *Two Thousand Seasons* calls 'a race of takers seeking offerers, predators seeking prey. It is a race that takes, imposes itself, and its victims make offerings to it' (p. 26). The Middle Passage motif is unavoidably linked to, indeed depends on, such a race of 'caretakers' (Armah). Thus, the intervening and benign comedy of *The Lion and the Jewel* notwithstanding,

Wole Soyinka had even earlier than 1963 set out to temper exuberance over the political enterprise in the metaphors of the Middle Passage. We see this response in that historical, ironical jab of a parable, *A Dance of the Forests* (1960), which Soyinka wrote in response to a commission to write a drama to be 'performed as part of the Nigerian Independence Celebrations, October, 1960'. In the play, a flashback from a corrupt and blindly naïve present takes us centuries back to the Court of Mata Kharibu (*CP 1*, pp. 46–57). It is a step back the purpose of which Armah's *The Beautyful Ones Are Not Yet Born* makes clear in the succinctness of 'New people, same style, old dance' (p. 156), and in the resigned clarity of 'Endless days, same days, stretching into the future with no end anywhere in sight' (p. 160).

Into Mata Kharibu's 'courtly' drama of political excess and sexual appetite Soyinka introduces the Slave Dealer; with bitter and profound irony, he is offered as a final solution. I have elsewhere, in 'History and dystopia in Alejo Carpentier and Wole Soyinka' (1977a, p. 12), offered the following view of the Slave Dealer and of his historical and moral significance:

> The weight of the intractable in Man and History finally results in weariness ... In *A Dance of the Forests* that intractability in Man and Time is incarnate in the Slave Dealer, scavenger of the roads to Dystopia. He is the perversion which is born when men acquire power over one another, and their instincts are fulfilled.

His ship, by extension the ship of state, is the 'slight coffin into which he stuffs his victims'. Doppelganger to the political ruler, the Slave Dealer is conceived of as an extension of the Emperor's excesses. The connection is underscored when Soyinka makes the Emperor vent his anger against the Warrior with 'Sell that man down the river. He and his men. Sell them all down the river'. For his part, the Slave Dealer insists, perhaps heavy-handedly, on the permanent and transcendent sea-worthiness of his slave ship: 'My new vessel is capable of transporting the whole of Mata Kharibu's court to hell.' Soyinka's political suspicions are all the more emphasized when the play's blustering and opportunistic Historian, grandiose in his ingenuousness, tells us that 'Mata Kharibu and all his ancestors would be proud to ride in such a boat'. The historical vision is an unhappy one; and the play anticipates Soyinka's later expression of concern with 'reactionary sperm' and 'the rape of the nation'.

There is, it now becomes clear, a fateful pointedness to Soyinka's introduction of the Warrior's wife: (*A woman, dishevelled, rushes in, followed by a guard ... The woman is pregnant. She is the Dead Woman.*) History, in sum, is marked and is determined by the 'stubborn continuity' of aborted or mutant expectations. Conception takes place in, and birth comes from, 'branded womb to branded womb'. *A Dance of the Forests's* Dead Woman/Pregnant Woman is therefore thematically and dramatically significant, serving here as a logical introduction to the *abiku/ogbanje* vision of the rites of passage which will be developed later in this essay. Fittingly, her prostrated condition closes the Mata Kharibu flashback, opening the play to the chaotic present. Thus, at the enslavement order from Mata Kharibu, 'Guard. You know my sentence. See that you carry it out.' (*The Woman clasps her womb, gasps and collapses. Sudden blackout. Immediate light to reveal Aroni and Forest Head, who continue to stare into the spectacle.*) And so, the birth of a nation.

A Dance of the Forests's 'Sell that man down the river ... Sell them all down the river' is also of some significance for other historical and literary reasons. Soyinka's flashback is an allegorical and sensitive compass whose 'true North' will be dramatized in the brutal Middle Passage of Ouologuem's *Bound to Violence*. To the south and down the river, a brutal slave revolt on a slave ship climaxes Armah's *Two Thousand Seasons*, as we shall see later. Historically, the compass also points out motifs, slave dealer, slave ship and passage, toward the diaspora consciousness with which this essay begins. Thus, centuries later and farther down the coast from Mata Kharibu's court, Captain Canot's *Adventures of an African Slaver* (1854) strains incongruously after poetic aptness as it provides a passage into Armah's fiction and Hayden's poetry. Canot's ship, with the 'bright, ironical name' (Hayden) of *Esperanza*, is becalmed in West African waters. There follows a scene pregnant with that 'living nightmare' which the literature of the Middle Passage seeks to exorcise – be the exorcism political, historical or, as with the *abiku* motif, metaphysical (p. 207):

There we hung –
A painted ship upon a painted ocean!
I cannot describe the fretful anxiety which vexes a mind under such circumstances. Slaves below; a blazing sun above; the boiling sea beneath; a withering air around; decks piled with materials of death; escape unlikely; a phantom in chase behind; the ocean like an unreachable eternity before; uncertainty everywhere; and, within your skull, a feverish mind, harassed by doubt and responsibility, yet almost craving

for any act of desperation that will remove the spell. It is a living nightmare, from which the soul pants to be free.[1]

Robert Hayden, for his part, resorts to a dark lyricism to capture the sense of history which the various contradictions of the Middle Passage engender:

> Shuttles in the rocking loom of history
> the dark ships move, the dark ships move
> their bright ironical names
> like jests of kindness on a murderer's mouth.

In Ouologuem, the contradictions are bound to violence in a less subtle expression.

Ouologuem's 'Grinning, Tutelary Gods'

> So among us the ostentatious cripples turned the honoured position of caretakers into plumage for their infirm selves.
> *Two Thousand Seasons* (p. 99)

Like Armah and Soyinka, Ouologuem is unrelenting when he traces the political woof and warp in the 'rocking loom' of the Middle Passage. Rather fittingly, one of the praise-names which *Bound to Violence* confers on Madoubo, son of the 'dreaded and magnificent Said ben Isaac Al-Heit', African emperor, is 'a man so strong that with a single stroke of his sword he could split a slave in two or sever the head of a bull' (p. 45). Given the literary ancestry of *Bound to Violence*, it is not at all surprising that 'bright, ironical names' are inseparable from the orgiastic flamboyance with which Ouologuem explores and interprets our motifs.

Heretically exuberant with both Koranic exultations and western thought, Ouologuem's novel, as he more calmly explains it in an interview with the *Guardian*, is an attempt 'to "restore an historical dimension" to the Negro problem. His thesis is that three historical periods of colonialism have been responsible for the Negro "slave" mentality. First, domination by African notables (like his own family); then the Arab conquest; and, since the mid-nineteenth century, British and French colonization. "After all, the white slave trader only proposed – it was the African notables who disposed." [2]

The novel itself resists calm statement, however. It is in the rhetoric of a highly crafted and often grotesque iconoclasm that *Bound to Violence* presents its thesis: 'the rush for that precious raw material, the nigger-trash ... At that early date! So be it! Thy work be sanctified, O Lord. And exalted' (p. 24). There is the same focus on the 'rush' and that 'early date' in Armah's *Two Thousand Seasons*. As may be expected, Armah's outrage is, by contrast, declaratively and fiercely unequivocating: 'We are not so warped in soul, we are not Arabs, we are not Muslims to fabricate a desert god chanting in the wilderness, and call our creature creator. That is not our way' (p. 5). Both writers none the less confront the Middle Passage significance of the alien's 'way'. 'Reactionary sperm' and 'the rape of the nation' are elaborately detailed in the suggestive but succinct identity of 'Hussein, twin brother of Hassan the Syphilitic' (*Two Thousand Seasons*, p. 34) as well as in Ouologuem's series of dynastic agonies and ecstasies (p. 16):

On April 20, 1532, on a night soft as a cloak of moist satin, Saif al-Haram, performing his conjugal 'duty' with his four stepmothers seriatim and all together, had the imprudent weakness to overindulge and in the very midst of his dutiful delights gave up the ghost ... The next day his raven-eyed minister Al Hadj Abd al-Hassana, having established a stripling boy and Hawa, the most beautiful of Saif's stepmothers, in his bed, was stung by an asp which he was caressing in the belief that he was holding something else, opened his mouth wide three times, and died ... His successor was his cousin Holongo, 'a horrible biped with the brutal expression of a buffalo', humped in front and in back; after a reign of two years, moaning in enviable torment, he died in the arms of the courtesan Aiosha, who strangled him as he was crying out in ecstasy. His successor was Saif Ali, a pederast with pious airs, as vicious as a red donkey, who succumbed six months later to the sin of gluttony, leaving the crown to Saif Jibril, Ali's younger brother, who, slain by the sin of indiscretion, was replaced by Saif Yussufi, one of the sons of Ramina ... An albino notorious for his ugliness, he was twice felled by one of his wife's admirers; the third time – at last! – much to his amazement, he was carried off by an ill wind, ceding his place to Saif Medioni of Mostaganem, who was recalled to God ten days later, torn to pieces, so it is said, by the contrary angels of Mercy and Justice. Then the last children of the accursed Saif and of his stepmothers reigned successively: Saif Ezekiel, who was dethroned after four years; Saif Ismail, reduced to impotence for seven months, then forced to abdicate; and the third, Saif Benghighi of Saida, somnolent for five years: as though the Court were condemned to have no tongue but a forked one.

This identification of 'ostentatious cripples' with the 'ship of state' parallels Soyinka's vision, of course. The difference lies, however, in the matter of flamboyance and intensity. For example, the

Kadiye is 'crippled' with considerably more restraint in Soyinka's
The Swamp Dwellers (CP 1, pp. 93–4):

> (The drummer is now at the door, and footsteps come up the gangway.
> The drummer is the first to enter, bows in backwards, drumming praises
> of the Kadiye. Next comes the Kadiye himself, a big, voluminous
> creature of about fifty, smooth-faced except for little tufts of beard
> around his chin. His head is shaved clean. He wears a kind of loin cloth,
> white, which hangs over his left arm. He is bare above the waist. At least
> half of the Kadiye's fingers are ringed. He is followed by a servant, who
> brushes the flies off him with a horse-tail flick.)

The Kadiye is, however, easy enough to detect in any one of the
characters with which *Bound to Violence* explores rapacity. We see
this in the deformed and deadly sensuality of Saif (p. 58):

> There was dignity and strength in Saif's long, slow strides. Smiling, he
> caressed the cutlass under his dashiki and, soothed by the light breeze
> from the plains, sponged his square forehead beneath his graying
> short-cropped hair – the forehead of a warrior far more than of a religi-
> ous leader. A few steps from the threshold, he removed his head cover-
> ing with a somewhat theatrical gesture, revealing an aristocratic, dis-
> solute, and handsome face and the bald crown of his head – a sign of
> weariness or of early debauchery. His thick lips, his aquiline nose,
> indeed his every feature smacked unmistakably of vice.

The violence that results in Armah and Ouologuem is correspondingly greater and more explicit in thrust and form. As a corollary
development, the Middle Passage is spatially and temporally more
extensive in Ouologuem: 'more and more often, unfreed slaves and
subjugated tribes were herded off to Mecca, Egypt, Ethiopia, the
Red Sea, and America at prices as ridiculous as the flea-bitten
dignity of the niggertrash' (p. 18).

The Middle Passage is directly represented as a metaphor for
dispossession, displacement and exile. Ouologuem and Armah
soon enough come to focus on grotesque marches which transform
the continent into endless 'Trails of Tears' and sadism. They all
lead, ineluctably, to final solutions in 'factories' and ships. The
most important and celebrated of these factories, 'castles', still
stand along the 'gold coast' of Ghana. This fact gives to Armah's
political vision an especial immediacy when, as a Ghanaian novelist, he insists that 'the beautyful ones are not yet born', the new
dispensation notwithstanding (p. 91):

> After a youth spent fighting the white man, why should not the presi-
> dent discover as he grows older that his real desire has been to be like

the white governor himself, to live above all blackness in the big old slave castle.

To get to factory, castle and ship Ouologuem transforms his landscape into trail upon trail which are made to cross and parallel each other in bewildering yet indeflexible symmetries. Throughout, the various incarnations of Mata Kharibu repeat his 'sentence' because, like him, they are bound to violence and violation (p. 27):

> When they get to Gagol Gosso, which has surrendered, they ask for food and huts for their slaves; the Chief's answer: 'Sell them.' They sold them. Those whom nobody wanted were drowned to save ammunition. And the march continued, a nightmare.

'Time passes; once more tornadoes send down sheets of water, roads and trails are drowned in mud' (loc, cit.). But, as in *Two Thousand Seasons* where the marches threaten to make of time 'same days stretching into the future with no end in sight', *Bound to Violence* picks up the trail and its victims. A compulsive *right* of passage is insisted upon in spite of wind, water and mud: 'And yet, at infrequent intervals, a caravan traversed those dismal and endless plains: slave traders driving wretched files of men, women, and children, covered with open sores, choked in iron collars, their wrists shackled and bleeding' (p. 28). The novel's vision is unflinching; its point of view is obsessively detailed. Our motifs are therefore sharply etched out with naturalistic insistence in Ouologuem − as compared to the allegorical orientation of Soyinka's *A Dance of the Forests*. Soyinka's 'reactionary sperm' and Pregnant Woman/Dead Woman are suggestive of things that Ouologuem is more than ready to render explicitly (p. 27):

> The children, the sick and disabled are killed with rifle butts and bayonets, their corpses abandoned by the roadside. A woman is found squatting. Big with child. They push her, prod her with their knees. She gives birth standing up, marching. The umbilical cord is cut, the child kicked off the road, and the column marches on, heedless of the delirious whimpering mother, who, limping and staggering, finally falls a hundred yards farther on and is crushed by the crowd.

Before the climactic expression which comes in *Two Thousand Seasons*, Armah's *Fragments* gives a form to these recurrent metaphors of birth and death which makes it easier to elucidate the rites of passage metaphysics in the literature of the Middle Passage. Wole Soyinka's triad, sperm, birth and death, thus comes to full term through an elaboration of the *abiku* motif.

'The Beautyful Ones Are Not Yet Born'

As she buried one child after another her sorrow gave way to despair and then to grim resignation. The birth of her children, which should be a woman's crowning glory, became for Ekwefi mere physical agony devoid of promise. The naming ceremony ... became an empty ritual ... One of them was a pathetic cry, Onwumbiko – 'Death, I implore you'. But Death took no notice ... Ozoemena – 'May it not happen again'. She died ... Onwuma – 'Death may please himself'. And he did.

Chinua Achebe, *Things Fall Apart* (p. 74)

In the silence of webs, Abiku moans, shaping Mounds from the yolk.

Wole Soyinka, 'Abiku'

The Middle Passage concerns, so obviously aimed at birth and death in the political process and at historical commentary, do more than that. The foreshortened cycle of birth and death involved is also seen as a violation of certain metaphysical and biological rhythms which, precisely because of their cyclical nature, make conception, birth, death *and* ancestral reintegration the bases of temporal and spiritual order. In the language of Chinua Achebe's *Things Fall Apart* (p. 115), 'The land of the living was not far removed from the domain of the ancestors. There was coming and going between them ... A man's life from birth to death was a series of transition rites which brought him nearer and nearer to his ancestors'. The Middle Passage in its resistance to such beginnings and endings is a state of permanent exile, a wandering in limbo. In the metaphysics of *Things Fall Apart* (p. 74) we are faced with the incarnation of a 'wicked tormentor' and an 'evil cycle of birth and death'. It is also appropriate here to highlight a sequence of references in that vision of disturbance in the cycle of fertility and regeneration which Wande Abimbola derives from the metaphysics of *Ifa Divination Poetry* (1977, p. 3):

> Pregnant women could not deliver their babies;
> Barren women remained barren.
> Small rivers were covered up with leaves.
> Semen dried up in men's testicles
> Women no longer saw their menstruation.

J. B. Danquah's *The Akan Doctrine of God* provides us with a formulation which integrates rites of passage, metaphysics and politics. We can therefore more readily understand the profane thrust of the politics of the Middle Passage when it turns 'the

honoured position of caretakers into plumage for infirm ... selves'
(Armah):

> Akan knowledge of God (Nyame) teaches He is the Great Ancestor. He is
> a true high God and manlike ancestor of the first man. *As such ancestor*
> *He deserves to be worshipped in the visible ancestral head, the good*
> *chief of the community* ... All ancestors are in the line of the Great
> Ancestor ... Life, human life, is one continuous blood, from the
> originating blood of the Great Source of their blood.
>
> (Johnson, 1971, p. 24; my emphasis)

Armah's *Fragments* mutes the political thrust of the view to
emphasize in the character of Naana the historical and cultural
significance of the rites of passage. The very structure of the novel
is, as a matter of exegesis, better understood in the light of the
perspective which Danquah gives us. That perspective shapes the
narrative and thematic rhythms which unite the first chapter and
first paragraph with the last chapter and last paragraph. As a
corollary feature, the novel's tragic lyricism is more fully
appreciated when we understand why and how Naana's condition
determines its expression. She awaits her grandson Baako's return
from 'exile' abroad; her desire is for a return which affirms 'one
continuous blood, originating from the blood of the Great Source'
(Danquah). But the times are not propitious for a traditional 'Incantation to Cause the Rebirth of a Dead Child'.[3] The novel's frame
therefore stands as an ironic and defiant affirmation of order and
rhythm in the face of the madness which the narrative seeks to
contain. In a sense, in so far as Naana at least completes near-
normative rites of passage, one madness (disruption of the 'line of
the Great Ancestor') is, in fact, contained. Thus Naana, as *alpha* and
omega – and *alpha* (pp. 11, 286):

> Each thing that goes away returns and nothing in the end is lost. The
> great friend throws all things apart and brings them together again. That
> is the way everything goes and turns around. That is how all living
> things come back after long absences, and in the whole great world all
> things are living things. All that goes returns. He will return.
>
> I am here against the last of my veils. Take me. I am ready. You are the
> end. The beginning. You who have no end. I am coming.

The 'line of the Great Ancestor' has, however, been warped, if not
actually broken. Under the pressure of political disenchantment
Armah insists again and again that the rites of passage – conception
and birth especially – have been profaned or violated. In sum, in

Soyinka's inelegant expression, the sperm is a 'reactionary sperm'. Armah is ready to be even more inelegant. He insists, often in angrily explicit metaphors, that birth and anal canals (passages) have fused into a 'marvellous rottenness'. Consider how the motif is developed in the following sequence from *The Beautyful Ones Are Not Yet Born*; we move from what seems mere, even if crude, invective to excremental birth. I resort to full documentation for effect (pp. 9, 97, 133):

> 'Your mother's rotten cunt!'

> The man put out his hands and touched the body in between the thighs, just below the genitals. The flesh yielded too readily, and the dreaded sense of familiarity threatened to return. The hand moved up. The vagina itself was harder, more resisting, almost abrasive in the sharpness of its hair and the dryness of outer skin. Wanting a satisfying moistness of a woman aroused at last, the man pushed his hand farther up and then bent it, searching for the hidden knob of flesh. But the movement had brought his wrist against his wife's belly, and the long line of a scar took the man's mind completely away from any thought of joy.
> The last child had had to be dragged out of his mother's womb ...

> The two men left their women and went off toward the bathroom and the latrine. The cement of the yard was slippery underfoot with a wetness that increased as they got closer to their goal. When they came to the latrine, they found its door locked, and had to wait outside. The agony and the struggle of the man inside were therefore plainly audible to them, long intestinal wrangles leading to protracted anal blasts, punctuated by an all-too-brief interval of pregnant silence. It was a long battle, and the man within took his time ... Finally the harsh sound of the old dry newspaper came at the end of a long, tearing, unambiguous sound and the two relaxed in readiness. Then a small boy emerged.

With that distinctive gift for climactic codas which he displays in each one of his novels, Armah moves to a resolution. A coup has taken place; it is, for *The Beautyful Ones Are Not Yet Born*, merely a 'change of embezzlers'. Ex-minister Koomson seeks to escape, but the only passage open is through the latrine. With a small shudder Koomson lowers his head till it is just above the hole, then in a rapid sinking action he thrusts it through. But then movement stops, for this is to be a battle from which one emerges only at the end of long tearing. This 'last child' (meaning only the *latest* of a breed) has to be dragged out – to be dragged through (p. 166):

> Koomson ... went down the hole again, the disgust returning to share his face with his resignation.

This time Koomson's body slipped through easily enough, past the shoulders and down the middle. But at the waist it was blocked by some other obstacle. The man looked at the hole again, but there was space there. Perhaps the latrine man's hole was locked. The wooden latch securing it would be quite small, and should break with a little force.

'Push!' the man shouted ... Quietly now, he climbed onto the seat, held Koomson's legs and rammed them down. The man pushed some more, and in a moment a rush of foul air coming up told him the Party man's head was out. The body dragged itself down ...

It is obvious that the trails and trials of such passages can not lead to that rhythm of integration and cycle which underlies Naana's vision. What we do have is a heretical birth, in effect, a growth whose stubborn metastasis is from 'branded womb to branded womb', to return to Soyinka's language. This sense of the tragically intractable is an expression of historical consciousness; it is also an invitation to, or a recognition of, the fatalistic. The theme is aptly rendered in the literature which concerns us here through Abiku, a 'spirit child' fated to a cycle of early death and rebirth to the same mother. Soyinka's suspicion that the human condition is beyond redemption affects his use of the motif. The voice in 'Abiku' shows a defiant insouciance in its stubborn continuity; indeed, it mocks the traditional ritual of mutilation and healing (1966, p. 152):

> In vain your bangles cast
> Charmed circles at my feet;
> I am Abiku, calling for the first
> And the repeated time ...
>
> So when the snail is burnt in his shell
> Whet the heated fragment, brand me
> Deeply on the breast. You must know him
> When Abiku calls again.
>
> ... Mothers! I'll be the
> Suppliant snake coiled on the doorstep
> Yours the killing cry.

J. P. Clark's 'Abiku' is a lyrical plea for release from a Middle Passage ('doorstep', 'threshold') existence, an existence exiled between life and death (1966, p. 117):

> No longer then bestride the threshold
> But step in and stay
> For good. We know the knife-scars
> Serrating down your back and front
> Like beak of the sword-fish,
> And both your ears, notched
> As a bondsman to this house,

> Are all relics of your first comings.
> Then step in, step in and stay
> For her body is tired,
> Tired, her milk going sour
> Where many more mouths gladden the heart.

In Armah's angrier contexts when rite of passage thus becomes the 'wicked tormentor' with an 'evil cycle' (Achebe), history is measured by the cumulative weight of an 'unconquerable filth'. It is 'unconquerable filth' quickened by an ectoplasmic and therefore lower form of life, 'made moist and covered over thickly with the juice of every imaginable kind of waste matter' (*The Beautyful Ones Are Not Yet Born*, p. 7). Much like Ouologuem's slave-raiding trails which are marked out in wind, water and mud, Armah's ectoplasmic wasteland seems a natural, and permanent, process of birth by excretion (p. 40):

> More than halfway now, the world around the central rubbish heap is entered, and smells hit the senses like a strong wall, and even the eyes have something to register. It is so old it has become more than mere rubbish, that is why. It has fused with the earth beneath.

Appropriately, one of the cries of despair which bondage to such a state of affairs provokes is 'But slavery ... How long?' (p. 85). But the despair is also a cry of defiance which provokes Armah into a series of extraordinary acts of exorcism in *Two Thousand Seasons*. It is an exorcism of sufficiently effective catharsis to engender his latest novel, *The Healers*. *Two Thousand Seasons*' climax thus comes in an act of individual and collective purgation: a slave rebellion in the very bowels of a slave ship. Its ferocity is responsive to, and is a reflection of, both a curse and a tradition of healing which brooks neither compromise nor charlatan expression. The ritual mutilation to break the *ogbanje* cycle in Achebe's *Things Fall Apart* can thus be conceptually related to that search for release from stubborn continuity which quickens the consciousness in *Two Thousand Seasons*:

> He brought out a sharp razor from the goatskin bag slung from his left shoulder and began to mutilate the child. Then he took it away to bury in the Evil Forest, holding it by the ankle and dragging it on the ground behind him. After such treatment it would think twice before coming again, unless it was one of the stubborn ones who returned, carrying the stamp of their mutilation – a missing finger or perhaps a dark line where the medicine man's razor had cut them.
>
> (*Things Fall Apart*, p. 75)

Conclusion: 'People of the Way'

The extraordinary coda into which *Two Thousand Seasons* concentrates the various features of our Middle Passage theme begins with studied inelegance, and does so calmly enough, in Armah's first novel. Thus, in *The Beautyful Ones Are Not Yet Born*, 'The man thought he would surely vomit if he did not get out from this foul smell' (p. 161). The catatonic melancholia which afflicts 'the man' is further intensified into outright madness in *Fragments'* Baako. That madness, which comes at the end of the novel, is anticipated by the intense response to a mad dog early in the novel:

> On this hot Atlantic day there was something inside the dog making him so cold he seemed to be searching for the whole feel of the road's warm tar under him, and he was turning round and round in circles trying to reach and touch every bit of skin he had all in one impossible movement his limbs and bones were not soft enough to give him.

The child's perception provides the link to that search for a purgative which *Two Thousand Seasons* will soon resolve (p. 33):

> the dog belonged to him and was his best friend in the world ... that he was suffering and shivering with coldness because perhaps he had swallowed something bad that he couldn't vomit yet.

The protagonists of *Why Are We So Blest?* are afflicted with the same bitter and choking need for relief. 'We have swallowed the wish for our destruction,' Solo writes (p. 159). As he tells us himself, 'All my apertures ran with fluid, living and dead, escaping a body unwilling to hold them: blood, urine, vomit, tears, diarrhoea, pus' (p. 114). But this is merely a morbidly suicidal and non-revolutionary consciousness of self.

The stage is thus set for *Two Thousand Seasons* to incorporate the references above into that symbolic and also pathologically brutal act of revenge and purgation with which Armah seeks relief from exile in the Middle Passage. The catharsis extends beyond the demands of our motif, however, to underscore a significant change in Armah's narrative point of view. The morally paralysed and catatonic protagonists of his three earlier novels are replaced by a collective identity and voice, by the migratory 'We' who endure the slave marches and embarkation of *Two Thousand Seasons*. Rage and suffering do not now implode, reducing and trapping the individual protagonist in an in-growing and self-damaging estrangement. The novel is emphatic about this change in perspective: 'How infinitely stupefying the prison of the single, unconnected viewpoint, station of the cut-off vision' (p. 210). The collective voice may thus be seen as a further illustration of what Danquah calls 'the line', or the 'one continuous blood, from the originating blood of the Great Source of their blood'. This vision is strategically insisted upon at just that historical juncture where the Middle Passage threatens exile and separation. We are thus intro- duced to a special 'poetics' of narration. In addition, the narrative mode is a thematic illustration of Naana's rites of passage search for 'the peace and understanding of those ancient words': ''There are no humans born alone . . . A piece of us, go/and come a piece of us/. . . There are no humans who walk this earth alone':

> A human being alone
> is a thing more sad than any lost animal
> and nothing destroys the soul
> like its aloneness
>
> *(Fragments*, pp. 15–16)

For these reasons, *Two Thousand Seasons*, though the most extravagantly violent of Armah's novels, anticipates rather directly the role of Damfo the Healer, with his passionate sense of com- munity, in the new work *The Healers, A Historical Novel*:

> You, Densu, growing up, have been told you belong to the Fantse people, like everyone else at Esuano. No one told you the Fantse people are no people at all but a single fragment of one community that misfortune blew apart. Of that exploded community the Asante are also a part. The Denchira, the Akim, the Wassa, the Sewhi, the Aowin, the Nzema, the Ekuapem – all these are merely scattered pieces of what once came together.
>
> Not only that. The Akan community itself was just a little piece of something whole – a people that knew only this one name we so seldom hear these days: Ebibirman. (1977, p. 62)

Here, too, the roll call and invocation to union are also explainable in categories derived from Danquah and from Naana's lyricism:

> And you, traveller about to go,
> Go and return,
> Go, come.
>
> *(Fragments*, p. 18)

Appropriately, it is when the various trails of the Middle Passage finally converge in the Slave Dealer's 'coffin' that *Two Thousand*

Seasons most powerfully activates the sense of community. The numbing shock of marches and trails gives way to collective revolt amid, as Hayden's 'Middle Passage' puts it, the 'charnal stench, effluvium of living death' of the ship's hold:

> where the living and the dead, the horribly dying
> lie interlocked, lie foul with blood and excrement.

One of the weapons whose 'fluid' preparation we have traced through all of Armah's other novels is fashioned out of long-gathering nausea and disgust.

'With worms eating him so near the surface of his skin', the 'soft-voiced one', one of the slaves, chuckles in the ship's hold: 'I will not reach their destination, I am dead already' (p. 109). He soon appears to be dead, and is then about to be dragged up to the deck and thrown overboard by John, 'zombi', 'slavedriver', 'overfaithful dog' to the white traders. John is, in this respect, a clear enough prototype of those latter-day political and 'ostentatious cripples' who turn 'the honoured position of caretakers into plumage for their infirm selves'. The rejection of this corruption in *Two Thousand Seasons* is, as I have put it elsewhere in a response to another of Armah's climactic scenes, 'what must surely be one of the most brutal of literary codas, one in which all the various levels of significance we have thus far developed are pushed to their narrative, aesthetic, and conceptual limits' (1977b, p. 26).

It begins when the soft-voiced one suddenly, 'and in a movement too swift for the following eye', comes to life. He braces his legs around the slavedriver's trunk. His left hand, no longer flopping like a dead thing, 'took the back of the slavedriver's head while the free right hand groped for and soon found his chin' (pp. 105–6):

Now the soft-voiced one held open the slavedriver's mouth and in one movement of amazing speed swung his own exhausted, emaciated, tortured body upward so that the two heads were on a level, his mouth next to the slavedriver's. The slavedriver gave a shuddering jerk, but the grip of the soft-voiced one was strong. The soft-voiced one brought his mouth exactly together with the slavedriver's and then – incredible obedience to will – we saw him with our own eyes bring up all the bile and dead blood from within his body into his mouth, and this mixture he vomited forcefully into the slavedriver's now captive mouth. The slavedriver ... heaved, refusing at first to swallow the deadly vomit from the sick man's mouth. In vain: the sick man's mouth was stuck to the slavedriver's like a nostril to its twin ... The deadly vomit was twice rejected by the struggling slavedriver. Three times the dying man refused to let it escape harmless on to the ship's wood below. Three times the dying man held the virulent juices, rejected, in his own mouth and throat. Three times with increasing force he pushed them down the slavedriver's reluctant throat. The third time the slavedriver's resistance was broken and the sick man shared death with him. Choking, the slavedriver fell to the floor with the soft-voiced one still inseparable from him.

The revolt that follows is bloody and brutal. 'The twin blows had pushed that askari's eyeballs out from within his head. His body lay prone under us, the tongue hanging out a hand's length from its mouth, the eyeballs fallen so far they almost touched the hanging tongue' (p. 222). The revolt is successful in a way that counterpoints the nature of another man's memories as Hayden's 'Middle Passage' will record it later: 'we were no match for them./Our men went down/before the murderous Africans':

> It sickens me
> to think of what I saw, of how these apes
> threw overboard the butchered bodies of
> our men, true Christians all, like so much jetsam.
> . . . I tell you that
> we are determined to return to Cuba
> with our slaves and there see justice done.

But from that port of call also comes Esteban Montejo's memory of a distant metaphysics and of a broken community, underscoring once again our diaspora framework:

> The strongest gods are African. I tell you it's certain they could fly . . . I don't know how they permitted slavery. The truth is . . . I can't make head or tail of it. To my mind it all started with the scarlet handkerchiefs, the day they crossed the wall. There was an old wall in Africa, right round the coast, made of palm-bark and magic insects which stung like the devil.
>
> (*Autobiography of a Runaway Slave*, p. 16)

Wole Soyinka, Yambo Ouologuem and Ayi Kwei Armah examine the breach of community which the Middle Passage represents, and they respond in various ways to the implications of that breaching of the wall. They have on the one hand written historical works which are expressions of outrage over political foolishness and exploitation. These works are a dark look at the grotesque dance of joy of crippled 'caretakers' over 'rolls of cloth some red as daytime blood, some a deep blue close to the colours of the most ancient of our cloths, [and] other things impossible to give a name to or describe, except that they all shone fiercely in the sun' (*Two Thousand Seasons*, p. 126).[4] At the same time, this African literature of the Middle Passage is also an artistic and conceptual initiation into ancestral rhythms and into that consciousness of man and his condition which those rhythms engender:

> Now too we began to understand descent. We thought of descent of the body, blood line running through mothers, life's creators here. We thought of descents of the spirit, descent of skills passing through experts to novices; descent of the mind, the mental line through teachers, passers on of knowledge about paths, knowledge about the way along which the people in body will be kept together with the people in spirit, the body of our people with our soul...
>   Then began that initiation beyond initiations of which the fundis had spoken.
>
> (*Two Thousand Seasons*, p. 138)

In essence, as Armah in his role of fundi puts it, the literature is engaged in a search for an end to 'absence of connectedness'. This is why, although prostrate in the coffin of the ship's hold, the voices of *Two Thousand Seasons* merge in antiphonal epiphany to underscore the dual vision which comes in the Middle Passage (p. 199):

> 'What will they do to us if we die so?'
> 'They will throw us into the sea.'
> 'Ancestors, this death is so new. We cannot join you.
> We cannot even be wandering ghosts.'
> 'No. This is a complete destruction, death with no
> returning.'

The literature of the Middle Passage is passionately lyrical in its concern and ferocious in its rage. In this way, its purpose and effect are suggestive of the myth in Esteban Montejo's 'There was an old wall in Africa, right round the coast, made of palm-bark and magic insects which stung like the devil'. Accordingly, 'descent' into these narratives of ships, coffins and branded wombs also supply us with a vision of an 'angle of ascent' (Hayden). In their treatment of history and politics, Soyinka, Ouologuem and Armah thus demonstrate their interpretation of that 'special responsibility' which conditions the modern African writer's attitude to his art.

NOTES

1. As in Canot, the following 'calm' precedes Armah's uprising:
   ...the white destroyers were waiting for a wind.
   It came fitfully when it came at all, the wind. Where we were trapped the strongest wind could only reach us as the languid motion of our own used air, but even that was a merciful thing compared to the total stillness of these days. (*Two Thousand Seasons*, p. 197)

2. This excerpt from the *Guardian* is featured on the back cover of the Heinemann edition of *Bound to Violence*.

3. 'Incantation to Cause the Rebirth of a Dead Child', *Poems of Black Africa*, ed. Wole Soyinka, New York, Hill & Wang, 1975, pp. 162, 163.

   > You my child
   > Oludande, you born-to-die,
   > Return from the red soil of heaven,
   > Come and eat the black soil of this world.

4. The common reference to red cloth by Armah and Esteban Montejo does make for an interesting reading of 'Oyeku Meji red cloth is never used to cover the dead' from Abimbola's *Ifa Divination Poetry* (pp. 49–50):

   > A small walking stick goes in front of he who wades through a
   >   foot-path on a wet day.
   > The two soles of the feet,
   > Struggle persistently for possession of the narrow path.
   > Ifa divination was performed for one hundred and sixty four cloths
   > When they were coming from heaven to earth.
   > All of them were told to perform sacrifice.
   > But only Red Cloth performed sacrifice.
   > After performing sacrifice,
   > He started to have honour and respect.
   > After a man has used Red Cloth for a long time,
   > On the day the man dies,
   > Red Cloth is removed from his corpse.
   > Only white and other shades of cloth go with the dead to heaven.
   > Red Cloth must never go with him.
   > Only Red Cloth performed sacrifice.
   > Only Red Cloth offered sacrifice to the divinities
   > Red Cloth does not go to heaven with the dead.

After deceiving the dead for a while (on earth),
It turns away from him (on the road to heaven).

Abimbola suggests something of the sacral danger involved: 'The Yoruba do not use red cloth to cover up the dead. To them, red signifies danger and restlessness. Since what the dead need is peace, it is not surprising that the Yoruba will not cover the dead with a cloth that has any red colour whatsoever' (op. cit., p. 156). Rite of passage and red cloth are linked thereby.

REFERENCES

Abimbola, Wande (1977) *Ifa Divination Poetry*, New York, Nok Publishers.

Achebe, Chinua (1959) *Things Fall Apart*, London, Heinemann.

Armah, Ayi, Kwei (1971a) *The Beautyful Ones Are Not Yet Born*, New York, Collier. London, Heinemann.

Armah, Ayi Kwei (1971b) *Fragments*, New York, Collier. London, Heinemann, 1974.

Armah, Ayi Kwei (1973a) *Why Are We So Blest?*, New York, Anchor/Doubleday. London, Heinemann.

Armah, Ayi Kwei (1973b) *Two Thousand Seasons*, Nairobi, East African Publishing House. London, Heinemann.

Armah, Ayi Kwei (1977) Excerpt from *The Healers: A Historical Novel* in *First World: An International Journal of Black Thought*, Premier Issue, January/February, 1977.

Canot, Captain Theodore (1854, 1969) *Adventures of an African Slaver*, New York, Dover Publications.

Clark, J. P. (1966) 'Abiku', in *Modern Poetry from Africa*, ed. Gerald Moore and Ulli Beier, Baltimore, Maryland, Penguin.

Equiano, Olaudah (1789, 1972) *Narrative*, in *Black Writers of America*, ed. Richard Barksdale and Kenneth Kinnamon, New York, Macmillan.

Hayden, Robert (1975) *Angle of Ascent: New and Selected Poems*, New York, Liveright.

Johnson, Lemuel (1971) *The Devil, the Gargoyle and the Buffoon: The Negro as Metaphor in Western Literature*, New York, Kennikat.

Johnson, Lemuel (1977a) 'History and dystopia in Alejo Carpentier and Wole Soyinka', Afro-Hispanic Symposium paper, in *Studies in Afro-Hispanic Literature*, ed. Clementine Rabessa and Gladys Seda-Rodriquez, New York, Medgar Evers College.

Johnson, Lemuel (1977b) 'Anti-politics and its representation in the Cuban and African political novel: Edmundo Desnoes and Ayi Kwei Armah,' ASA/LASA paper; in press: *History of African Literature in European Languages, Vol. IV: Comparative*, ed. Albert Gerard, Liège, Brussels.

Montejo, Esteban (1973) *The Autobiography of a Runaway Slave* (Biog-

rafía de un Cimarron trans. Jocasta Innes, ed. Miguel Barnet), New York, Vintage.

Ouologuem, Yambo (1971) *Bound to Violence* (trans. Ralph Manheim), London, Heinemann.

Soyinka, Wole (1964) 'Abiku', in *Modern Poetry from Africa*, ed. Gerald Moore and Ulli Beier, Baltimore, Maryland, Penguin.

Soyinka, Wole (1967) *A Dance of the Forests*, London, Oxford University Press.

Soyinka, Wole (1967) *Kongi's Harvest*, London, Oxford University Press.

Soyinka, Wole (1971) *The Lion and the Jewel*, London, Oxford University Press.

Soyinka, Wole (1972) In 'Man Alive', John Goldblatt, the *Guardian*, 27 November.

Soyinka, Wole (1973) *Collected Plays 1*, London, Oxford University Press.

Soyinka, Wole (1974) *Collected Plays 2*, London, Oxford University Press.

Soyinka, Wole (1975) (ed.) *Poems of Black Africa*, New York, Hill & Wang. London, Heinemann.

Armah's Histories

Bernth Lindfors

W hen Ayi Kwei Armah went to live in Tanzania in 1970, some readers wondered what effect this move might have on his fiction. He had already registered his revulsion against human corruption in his native Ghana in the two anguished novels that had established his reputation as a significant writer, *The Beautyful Ones Are Not Yet Born* and *Fragments*, and in his next and perhaps most cynical work, *Why Are We So Blest?*, published in 1972,[1] he broadened the scope of his satire to include mortals elsewhere, particularly the featherbedded leaders of the revolutionary movement in Algeria and the naïve, misguided, racist liberals, white and black, in the United States. It was clear that the attitudes informing these misanthropic narratives had been shaped by his own experiences in the three societies depicted: his years at Harvard, his return to Ghana and his months in Algiers lay reflected in the background like subterranean raw material out of which valuable gems of social insight had been mined and brought to light. The question was: what would he dig up in Tanzania? What could he find to be disillusioned about there? What targets would he choose for his next attack?

There had been some concern expressed by African intellectuals that Armah's vision was warped, that his stony view of African society, though brilliantly lucid, perpetuated the kind of distortion of reality that had existed throughout the colonial era and could ultimately prove harmful to the African revolution. Ama Ata Aidoo, in the preface to an American edition of *The Beautyful Ones Are Not Yet Born*, complained that 'whatever is beautiful and genuinely pleasing in Ghana or about Ghanaians seems to have gone unmentioned'; some of Armah's countrymen, she said, 'could find it difficult to accept in physical terms the necessity for hammering on every page the shit and stink from people and the environment'.[2] Ben Obumselu, commenting on the same novel, suggested that in his reaction to the offensive sights and smells of mother Africa, Armah was expressing 'the aesthetic discomfort of an American tourist' and a 'misanthropic neurosis' that was characteristic of an 'exiled imagination'.[3] Chinua Achebe said that he had found the first novel 'a sick book'[4] and the second 'worse than the first and the third ... worse than the second';[5] he described Armah as an 'alienated native ... writing like some white District Officer'.[6] Toward what kind of social transformation, he asked, could a writer overwhelmed by such existential despair and projecting such destructive, negative images of Africa be committed?[7]

Armah has now answered some of the questions raised about his art by writing two novels which attempt to put the accent on the positive. To do this, he has had to retreat into history, first into a figmental past stretching back a full millennium in *Two Thousand Seasons*,[8] then into the well-documented events a century ago that led to the downfall of the Ashanti Empire, as re-created in *The Healers*.[9] At a moment when other African writers were insisting that the creative artist come to terms with contemporary African realities, Armah appeared to be swimming against the tide by immersing himself in times gone by. Yet his was a Janus-like view for it looked forward at the same time as it fixed its gaze on the past. In fact, these novels are really more concerned with tomorrow than with yesterday or today. They are visionary myths rather than historical chronicles.

It is tempting to read current Tanzanian political ideology into such fictions because the emphasis in both is on brotherhood, sharing, self-reliance and unity. Basic to the argument of each are certain philosophical assumptions: that wealth should be distributed equitably in a society, that the welfare of the community as a whole is more important than that of any single individual in it, that institutions of kingship, chieftaincy or any other arbitrary forms of hierarchical social order that place one man above others are unnatural and exploitative, that true socialism is, always has been, and ever shall be a guiding principle in indigenous African life. It looks almost as if Armah were trying to justify the ways of TANU to man by creating a legendary prehistory of Ujamaa.

The events recorded do not take place in East Africa, however. Both novels are set in West Africa, *The Healers* quite specifically in nineteenth-century Ghana, *Two Thousand Seasons* more generally in a green area bounded on one side by a great desert and on the other by a great sea. The peoples living in this peaceful sub-Saharan haven are subjected to attacks from hostile strangers who invade their territory, taking advantage of their trustfulness, generosity and the internal political divisions that make them vulnerable to foreign aggression. In other words, both books present Africa as a victim of outside forces that it resists but cannot contain. These depradations of the past are responsible for the chaos one sees in Africa at present, and only by properly understanding that past and present will Africans collectively be able to tackle the problems of the future: how to get the victim back on its feet, how to raise the materially oppressed and down-trodden, how to heal the spiritually sick. Instead of merely cursing various symptoms of the colonial disease, as he had done in his first three books, Armah now wants to work towards effecting a cure.

The strategy in *Two Thousand Seasons* is to take the longest possible view by moving backwards in time to that distant point when an alien civilization first impinged upon African existence. According to Armah, this would have been the period of the Arab incursion into the Sudanic grasslands, the aboriginal home of happy, self-sufficient African communities. Armah calls the Arabs 'predators', saying they first came out of the desert in the guise of parasitic beggars and then, after being sustained and nursed to greater strength by their African hosts who were by nature noble, hospitable and far too charitable, they turned their innate fury against these very benefactors, massacring and enslaving them. The predators, their minds debased by a perverted religion, their bodies yearning for every variety of sybaritic self-gratification, were capable only of depravity and destruction. Whatever they touched, they maimed or killed. The Arab way was the way of annihilation, of absolute obliteration of all that was good, whole-some and creative. For them (pp. 62–3):

> force is goodness. Fraud they call intelligence ... In their communion there is no respect, for to them woman is a thing, a thing deflated to fill each strutting, mediocre man with a spurious, weightless sense of worth. With their surroundings they know but one manner of relation-ship, the use of violence. Against other peoples they recommend to each other the practice of robbery, cheating, at best a smiling dishon-esty. Among them the sphere of respect is so shrunken they themselves have become sharp-clawed desert beasts, preying against all.
>
> They plant nothing. They know but one harvest: rape. The work of nature they leave to others: the careful planting, the patient nurturing. It is their vocation to fling themselves upon the cultivator and his fruit, to kill the one, to carry off the other. Robbery with force: that is the predators' road, that is the white destroyers' road.

Contact with so pathological an evil inevitably led some suscep-
tible Africans to follow the predators' road. This they did by becoming devotees of the new religion, or by trying to raise themselves above others through displays of impressive splendour, or
simply by enforcing the slave laws of the conquerors. Armah has a
name for each traitorous group: the first he calls 'zombis', the
second 'ostentatious cripples', the third 'askari zombis'. The initial
schism in African society thus developed as a consequence of the
Arab invasion and the concomitant spread of Islam. Africans who
had been won over to the new faith or who had chosen to serve the
conquerors turned against their own kith and kin.

The more resilient Africans, those who steadfastly refused to be
converted or corrupted by the new forces in their world, decided
that the best way to counter such disintegrative pressures was not
to confront them in a suicidal counter-attack but rather to remove
themselves from the sphere of their harmful influence. So a migration took place – long, arduous, lasting many seasons, covering
great distances. Grassland gradually gave way to forest and swamp,
and the pilgrims, archetypal refugees from religious and political
oppression, finally reached their promised land a short distance
from the sea. Here they hoped to be left undisturbed by marauders,
but almost immediately they met a new alien force – the white
invaders from the sea.

These European 'destroyers' turned out to be even worse than the
Arab 'predators', for their unlimited greed was backed by a tech-
nology of death more devastating than anything Africa had pre-
viously known. At one point a spokesman summed up the base
desires of these monsters (pp. 130–1):

> The white men wish us to destroy our mountains, leaving ourselves
> wastes of barren sand. The white men wish us to wipe out our animals,
> leaving ourselves carcases rotting into white skeletons. The white men
> want us to take human beings, our sisters and our sons, and turn them
> into labouring things. The white men want us to take human beings, our
> daughters and our brothers, and turn them into slaves. The white men
> want us to obliterate our remembrance of our way, the way, and in its
> place to follow their road, road of destruction, road of a stupid, childish
> god.

To accomplish these goals the white men offered African kings and
their courtiers worthless, glittering gifts, thereby bribing them with
trinkets to collaborate in the enslavement of their own people.

The rest of the novel focuses on one small band of Africans who
get sold to European slave traders but stage a successful shipboard

revolt and then form themselves into a pioneer liberation army which wreaks vengeance against the white destroyers and their black lackeys. This group of guerrillas, self-trained and splendidly disciplined, dedicates itself to the destruction of Africa's enemies, the most creative vocation possible for freedom fighters intent on purging their world of the debilitating malignancies inflicted upon it by European and Arab imperialism.

It is an interesting scenario and a fascinating contrast to Armah's earlier fiction. Instead of watching one man struggle fruitlessly to maintain his purity or sanity in an atmosphere of rank corruption, we see a communal group, activated by the highest ideals, actually *succeed* in their military manoeuvres against extraordinarily powerful antagonists. Instead of witnessing the anguish of a doomed, fragmented individual, we are shown the joy of a mini-tribe united in the struggle against evil. Instead of existential despair, there is revolutionary hope. Instead of defeat, victory.

But the optimism in Armah's new view of man and society in Africa is predicated on certain assumptions which it is difficult to credit as reasonable. Foremost among these is the belief that Africa, before being polluted by contact with the outside world, was a Garden of Eden, at least in terms of social organization. People lived in harmonious communities, sharing the fruits of their labour and never striving to compete against their neighbours for the acquisition of superior status or material goods. Rulers did not exist; the communities were acephalous, completely democratic and devoted to the principle of reciprocity. This principle was the very essence of what Armah calls 'our way, the way'. Here it is in one of its most compact formulations (p. 62):

> Our way is reciprocity. The way is wholeness. Our way knows no oppression. The way destroys oppression. Our way is hospitable to guests. The way repels destroyers. Our way produces before it consumes. The way produces far more than it consumes. Our way creates. The way destroys only destruction.

So Africans were a creative, productive, hospitable, non-oppressive, healthy and sharing people – until the invaders came. Africans should now strive to return to 'our way, the way' by destroying the destroyers of their former paradise.

The villains in this stark melodrama are portrayed as the obverse of the heroes. This may be a dramatic necessity, in as much as one needs very potent Manichean forces to overwhelm such a superabundance of virtue as is said to have existed in prehistoric

Africa. But it also assumes that entire races of people can be reduced to the level of primal forces, that one can be characterized as inherently predisposed towards good, another addicted to evil. This kind of xenophobic oversimplification used to be found in B-grade films manufactured in Hollywood during the Second World War, in which fanatical kamikaze pilots and fat, stupid, goose-stepping German generals represented all that was reprehensible in the world. The 'Japs' and 'Krauts' in such celluloid fantasies performed essentially the same function as the 'predators' and 'destroyers' in Armah's fiction: they were crude, simplistic symbols towards which a chauvinistic audience could direct the energy of its hatred while waiting for the satisfying *dénouement* in which vice would be vanquished and virtue rewarded. The good guys might lose a few battles but they always won the war.

The trouble with Armah's cartoon history of Africa is that it ultimately is not a positive vision, even though it promises future happiness. All it really offers is negation of negation. The most creative act imaginable is destruction of the destroyers. The last pages of *Two Thousand Seasons* reiterate this theme with evangelical fervour (pp. 316–20):

> Destruction of destruction is the only vocation of the way ... The liberator is he who from a necessary silence, from a necessary secrecy strikes the destroyer ... Nothing good can be created that does not of its very nature push forward the destruction of the destroyers ... Whatever thing, whatever relationship, whatever consciousness takes us along paths closer to our way, whatever goes against the white destroyers' empire, that thing only is beautiful, that relationship only is truthful, that consciousness alone has satisfaction for the still living mind.

This is a philosophy of paranoia, an anti-racist racism – in short, negritude reborn. In place of a usable historical myth, *Two Thousand Seasons* overschematizes the past, creating the dangerous kind of lie that Frantz Fanon used to call a 'mystification'.

Compare, for example, Armah's treatment of history with Chinua Achebe's. In *Things Fall Apart* and *Arrow of God* Achebe shows us complex human beings entangled in a web of circumstances that ultimately brings disaster to rural Igbo society. The individuals portrayed cannot be divided into two camps – the saints versus the sinners – but rather can be recognized as quite ordinary people motivated by fairly commonplace ambitions and desires. Moreover, the communities in which they live are not perfect or even remotely perfectable; they are rife with conflicts ranging from the petty to the profound, conflicts which are exacerbated when an alien civilization intrudes into their relatively encapsulated world. The ensuing interaction between Europe and Africa is not really a species of all-out war but rather an uneasy, and at times unpeaceful, coexistence of differing world-views in which the inability of one side to comprehend the perspective of the other precipitates tragedy. Achebe perceives that it was a failure of communication, not an absence of humanity, that was responsible for certain of the catastrophes of the colonial period. In documenting the numerous ironies of this confused era with such compassion and lucidity, Achebe proves a more convincing historian than Armah. Achebe deeply understands ethnocentrism, whereas Armah shallowly advocates it.

In his latest novel *The Healers* Armah moves a step closer to fleshing out his nightmare vision of the past by substituting concrete substance for abstract symbol. If *Two Thousand Seasons* was his theory of history, *The Healers* is an adumbration of the theory using actual recorded events as proof of the hypotheses advanced. Armah takes the fall of the Ashanti Empire as emblematic of Africa's destruction, and he attributes the calamity not only to the rapacity of the West but also to the disunity within Africa itself. It is towards the reunification of Africa tomorrow that Africans must work today if they wish to repair the damage done yesterday. History is again seen as a guide to a better future.

The novel itself is unified by the imagery of disease. Africa has been prostrated by a foreign plague against which it had no natural immunity, and some of its members, infected beyond all possibility of recovery, have turned against the parent body itself, spreading the disabling disorder still further. Any manifestation of division in society is regarded as a symptom of the malady, a crippling indisposition requiring a cure.

Notice how smoothly this imagery of illness is employed to elucidate Armah's underlying political philosophy in the following passage (pp. 100–1):

Healing an individual person – what is that but restoring a lost unity to that individual's body and spirit?
   A people can be diseased the same way. Those who need naturally to be together but are not, are they not a people sicker than the individual body disintegrated from its soul? Sometimes a whole people needs healing work. Not a tribe, not a nation. Tribes and nations are just signs that the whole is diseased. The healing work that cures a whole people is the highest work, far higher than the cure of single individuals ...
   The ending of all unnatural rifts is healing work. When different

groups within what should be a natural community clash against each other, that also is disease. That is why healers say that our people, the way we are now divided into petty nations, are suffering from a terrible disease.

Fortunately, there are a few remarkably perceptive hermits living a pure life on the fringes of this sick society who are devoted to the art of healing. They function simultaneously as physicians, psychoanalysts and social theorists, for they are committed not only to restoring the physical and mental health of ailing individuals but also to purging the body politic of all its ills. Because they possess the ability to see, hear, understand and act more truly than ordinary human beings, they are the seers and prophets who can lead Africa back to wholeness (p. 102):

> A healer needs to see beyond the present and tomorrow. He needs to see years and decades ahead. Because healers work for results so firm they may not be wholly visible till centuries have flowed into millennia. Those willing to do this necessary work, they are the healers of our people.

Naturally, Densu, the hero of the novel, is one of these, or rather is an idealistic young man who, aspiring to join this elite fraternity, begins to undergo the long process of initiation and apprenticeship required. Certainly he seems to have all the necessary qualifications. Intelligent, sensitive, honest, courageous, hardy, persevering, self-sacrificing, totally dedicated, yet becomingly modest about his many prodigious achievements, he is the model pre-med. student, the pluperfect seer-in-training. One searches in vain for the tiniest flaw in his character.

At this point one is tempted to pause and ask why so many of Armah's heroes are of this saintly breed. Why does he feel compelled to make his protagonists supermen? Are such beautiful ones ever born? Is Armah bent on creating a new type of utopian fiction? Or is he merely rewriting a modern secular version of *The Pilgrim's Progress* in which an upright unChristian soldier, beset by numerous temptations, goes singlemindedly marching on to social salvation, never veering from the straight and narrow path, 'our way, the way'?

Densu, a bit younger than most of Armah's puritanical protagonists, is introduced to us as an unsullied boy scout. In village games testing physical and mental prowess, he invariably is the overall champion, losing only when he defaults by refusing to participate in wrestling and pigeon shooting – violent sports that violate his higher moral principles. It is true that he is beaten in a few short sprints by a more muscular Adonis, but he reigns supreme in the long-distance races demanding greater stamina and controlled efficiency of effort. However, even though he is a consistent winner, he dislikes such competitions because they set one individual against another – indeed, against his whole community. Densu, you see, believes in equality, brotherhood and reciprocity, not in individual achievement. But Armah lets us know that there is no prize, no merit badge that this paragon, born of noble blood, could not win if he really wanted to. Some socialists, as Orwell pointed out long ago, are more equal than others.

Densu serves his apprenticeship under Damfo, a master healer and supreme scoutmaster who lives, significantly, in the *eastern* forest. Damfo teaches him the seven commandments of the healer's faith and helps him to distinguish between two crucial concepts: 'inspiration' and 'manipulation' (p. 99):

> The healer devotes himself to inspiration. He also lives against manipulation [which is] a disease, a popular one. It comes from spiritual blindness. If I'm not spiritually blind, I see your spirit. I speak to it if I want to invite you to do something with me. If your spirit agrees it moves your body and your body acts. That's inspiration. But if I'm blind to your spirit I see only your body. Then if I want you to do something for me I force or trick your body into doing it even against your spirit's direction. That's manipulation. Manipulation steals a person's body from his spirit, cuts the body off from its own spirit's direction. The healer is a lifelong enemy of all manipulation. The healer's method is inspiration.

The major manipulators, of course, are the local court politicians and foreign imperialists whose greed is dividing Africa against itself. Discord and disunity are seen as by-products of the kind of political system that sets one man above others, that concentrates power in the hands of a few. Even the healers themselves are cautioned by Damfo against the dangers of elitism and power politics in their own work (p. 329):

> We healers do not fear power. We avoid power deliberately, as long as that power is manipulative power. There is a kind of power we would all embrace and help create. It is the same power we use in our work: the power of inspiration. The power that respects the spirit in every being, in every thing, and lets every being be true to the spirit within. Healers should embrace that kind of power. Healers should help create that kind of power. But that kind of power – the power that comes

from inspiration – can never be created with manipulators. If we healers allow the speedy results of manipulation to attract us, we shall destroy ourselves and more than ourselves, our vocation ... Are we forgetting that for healers the meaning of the span of life takes in our whole people, not just our single separate lives?

So the struggle continues, not just here and now, but for generations to come. It may take another two thousand seasons for Africa to be healed through the power of inspiration.

It is clear that Armah himself wants to assist in the healing process. The role of the writer, he seems to be saying, is to inspire Africa to be true to its own spirit so it can be reunited as the harmonious community it once was before the predators and destroyers came. This is a noble goal, even if the 'paradise lost' theme is rather naïve as an interpretation of human history. Armah evidently is trying to do something constructive in his fiction, something far more positive than he had done in his first three novels. Giving Africa a new, clean image of itself is a much more wholesome occupation than rubbing its nose in dung.

And, indeed, The Healers is a better-balanced book, a saner piece of fiction, than Two Thousand Seasons. Gone, but not totally forgotten, are the Arab and European demons who were objects of such intense hatred in Armah's earlier venture into history. Gone, too, are the scenes of sexual perversion and the almost Homeric descriptions of bloodshed, gore and corporeal mutilation, descriptions which told in gleeful, gloating detail exactly where a bullet or blade entered an enemy's body and where it exited. Gone as well is the over-idealized band of forest guerrillas, those glamorous outlaws descended from a romantic blend of Mao, Mau Mau and Robin Hood, who, instead of offering the reader some semblance of fidelity to African life, gave imaginary life to African fidelity. Gone, in short, are the delirious fantasies that pushed Two Thousand Seasons beyond the dimensions of viable myth into the wilder liberties of nightmare.

The Healers, it must be admitted, also has its good guys and bad guys, its heavy-handed moralizing and its propensity to force history to fit a predetermined ideological paradigm, but it is not a harmful book to put into the hands of young people. For one thing, it does not encourage xenophobia. For another, it emphasizes creativity ('inspiration') rather than destruction. And by concentrating on real events and weaving fiction into the fabric of fact, it could help young Africans to reshape their perspective on the past and come to a better understanding of the world in which they currently live. In other words, it offers an interpretation of human experience that seems valid because it is rooted in an imaginable reality.

Yet it is still a cartoon, still comic-strip history. It will not persuade many adults because it falsifies far more than it authenticates and in the process fails to avoid the pitfalls of oversimplification. Nevertheless, some grown-ups will be able to enjoy it at the level of popular fiction, for it is good cops-and-robbers, cowboys-and-indians stuff. It even includes a murder mystery to bait the reader's interest. But basically it is juvenile adventure fiction of the *Treasure Island* or *King Solomon's Mines* sort, the only major difference being that it is thoroughly *African* juvenile adventure fiction. Densu is the new Jim Hawkins or Allan Quatermain, the young man with whom generations of schoolchildren will readily be able to identify. And he is a fine model for them, a decent and wholesome youth who, as Mark Twain is alleged to have said of James Fenimore Cooper's heroes, never gets his hair mussed and never farts. If the mission schools could somehow manage to forgive or forget Densu's tumbles in the grass with Ajoa, sales to high schools could be quite brisk. It might even become a set book for school certificate exams.

I am not saying this to belittle the novel's importance. Obviously, *The Healers* is a major attempt by a major African writer to reinterpret a major event in African history. But I think it will have its major impact on young people, and this is as it should be in any remythologizing of Africa. One must aim at winning the hearts and minds of the young, imbuing them with the highest ideals and making them proud and happy to be Africans. This *The Healers* does better than any other novel Armah has written. And this is why it is potentially his most important book and certainly his healthiest. One can no longer complain that his vision is warped or his art sick.

So the Tanzanian years have been good ones for Armah, helping him to emerge from the destructive negativeness of cynicism and despair, turning him in a more confident, affirmative direction. The would-be healer gives signs of having himself been cured. One waits now to see what the Lesotho years will bring.

NOTES

1. This novel, which Armah started writing in Ghana in the mid-1960s, was not completed until after he had arrived in Tanzania in August 1970. Since it was published in 1972, and since Armah began writing *Two Thousand Seasons* in October 1971, one can assume that much of *Why Are We So Blest?* had been written in the 1960s and that Armah was able to finish it during his first year in Tanzania. In other words, it does not owe its inspiration to his Tanzanian experience in quite the same way as the next two novels apparently do.

    Biographical information on Armah can be found in his essay 'Larson, or fiction as criticism of fiction', *First World*, vol. 1, no. 2, 1977, pp. 50–5. This essay has been reprinted in *Asemka*, 4, 1976, pp. 1–14; *New Classic*, 4, 1977, pp. 33–45; and *Positive Review*, 1, 1978, pp. 11–14. The period during which *Two Thousand Seasons*, Nairobi, East African Publishing House, 1973, London, Heinemann, 1979, was written is recorded on page 321 of that novel.

2. Ama Ata Aidoo, Introduction to *The Beautyful Ones Are Not Yet Born*, New York, Collier-Macmillan, 1969, p. xii.

3. Ben Obumselu, 'Marx, politics and the African novel', *Twentieth Century Studies*, 10, 1973, pp. 114–16.

4. Chinua Achebe, 'Africa and her writers', in *Morning Yet on Creation Day*, London, Heinemann, 1975, p. 25. The same essay appears in a slightly different form in *In Person: Achebe, Awoonor and Soyinka at the University of Washington*, ed. Karen Morell, Seattle, African Studies Program, Institute for Comparative and Foreign Area Studies, University of Washington, 1975, pp. 3–23.

5. 'Class Discussion', in Morell, op. cit., p. 52.

6. Achebe, op. cit., p. 26; Morell, op. cit., pp. 15–16.

7. Chinua Achebe, 'Panel on Literature and Commitment in South Africa', *Issue*, vol. 6, no. 1, 1976, p. 37.

8. *Two Thousand Seasons*, Nairobi, East African Publishing House, 1973. All quotations are taken from this edition. London, Heinemann, 1979.

9. *The Healers*, Nairobi, East African Publishing House, 1978. All quotations are taken from this edition. London, Heinemann, 1979.

'As Grasshoppers to Wanton Boys': The Role of the Gods in the Novels of Elechi Amadi

Niyi Osundare

Elechi Amadi's treatment of the supernatural is remarkable but not unique. Nearly all African novelists portray man as existing in mutual co-operation with other men, and in communion with the gods. This communion and co-operation between the human and the divine is important, and indeed, indispensable, for the realization of what Soyinka (1976, p. 3) describes as 'cosmic totality', a relationship compounded by fellow men and supernatural essences, a relationship that is particularly vital for the African world-view.

However, in no other Nigerian novels have the gods been more dominant than in those of Amadi. Here the gods, uncanny, implacable and ubiquitous, are not only an essence but a presence, woven as it were into every aspect of human relationship. In *The Concubine*, the sea-king intervenes even before the beginning of the story, and throughout remains the paramount but unseen force manipulating human life and orchestrating the painful course of men's tragic drama. The dreaded Ogbunabali breaks in halfway through *The Great Ponds*, and thereafter his power dominates human thought and action and pilots the very movement of the story. Consequently, in a vein reminiscent of early Greek tragedy and Victorian fiction, fatalism and its episodic surrogates of coincidence, omens and premonitions loom large in the narrative. My task in this essay is to examine how these and other supernatural forces shape human action and situations, and control the very plot and structure of Amadi's novels.

In both The Concubine and The Great Ponds, the supremacy of the gods is openly acknowledged. In the latter novel, Olumba's deferential adulation of the gods is something of a sonorous and tragically ironic refrain: 'I would rather face a whole village in battle than have the weakest of the gods after me' (p. 3). In The Concubine, the dibia, as veritable mediums between man and god, constantly remind the inhabitants of Omokachi about the potency of the gods. Emphasis, therefore, shifts from human action to divine action. In The Concubine, especially, human characters are, to use Lattimore's words, 'puppets moved by creatures of over-whelmingly superior force' (1969, p. 38). Ihuoma, wife of a sea-god before her reincarnation into human form, becomes the uncon-scious tool of a man-killing god. She has all the qualities to attract men to her, and through her to their death. She is beautiful, level-headed, liberal-minded and finickily decent. Her godly virtues are unconsciously acknowledged by Ekwueme when he confesses, 'You are above any form of ridicule, Ihuoma' (p. 197) and by the author when he comments (p. 199):

> As her prestige mounted its maintenance became more trying. She became more sensitive to criticism and would go to any lengths to avoid it. The women adored her. Men were awestruck before her. She was becoming something of a phenomenon.

The sea-king has therefore chosen an extraordinary bait to lure men to their death. And his catch is the cream of the village manhood. First Emenike, a handsome, hard-working and considerate young man, next Madume, who gets more than he deserves for his 'big eye', and lastly Ekwueme, a promising young singer and trapper whose relationship with Ihuoma forms the crux of the tragedy in The Concubine.

The very moment Ekwueme gets interested in Ihuoma, he becomes a 'marked' man, a mortal involved in tragic rivalry with a god. Ekwueme's reluctant marriage to Ahurole merely causes a temporary postponement of his fate. In fact, the failure of this marriage and Ekwueme's consequent return to Ihuoma is traceable to both human and divine causes. Ahurole is a peevish young girl who stands as a clear foil to Ihuoma. While the former is too old for her behaviour, the latter is too mature for her age, thereby satisfying Ekwueme's quest for a mother-figure. Moreover, in a bid to attract her husband's heart from Ihuoma, Ahurole and her mother seek a supernatural means which, ironically, engenders the collapse of Ahurole's marriage and a further deepening of Ekwueme's involvement with Ihuoma.

A number of questions arise from the collapse of the Ekwueme–Ahurole marriage and Ekwueme's later insanity. What kind of 'potion' did the *dibia* of Chiolu give to Ahurole? Is it the right love potion which only turns Ekwueme's head because he is subconsciously in love with someone else? Whatever may be the answer to these questions, Ahurole, her mother and the *dibia* are all tools of an 'overwhelmingly superior force', and Ahurole must be promptly removed as she seems to stand between Ekwueme and destiny. With Ahurole out of the way, the road is clear for Ekwueme to take possession of Ihuoma, beloved of a god. The painful irony here is that Ekwueme has broken off with a girl chosen according to human mores to be his wife, and has continued his pursuit of a woman who, by divine ordination, will lead him not into the matrimony he desires but a painful death he least expects.

Every event in *The Concubine* works towards this final show-down with the sea-god. Even the *dibia*, the grand seers with 'four eyes' who could have prevented the successive deaths of Omokachi's young men are themselves blinded by the gods. The *dibia* are human after all, and only hold their power on trust from the gods. A less vague divination by Anyika earlier in the story would have prevented Ekwueme's later death. But when Madume consults him about the strange toe injury in Ihuoma's compound, Anyika knows that 'The gods were behind it. It was a premonition' (p. 74). But the particular god does not appear to Anyika and his divination gets bogged in a flat generalization: 'Unknown spirits, some of them from the sea, teamed up to destroy you' (loc. cit.). The main source of Madume's problem, the spirit of the sea, is men-tioned in an ostensibly inconsequential parenthesis. The sea-god shuns the kind of focus that would have laid his machinations open at this stage of the story. His role as the major cause of Madume's tragedy is further befuddled by the *dibia*'s categorical confirmation of human responsibility: 'Let me see, oh yes, Ekwueme's father was among them' (loc. cit.).

Anyika's suspicion that 'The Sea-King himself probably con-fused me...' does not come until late in the story, during his divination for Ekwueme's parents. But even now that he has made a 'definite investigation into the matter' and 'everything is clear' (p. 254), he feels powerless to do anything to circumvent the foretold disaster. His eyes are now open but his hands are tied, for the sea-king is 'too powerful to be fettered' (p. 255). The divination terminates in an exchange that is oppressive in its finality:

'Is there nothing we can do to make the marriage work?'
'Nothing.'

But goaded by fate, humans hardly take 'nothing' for an answer, and so another *dibia* who can do something to save the marriage must be looked for. Agwoturumbe, the powerful *dibia* of Aliji, becomes that tragic alternative. Before turning to Agwoturumbe, Ekwueme's parents invent a rational basis for their doubt about Anyika's divination: his refusal of divination fees must have impaired his vision. For once, Anyika is distrusted, just like Tiresias in *Oedipus Rex* and Ahithophel in *II Samuel*. The fact is that these three 'counsels' are archetypal figures whose visions must be disregarded or defeated by a superior force so that fate can have its way.

Henceforth, Agwoturumbe replaces Anyika as a tool in the hand of the sea-king. His behaviour leaves a number of questions unanswered. Does he truly mean he can bind the sea-king? Is he a freak trying to 'out*dibia*' Anyika in his own territory? Anyika seems to have more knowledge about the way of the gods, and is therefore less likely to be a ready puppet than Agwoturumbe. He is cool, considerate and uncompromisingly frank. He remains the real *dibia* in the story and each time divination is sought from an alternative source, the result is disastrous. The fact is that *dibia* like the one in Chiolu who gives Ahurole the love potion, and Agwoturumbe who claims the power to bind the sea-king, are necessary proxies of fate among humans, and they are destined to hasten the tragic *dénouement* of the story.

Agwoturumbe does this in more ways than one. In an effort to reassure Ekwueme and his parents about his power to bind the god through sacrifice, he only ends up by further enraging the sea-king: 'All will be well my daughter, even if I have to make a journey to the bottom of the river myself' (p. 268). Who is Agwoturumbe, a mere mortal, to promise to go down to a god's domain and bind him? He is guilty of hubris and blasphemy, for he has flouted a condition similar to that laid down by the chorus in *Antigone* as the desideratum for a 'happy life': 'One must do the gods no impiety' (Lattimore, p. 16). It should be noted that Ekwueme himself has, in an equally hubristic manner, boasted that 'If Ihuoma was a sea-goddess then, he could very well be a sea-god himself' (p. 258).

Both Agwoturumbe and Ekwueme are thus proud challengers of the gods; convention demands that they must be brought low.

Because of the predominance of divine authority in The Concubine, human responsibility is considerably minimized. The characters hardly arrive at that critical moment of choice when there is a fork in the road, a moment when the question 'What shall I do?' tugs the human mind. They seem to have few of those doubts and hesitancies that put human will to the test and draw the audience's tears for the tragic consequences of a wrong but ignorant choice. The fact is that the 'master choice' (Lattimore, p. 31) belongs to the sea-king, and it is made long before the story begins. Tragedy is wrought not by human but by divine whims. It is not Ihuoma's choice that she should be the death-snare for men; it is not Emenike's choice that he should be killed by a jealous god. Ekwueme has something of an illusion of a choice: he could take Ihuoma or leave her. But he is a man destined to die, and a false assurance by a dibia merely spurs him towards sure doom. Rather than act, therefore, the characters in The Concubine are acted upon. The sea-god manipulates his human puppets and does not for one moment let go of the strings.

Emphasis therefore shifts from man-to-man relationship to man-to-god relationship, and in the latter unequal arrangement, the human being gets the worst of the deal. This is why one would find it difficult to accept Taiwo's (1976, p. 204) conclusion that The Concubine is 'concerned with the circumstances of a marriage which ends in disaster for reasons which are deeply human and universally valid'. Bolaji (1978, p. 2) also traces the source of the tragedy in The Concubine to 'an attempt by individuals and communities to pervert the course of order and the accepted norms in the society'. He goes on to say that 'Ekwueme's madness and subsequent death are necessary punishments' for his attempt to 'upset social order'. It is hard to see what aspects of social order Ekwueme has upset to warrant his death; marrying a widow is not the crime that Bolaji makes it out to be. Ekwueme's other 'offence', his divorce from Ahurole, is nothing of his own making; the erring woman runs off after her attempt to win Ekwueme's love by supernatural means has failed.

The impression one gets is that both Taiwo and Bolaji have tried to attribute human tragedy in Amadi to a kind of hamartia. Undoubtedly, there is ample evidence of this in The Great Ponds where human greed, graft and bestiality justifiably precipitate hardship and death. There we can say it serves them right. In contrast, humans have few flaws in The Concubine. In fact, human characters here are so good that the gods look bad for causing them unnecessary suffering. What we have, therefore, is not human but divine hamartia! The sea-king, jealous and vindictive, uses his superior strength to crush innocent humans, a clear case of abuse of power. The chief human characters, then, are Oedipal types (that is in the Attic-Sophoclean sense), fated even before their birth, more sinned against than sinning.

The gods not only control human beings and their affairs, they also direct the plot and the events mediated through it. Indeed, Lattimore's (p. 38) description of The Iliad as a story where 'fate is just the plot, the script, the traditional story, the given' is largely applicable to the novels of Amadi. Hence fatalism operates through mystery or surprise, an element which, according to Forster (1974, p. 95) is of vital importance in plot, occurring, as it does, 'through a suspension of time-sequence . . . and more subtly in half explained gestures and words, the true meaning of which dawns pages ahead'. Mystery and surprise in Amadi are realized through plot types such as mistaken identity, followed by discovery and recognition. The tragedy in The Concubine is predicated significantly on the dual identity of Ihuoma, a goddess-human operating as human in Omokachi community. Only the sea-king knows the whole truth about her; she herself is not even aware of her membership of two worlds. As one man after another drops dead upon 'assaulting' her, the village is anguished, but not surprised in the technical sense of the word. After all, the cause of each death has a plausible human explanation: Emenike's 'lock-chest' and Madume's 'big-eye'. Not until Chapter 28 (just two chapters from the end of the novel) do we know that 'Ihuoma is a little unusual' (p. 253). Surprise follows as the mystery of Ihuoma's circumstances is unravelled, a surprise born of breath-taking recognition.

The question to ask is: why does Amadi fail to clear the mytery until well into the close of the story? Can we accept Anyika's explanation that the sea-king 'probably confused' him? If so (and we have reason to, given the enormous potency of the sea-king in The Concubine), then some divine effort has helped Amadi prolong his story. But the weakness of this kind of plot-pattern is that the reader is as ignorant as the characters. Although the discerning reader might develop some vague suspicion about some happenings at the beginning of the story, the novelist never really takes him into his confidence. The result is that when discovery comes eventually, it explodes a volley of hidden truths, and we heave a retrospective sigh of grief for bygone victims. A similar retroactive explanation is given in The Great Ponds for Olumba's fall from a wasp-infested palm-tree (p. 107). It is not until twelve pages later that we know that Igwu, the dibia of the rival village, has been responsible for making him 'careless ... So that he may run into danger' (p. 119). This flashback technique of preceding cause with consequence tends to rob Amadi's story of that dramatic irony which mostly comes to full realization when the audience, by virtue of knowing more, is wiser than the character. The gods often take total control, wilfully 'confusing' the dibia, the agents of discovery and revelation whose duty it is to let the people into the full cosmic picture.

In both novels the story line is pegged with omens, premonitions and ostensibly inconsequential episodes that later turn into vital ingredients of tragedy. This is hardly surprising in novels pervaded by fatalism. The Great Ponds, for example, teems with inexplicable, potent happenings. Immediately after Wago has cut off the edge of Olumba's wrapper for a powerful medicine against him, the victim's path is crossed by a brightly coloured snake. On another occasion a huge snake frightens Okehi in his dream and drives him into a well. While Olumba lies 'cooking' on his bed, strange things happen: night birds flew past his compound 'flapping their wings ominously' (p. 135), a wild tortoise saunters into his reception hall, and an owl and a viper also make an appearance. As Eze Diali and others sit in his reception hall trying to iron out Olumba's problem, 'A spider let itself down from the roof by a thread. It remained suspended in the air at Diali's eye-level' (p. 156). In The Concubine, Ekwueme has a dream in which he is nearly lured away to the land of the dead by Emenike (p. 63); Madume receives a serious toe injury for visiting Ihuoma. As the dibia's divination after each episode reveals, the cause of these omens is cosmic disharmony: the sea-king is enraged by human attempts to seduce his wife; Ali the earth-god is annoyed because Aliakoro has been instrumental in the kidnapping and selling off of 'a woman with child' (p. 77).

However, some episodes are more parabolic than ominous, and serve as a kind of moral commentary on events in the story. For instance, in a desperate effort to crush the spider hanging menacingly down before his eyes, Eze Diali loses the 'bit of kola' he holds in his right hand; this sounds like a symbolic rehearsal of the loss of the highly prized and brutally contested pond at the end of the story. Okali's son's capture of the two flightless birds parallels

Aliakoro's unreasonable kidnapping of two Chiolu women, one of whom is pregnant. Furthermore, in both novels, Amadi portrays children playing with grasshoppers. In *The Great Ponds*, Okehi's son brings home a parcel of cocoyam leaves containing 'a collection of green and yellow grasshoppers disabled in one way or the other so that they could not fly. The youngster played with them intercepting them as they made a bid for freedom' (p. 64). In *The Concubine*, Ihuoma's second child (p. 107)

> had caught some grasshoppers and was feeding them limb by limb to some ants. He watched with undivided attention, the ants dragging their comparatively mighty burdens into the dark mysterious interior of their holes.

The helplessness of these insects, their desperate but fruitless 'bid for freedom', is a powerful analogue to the plight of humans in the hands of the gods. There seems to be a kind of cosmic chain of oppression in which those at the top thwart and toy with the lives of those below. As grasshoppers to wanton boys, so are we to the gods; they kill us for their sport.

Like those of Thomas Hardy and Charles Dickens, Amadi's plot pattern derives its strength from the depiction and elaboration of minutiae and seeming trivia, tiny incidents which gather immense significance through structural repetition and thematic stress. In *The Concubine* the lizard, which eventually causes the death of Ekwueme, sets off a sonorous resonance throughout the whole narrative:

> Ihuoma sat with her children watching the lizards playing on the walls of her house. (p. 14)

> 'He [Nwonna] is roaming around with bows and arrows trying to shoot lizards with other children.' (p. 100)

> '... look at your belly. It is as flat as that of a lizard.' (Wakiri to Ekwueme, p. 113)

Later in the story Ekwueme, who has always been associated with a lizard, gets killed by an arrow meant for one. The irony is tragic in its import. The 'lizard', therefore, becomes a word 'half explained ... the true meaning of which dawns pages ahead' (Forster, ibid.).

The tragedy of Ekwueme's death is further deepened by the ironic circumstances surrounding the hunt for a lizard. We would not now ask the question: why should the *dibia* have a lizard as one of the items for binding the sea-king? That would be tantamount to searching for the tap-root of the whole plot. But it must be pointed out that as the story hastens towards the end, the word 'lizard' comes in with an oppressive frequency. As fate would have it, it is the last, perhaps the most inconsequential item for the sacrifice (p. 276):

'The lizard.'
'Ah, yes I forgot about it.'

Ekwueme then instructs Nwonna on how to kill the 'big coloured male lizard' (loc. cit.):

'Don't shoot directly,' Ekwe said 'shoot along the wall and the wall will direct your arrows to the lizard.'

Little does he realize that he is offering a grand recipe for his own destruction.

The lizard establishes a tragically ironic link between Nwonna and Ekwueme. Why is it that Ekwueme is killed by Nwonna's arrow and not by any of those of 'his little friends' (p. 268)? His death at the hand of Nwonna is really 'wanton', considering the fact that the required lizard has already been killed by one of Nwonna's play-mates. But it is fate's grand design that the 'good shot' (p. 277) must disregard this so that he can shoot his own 'lizard' (p. 279):

'But you had caught one lizard already.'
'No, it was I who shot this one. Nwonna wanted to kill another by himself.'

There are now two lizards, one for the boastful Agwoturumbe and the juicier other for the sea-king whom he is seeking to bind. Thus, we have an archetypal tragic situation where every step taken to circumvent the wish of the gods ironically leads towards its ultimate fulfilment.

Such discrepancy between expectation and fulfilment, between human proposition and divine disposition, rules the lives of Amadi's characters, and directs the course of his plot. Just a few moments before Ekwueme is shot, he and Ihuoma plan for the future with ebullient optimism (p. 275):

'Just tonight and then we shall be married.'
'Yes.'

But this much-desired marriage is lost, as it were, between cup and lip. It is the moment when the elders of Chiolu think that the ponds are closest to being theirs that they realize that 'It would be an abomination to fish in a pond in which someone committed suicide' (p. 217). As in classical tragedy, the débâcle 'comes just after an outburst of false joy and hope' (Lattimore, p. 53). Margaret Lawrence (1968, p. 184) makes a perceptive observation when she posits that The Concubine contains an 'acute awareness of fate's ironies, for at the exact moment when we think the prize is within our grasp, the gods cut the thread'.

This brings us to the quality of the tragedy in Amadi's works. In great tragedy grave issues are at stake; characters undergo moments of conflict, psychological or physical, and sessions of rigorous self-examination. Few of these conditions can be found in the novels. Emenike gets snuffed out before we know anything of significance about him; Madume is too 'big-eyed' to be admirable; Ekwueme, the mother-dominated young man, has his fate cut and dried by the gods. The characters in The Concubine are, therefore, either too good or too bad. Moreover, as we said earlier on, the overwhelming presence of fate robs them of their will and power of choice. When a character opts for life and the gods impose their choice of death, we would be Attics to feel tragedy and not disgust. If The Concubine contains characters that are too good, The Great Ponds is a story of 'bad guys'. Both Chiolu and Aliakoro stake life and all on hazy claims. Wago epitomizes the consummate Machiavellism of Alikoro; he is not only a leopard-killer, he is also a conscience-killer. Olumba, though more scrupulous than Wago, is an impulsive patriot who sticks out his neck for a cause he is not quite sure of. His mental and physical atrophy draws little pity. The Great Ponds does not assume any tragic dimensions; the gory killings and near-holocausts orchestrated through its episodic plot-structure produce, not tragedy, but pathos of a very low kind.

This is why one would find it hard to justify the rather sweeping conclusion reached by Alastair Niven (1971, p. 188) about the tragic quality of Amadi's novels:

> Amadi, like Achebe, shows that man's priority in a rural community is to sustain his masculinity, but the heroes of both novels have feminine characteristics which may be one reason why the gods ultimately destroy Ekwueme and render Olumba a physical wreck. Amadi remains the most likely novelist to offer a version of tragedy for Africa.

This conclusion is hard to accept. The gods do not cut Ekwueme down because of his femininity, nor are we sure whether they directly have a hand in the wrecking of Olumba. Ekwueme's destruction is due to the vindictiveness of the sea-king, while Olumba's deterioration is a result of mental torture produced by fear and doubt. Besides, extreme masculinity is not an asset in either Achebe or Amadi. Does Okonkwo not fall because of a rather inordinate stress on masculinity and its concomitants of fierceness and war? In Amadi, Wago, the village hunter and warrior, possesses an unconscionable amount of strength and force that hastens his doom. In fact, contrary to Niven's interpretation, *The Great Ponds* is an allegory on the futility of war and its attendant masculinity — especially the kind of masculinity shorn of reason and consideration for others. The deterioration of masculinity is not, therefore, a source of tragedy in Amadi, and we cannot brand it a 'version of tragedy for Africa' any more than we can enlarge Hardy's overworked fatalism into a veritable version of tragedy for Europe.

Hitherto, we have seen how the gods treat human characters in Amadi. Now we should ask: how does the author in turn treat the gods? What can we say is his attitude to them? To my mind, Amadi portrays the sea-king as more Olympian than African — cold, indifferent and manipulative. He stays in his watery remoteness and toys with human lives. He is proud, ostentatious and sadistic, totally alien to what Soyinka (1973, p. 14) has called morality of reparation. Lost here are the principles of sane complementarity and coexistence that characterize African godheads and the human race. A god who does not want his shrine overgrown with weeds must seek to elicit a certain measure of fear mixed with a corresponding proportion of respect. The sea-king exacts fear but commands little respect. As Anyika confesses, other spirits are appeasable but (p. 255):

> 'With the Sea-King it is impossible. He is too powerful to be fettered and when he is on the offensive he is absolutely relentless. He unleashes all the powers at his command and they are fatal.'

Ogbunabali is another god who rules through fear and intimidation, but at first sight, he seems more terrestrial, more secular than the sea-king. He is regarded by the people as the bastion of morality and the ultimate arbiter of justice. This explains why he is evoked to settle once and for all a case that defies human memory and judgement. But Ogbunabali comes out at the end of *The Great Ponds* a crest-fallen god, a night tiger with blunted claws. The haze of doubt hanging over his power raises a number of questions:

Where is TRUTH? Which village is right? Is Olumba's survival a vindication of Chiolu's claim to the ponds? This latter cannot be because *wonjo* through its killing power has elbowed out Ogbunabali and deified itself as the god of the moment. It is, therefore, hard to agree with Taiwo (p. 206) that 'It is Wago's attempt to kill Olumba and thus prejudge the result of the latter's oath to the dreaded Ogbunabali that brings *wonjo* to the two villages and paralyses social life'. *Wonjo* is not brought by Ogbunabali; *wonjo* strides in to rival the god of night, to 'outgod' him. If *wonjo* is punishment on Aliakoro for tampering with the oath, then why are other villages unconnected with the pond dispute affected?

Further issues arise as regards the author's treatment of Ogbunabali *vis-à-vis* the outbreak of *wonjo*. The first is structural: *wonjo* crashes in on the story like a kind of technical *deus ex machina*, a rescue strategy to hasten a tortured plot to a restful conclusion. The second is thematic: a local conflict is resolved once and for all through the fortuitous intervention of a universal pestilence. But the most serious issue is the failure of Ogbunabali to function as 'affirmer of secular ethos' (Soyinka, p. 95), a failure amplified in Amadi's last but most obtrusive paragraph in *The Great Ponds* (p. 217):

> But it was only the beginning. Wonjo, as the villagers called the Great Influenza of 1918, was to claim a grand total of some twenty million lives all over the world.

Now we know that it is 'the Great Influenza of 1918' at work, not Ogbunabali. The historical accuracy of this commentary jars the fictive harmony of the whole novel, creates an authorial stance that undermines (or even ridicules) the beliefways of the characters, and reduces Ogbunabali (their god) to a mere superstition. The author seems to have been too informed for his characters.

In spite of this obvious authorial stance, however, the gods are a powerful presence in the collective consciousness of Amadi's characters. In the end, the sea-king is still the uncanny, 'absolutely relentless' spirit he used to be; Ogbunabali still remains 'a god powerful enough to clear whole families'. Like Achebe's Evil Forest, both gods 'kill a man on the day that his life is sweetest to him'.

REFERENCES

Texts

Amadi, Elechi (1966) *The Concubine*, London, Heinemann.
Amadi, Elechi (1970) *The Great Ponds*, London, Heinemann.

Critical Works

Bolaji, E. B. (1978) 'Culture and communication in the novels of Elechi Amadi', unpublished paper presented at the Third Ibadian Annual African Literature Conference, July 1978.
Forster, E. M. (1974) *Aspects of the Novel*, Harmondsworth, Penguin.
Lattimore, Richmond (1969) *Story Patterns of Greek Tragedy*, Ann Arbor, Michigan, Ann Arbor Paperbacks.
Laurence, Margaret (1968) *Long Drums and Cannons*, London, Macmillan.
Niven, Alastair (1971) 'The Achievement of Elechi Amadi', (in abstract form) in *Research in African Literatures*, vol. II, no. 1.
Soyinka, Wole (1976) *Myth, Literature and the African World*, Cambridge, Cambridge University Press.
Taiwo, Oladele (1976) *Culture and the Nigerian Novel*, New York, St Martin's Press.

The Essential Unity of Soyinka's *The Interpreters* and *Season of Anomy*

Juliet Okonkwo

There exist between *The Interpreters* and *Season of Anomy*[1] differences in texture and narrative method. Where the one is built on a complex structure and developed on a cyclic, and almost static, framework of revelation and reaffirmation, the other achieves progression in an unmistakable linear fashion. In *The Interpreters*, the characters are deeply individuated through their relationship with the various gods that make up the Yoruba pantheon which is being painted by one of them. Characters in *Season of Anomy* are allegorical throughout and represent ideas and theories some of which derive from classical and biblical mythology. These differences have misled a number of Soyinka's readers into assuming a greater gulf between the thematic concerns of the two novels than a close examination can sustain. Most people are impressed by the deep layers of meaning, especially as they relate to Yoruba mythology, which inform *The Interpreters*, and tend to dismiss *Season of Anomy* as a chronicle of Nigeria's disturbances during her deep crisis years. An anonymous reviewer categorizes *Season of Anomy* with the 'post-prison writings in its narrower margin of hope',[2] seeing the greatest affinity between it and *Madmen and Specialists*. Gerald Moore considers the period of August 1967 to October 1969 as 'marking a definite break in his [Soyinka's] career, both as a writer and as a man of the theatre. The first decade of his activity is thus clearly marked off from whatever developments may now reveal themselves.'[3]

Such severe compartmentalization of experience and artistic

vision would seem a violation of Soyinka's own conception of himself and his art, as expressed in the following dialogue at an interview:

> Agetua: At the source of every work there is an experience ... For you there was the war and your detention. Have not the last few years been the source of a new experience?
>
> Soyinka: One must never try to rigidify the divisions between one experience and another. All experiences flow one into another.[4]

Professor Eldred Jones's view in this matter seems much nearer the truth that 'Soyinka's ideas matured early. The seeds of his essential ideas are seen in his earliest work, and he has remained consistent throughout.'[5] There is a consistency in the thematic concern of the two novels, and *Season of Anomy* is conceived as a sequel to *The Interpreters*; or both of them as two sides of the same coin. Their common theme can be stated as 'the intellectual and his responsibility in a new nation'. His approach is comparable to the film technique whereby an audience is first given a possible development of a plot from beginning to end, and thereafter, another variation, using basically the same ingredients as the first, is gradually worked out. Such a technique has been particularly exploited by one recent English novelist, John Fowles, especially in his novel *The French Lieutenant's Woman*, London, Jonathan Cape, 1969. In this novel, the writer takes liberties at various points in his narration to suggest very many variants in the possible development of his plot.

In an article about the influence of western education on the psychology of its African recipients, a writer divides the African intellectuals into two categories: the psycho-passive intellectuals and the socio-active intellectuals. The psycho-passive intellectual's 'reliance is predominantly on himself, and his thoughts, ideas, decisions, sense of well-being, and humour are all self-centred or egoistic. If he thinks that there is need for development and progress, he will limit these to himself and only in the direction his personality directs him.' The socio-active are 'marginally ethnic elites ... who think about the city, the people and progress as they affect the whole heterogeneous population'.[6] Soyinka has maintained this distinction in the characters whom he projects in *The Interpreters* and *Season of Anomy*, and this has inevitably affected the action in each of the novels. In *The Interpreters*, Soyinka projects the mainly passive intellectuals whose preoccupations are a hedonistic indulgence in self-questionings and in the exercise of their individual hobbies and interests. Their response to the hostility of their social context is an alienated withdrawal into art and the search for experience. On the other hand, Ofeyi and the Dentist of Season of Anomy are socio-activists who occupy themselves with schemes through which they hope to counter the offensive of the establishment in the interest of the populace. This differentiation, however, is a convenient one which Soyinka has employed in order to investigate the two related roles of his chosen subject. For it is the same characters who are projected in the two books, first in their passive and, subsequently, in their active roles. This idea is sustained by an examination of some of the features in both novels.

Although in The Interpreters, Soyinka has projected five central characters – Egbo, Sagoe, Bandele, Kola and Sekoni – Egbo emerges as the dominant character who influences all the others. Sekoni's masterpiece, 'The Wrestler', had its gestation from an action that was initiated by Egbo. Kola confesses that his painting of the Yoruba pantheon was inspired by Egbo who 'started me on it, unwittingly, of course, and in fact he should be labouring it out not me ...' (p. 227). At another time '... Kola found he was thinking about what Egbo had said. For Egbo saying it, made it sound almost like experience, and Kola had often felt from this point alone, if for no other, that his role and Egbo's should be reversed' (p. 218). Egbo's problem, his inability to direct his life with a clearly formulated policy, is stressed at the beginning of the novel and becomes a unifying theme – that of apostasy. He is aware of this negative aspect of himself and confesses this to his undergraduate girl acquaintance at his grove sanctuary that his friends are 'all busy doing something but I seem to go only from one event to the other. As if life was nothing but experience' (p. 133).

Egbo reappears in Season of Anomy, now in his active role as Ofeyi. It may not be entirely a printer's error that on page 152 of Season of Anomy the name Egbo is substituted for Ofeyi. It is symptomatic of the relationship between the two characters in the writer's mind. Ofeyi is as addicted to women as Egbo. A conversation between him and Iriyise establishes this beyond doubt (p. 68); and to her he is 'just a woman wrapper'. Iriyise herself is a transplantation of Simi 'of the slow eyelids' from The Interpreters. Simi is 'Queen Bee' who 'has the eyes of a fish'. She has the same devastating effect on men as Iriyise who is also 'Queen Bee' who 'occupied a cell in a deep hive' (p. 58). Iriyise is a goddess, just as

Simi is a 'Mammy Watta'. Both of them practise the disdainful detachment from men which comes from an arrogant consciousness of their beauty and its effect on their admirers. The exclusively sexual relationship between Egbo and Simi in The Interpreters is transformed into a more useful co-operation between Iriyise and Ofeyi, as partners in a serious venture. Sir Derinola's vaguely insinuated misdemeanour in The Interpreters where he confesses 'These politicians; you can never trust them. Oh, how they betrayed me' (p. 64) is expatiated in Season of Anomy into the corrupt judge who is harassed and finally eliminated by the Dentist for his alliance with the leader of the Jeku Political Party. His sin is that of 'sanctification of crimes from the bench, even of murder, obeying a call on the telephone or a whisper from the leader of Jeku' (p. 115). Spyhole, the journalist of Season of Anomy, like Sagoe of The Interpreters, has a weakness for drink and 'never left a party until the shaming light of day shone on the last empty bottle' (p. 37). Some affinity can be detected between Egbo's undergraduate and Ofeyi's Taiila.

In The Interpreters, Egbo battles with the problem of reconciling his past with the present. Ossa, his grandmother's kingdom, offers him privileges which fascinate him and cause him agonized moments of struggle. This problem appears in Season of Anomy with Ossa transformed into an idealized Aiyero. Like Egbo, Ofeyi shrinks from submerging himself in such 'an anachronism' but he is able to reconcile the claims of the old with the new, the past with the present. While he rejects the offer of the Custodianship of the Grain, protesting that 'the waters of Aiyero need to burst their banks, the grain must find new seminal grounds or it will atrophy and die', he nevertheless proceeds to extract from it seeds that will help in revitalizing the rotten present. In all these parallels, the negative, the passive, the ineffectual have become positive, active and effective weapons with which the intellectual can now assume the full responsibility which his status imposes on him.

Most original thinkers, from the time of Plato, have reserved for the intellectual the mission of setting standards and giving leadership to the nation. The exception is Marx. Even Rousseau's social contract never absolved the elite from this essential responsibility; and Nietzsche, with whom Soyinka has considerable affinity, felt that 'society needs an elite that will set a pattern and curb the thoughtlessness of the mass'. Among Third World revolutionary thinkers, Frantz Fanon in The Wretched of the Earth clearly prescribes that the task of fashioning a new consciousness among the oppressed citizenry belongs to the elite. And in spite of his theory of 'collective leadership', Amilcar Cabral stresses the need for a 'hierarchical structure dominated by the leaders'. Soyinka is restating the same with some modifications. His preoccupation with the intellectual and his place in society is seen in such early works as *The Lion and the Jewel, Kongi's Harvest* and *The Road*. It reaches its utmost cynical expression in *Madmen and Specialists*. In *The Interpreters* and *Season of Anomy* he suggests the necessary steps which the intellectual must take towards the achievement of his prescribed goal.

The characters in *The Interpreters* engage themselves in the task of clarification of very many preliminary issues before an actual confrontation with the malignant forces in their society. The novel is therefore a type of clearing-ground or, in military terms, a reconnoitre. Self-knowledge is a prerequisite in this venture. They have to understand themselves, understand the forces that are ranged against them, their strengths and their weaknesses. So these intellectuals seek knowledge through discussion and dialogue. Inherent in their discussions is the non-acceptance of custom as sacrosanct and the creation of an atmosphere of liberty to probe in order to open up new vistas of life. Truth, to them is not ready-made but must be sought at great cost, and they are extremely honest with themselves and with each other. Like Socrates, they believe in the use of reason to decide moral questions. They must think and decide for themselves so that any actions they may take can be guided by general principles that will bear close scrutiny. They skirt beyond, behind and beneath every issue brought up for examination so that, in the end, its many facets are illuminated and the result is the expansion of knowledge. An example of this type of scrutiny is the discussion about Noah's suitability for the role initially chosen for him both by Lazarus and Kola in his painting (p. 177):

> Egbo said, 'I cannot like the new apostle. He looks submissive, not redeemed. I find this air of purity just that – air. There is no inner radiance in the boy, only a reflection from the spill of zealots' flames.'
>
> Lazarus listened, open-mouthed. 'You are mistaken. That youth has received the holy spirit of God.'
>
> 'I do not like apostasy,' Egbo said. 'He has the smooth brass face of an apostate.'
>
> Bandele spun round, 'What was that twisted idea?'
>
> Kola said, 'I agree with Egbo. If I painted him, it would be as Christ.'
>
> 'You mean to say Judas,' Dehinwa corrected him.
>
> 'No. I mean Christ the apostate.'

'Wait a minute. I think we ought to get our definitions clear.'

'No need,' Egbo said. 'Kola is only trying it on. But don't start hanging your notions on mine. When I said apostate I meant the straightforward Judas type.'

'And I meant the Jesus type. And that is just how I would paint him.'

From this discussion, the idea of apostasy appears quite different from the common one that an ordinary man like Lazarus can understand. Even among the intellectuals themselves the idea is not a simple one, but complex, seen from various viewpoints which add to the enlargement of knowledge.

In this manner they discuss their individual natures and their responses to the varied experiences to which they are exposed. They spend a great deal of time in the exposure of the shortcomings of their society: the greed, the phoniness of men like Oguazor and Faseyi; the corruption of Sir Derinola and Chief Winsala; the capitalist set-up which encourages misdirection of the country's resources. Sekoni is confined to an office desk when he would be better employed as a practising engineer in the field; and Sagoe's zeal at enlightening the masses through his profession is completely negated.

The young intellectuals are thorough in their self-denunciation. Kola is aware of his limitations as an artist. Beside Sekoni's 'The Wrestler', his pantheon is a shadow because he is holding something back and 'dared not, truly, be fulfilled. At his elbow was the invisible brake which drew him back from final transportation in the act' (p. 218). They are even aware that, in formulating no counter-programme of reform, they are abetting the establishment and that criticism by itself, especially among themselves, is futile. In such a situation, Egbo wonders about the purpose in their lives (p. 13):

> 'Beyond propping up the herald-men of the future, slaves in their hearts and blubber-men in fact doing what? Don't you ever feel that your whole life might be sheer creek-surface bearing the burdens of fools, a mere passage, a mere reflecting medium or occasional sheer-mass controlled by ferments beyond you?'
>
> Bandele shrugged. 'I don't work in the Civil Service.'
>
> 'But you acquiesce in the system. You exist in it. Lending pith to hollow reeds.'

Open rebellion and direct confrontation with the oppressive forces meet with severe brutality. Sekoni learns this at great cost when his professional competence is set aside so that a corrupt minister can make money. And Sekoni becomes insane. Sagoe

manages to get his job in spite of many odds because of the excessive indiscretion of his oppressors. At other times, he works his
frustrations out of his system by flinging plastic fruits and flowers
out of the window or engaging in his absurd coprolitic philosophy
of voidancy. Egbo can only spit in the face of Dr Lumoye. To make
matters worse, the 'blood cruelty' of an already terrorized and
emasculated populace undermines the intellectual's capacity for
revolutionary action. Sagoe's article about the merging of three
ministries of Works, Electricity and Communication into one and
his speculations about a battle between the three incumbents for
the one ministry 'earned him his first family delegation, a clever
assortment of eleventh cousins whom Sagoe could not know.
Pleading caution. Please, don't make enemies' (p. 107).

To some, the brilliant exposition in The Interpreters leads
nowhere: 'one is forced to ask where they lead to, what they add up
to'.[7] Another criticism is that the novel offers no hope of retrieval
when it concludes, as it began, with Egbo still unable to make an
important choice.[8] Apart from the answer supplied by one of its
characters, 'Knowledge of the new generation of interpreters' (p.
178), the young men, as well as the writer, have taken stock of
themselves and the problems that face them, measured their
strength against the might of the oppressor, as a first step towards
the enactment of any strategies with which to confront these forces.
This is 'a crucial step in the self development of Africa. For if it is
not voiced, the beautiful ones will never be born'.[9]

Season of Anomy takes off where The Interpreters ends. It is
concerned with a search for how the beautiful ones can be born.
Soyinka's allegorical presentation in this work facilitates, to a
considerable degree, the interpretation of his meaning. Here, the
corrupt, excessively materialistic world of the establishment
which already existed in The Interpreters is represented by the
Cartel, whose predations on the land are symbolized in the
Corporation's desecration of cocoa from an ordinary life-giving
food to commercialized 'cocoa bix' and 'cocoa wax'. Cartel – an
alliance of big business, politics and the military – which controls
production, marketing and prices has set up a 'superstructure of
robbery, indignities and murder ... new phase of slavery' (p. 27),
and maintains a stranglehold that gradually suffocates the country.
The power and opulence of this cabal airs itself at the party organized to open the marble fountain of the corporation's Chairman,
one of the many powerful servants of the Cartel. The gadgets which
the newspaper chairman in The Interpreters collected in his

foreign travels abroad for his offices pale before the grandiose scale on which the fountain is conceived. Among the gathered guests are a representative of the military, in the person of the commandant himself, a brigadier; Skyros represents the mercantile group; the Lebanese 'who owned three quarters of this clientele, Skyros with his grand boutique that gleamed full of smuggled gold'. Other guests are 'trapped in vestments richer than the wildest dreams of Tutankhamen'.

The impression is of a 'Florentine moment in the heart of the festering continent' (p. 44). The fountain itself beggars the wildest dreams in extravagance and fantasy (loc. cit.):

> The fountain pool, itself a fish-pond was indeed scooped out in the shape of the cocoa-pod, floor and sides laid in tiny tiles of amber. From the centre of the pod rose a noble plinth, a marble arm from the enchanted lake, which for Excalibur upheld a blue marble platform upon which sat an armoured knight, equestrian. At the horse's feet writhed a monstrous dragon, scales of silver, tongue of bronze, fiery, fire-flashing eyes of onyx. It was transfixed by a ponderous silver spear and pounded by steel hooves of the noble steed.

The Chairman expresses his cynicism and that of his accomplices in his comment that 'St George seated on that horse there as you can see is representative of the new order which is battling the dragon which represents the forces of our greatest national enemy corruption' (loc. cit.). The Cartel's complete control over the bodies and minds of the populace, symbolized in the chance of their puppets' representations during Ofeyi's show at the same party 'a slow macabre dance of the magic circle, heads slowly turning side to side in contemplation of a prostrate world' (p. 46), must account for the final resolve of the intellectual to attempt its dissolution.

Ofeyi conceives his campaign against the Cartel in the guise of surreptitious re-education and reclamation of the exploited, corrupted, debased populace. The young in particular need a new sense of direction. He wants 'to effect restitution to many but also to create a new generation for the future' (p. 19). He plans to utilize 'the same powerful propaganda machine of the Cartel throughout the land, taking hold of undirected youth and filling the vacuum of their transitional heritage' with new invigorating ideas extracted from the philosophy of life in the traditional community of Aiyero. Since the problems of the present originated from the dislocation of traditional by western European educational patterns and life-styles and 'set the nation on the unpredictable and uneasy road into the future',[10] the dismantling of some of the prevailing institutions would be replaced by the restitution of some of those from the African past. Aiyero represents in this novel the egalitarian, morally incorruptible essence from the African past which was destroyed with the intrusion of foreign, excessively materialistic and exploitative ideologies. Ofeyi resolves here Egbo's irritating problem of how to reconcile the past with the present. To Ofeyi, the past in its entirety would be intolerable, as Soyinka's *A Dance of the Forests* demonstrated. The contentment which the Aiyero environment offers 'can become malignant', and 'the healing essence which soothes one individual . . . that happens to wander into Aiyero is not enough for the bruises of others . . . They require a very different form of healing' (p. 24). Even the young people from Aiyero venture out into the outside world for the material advantages it has to offer, but the miracle is that they always come back 'untouched by where they have been, by the plight of the rest of mankind' (p. 6). Ofeyi wants from Aiyero that 'essence of leaves or bark' which protects the Aiyero youth from contamination by 'temptations such as the Cartel can offer'. The earnestness, sense of responsibility, moral purity, honesty with which to counter the Cartel's programme of exploitation, greed, hypocrisy and enslavement of body and mind exist in the Aiyero community. Violent revolution, as an ally to humanistic education, may be necessary in this campaign since the Cartel itself uses violent methods.

Ofeyi's optimism in the ultimate success of his venture rests on the transformation which the immersion in Aiyero life already achieved in Iriyise. Within the short duration of their first stay, this notorious courtesan 'whose only knowledge of fulfilment . . . had been the aftermath of love' becomes fired with the prospects of a new spiritual type of fulfilment. From here, Iriyise ceases to be just the girlfriend of Ofeyi and symbolizes the life-restorative qualities of Aiyero. To Ofeyi she 'has become indissoluble . . . from the soil of Aiyero'. Her subsequent abduction by the officials of the Cartel suggests the Cartel's efforts at a complete liquidation of the idea which Aiyero represents – a reformative essence that certainly heralds the demise of its powerful reign. Temoko, her place of confinement, is identifiable with hell, where Pluto took the abducted Persephone.[11]

Ofeyi has no illusions whatsoever about the dangerous nature of his undertaking. To Ahime it is a 'form of aggression', and he warns about 'sowing the wind and reaping the whirlwind'. But Ofeyi has thought of all that and has decided on his action because 'our generation appears to be born into one long crisis'. The risks have to be faced. The intellectual now has his back against the wall. He loses nothing by staking all his resources; on the contrary, with some luck, something might be salvaged. 'The storm was sown by the Cartel, Pa Ahime. Unless we can turn the resultant whirlwind against them we are lost.' The brutal violence of the Cartel's reaction to the offensive propaganda against them surpasses Ofeyi's calculations and nullifies his carefully planned counter-measures. The carnage at Shage, his most cherished and promising centre for the taking-off of the new idea, represents the extent of the disaster throughout the land. But, destruction is part and parcel of a revolution and Soyinka's philosophy of revolution incorporates the fact of destruction and carnage:[12]

> I cannot sentimentalize revolution. I recognize the fact that it very often represents loss. But at the same time I affirm that it is necessary to accept the confrontations which society creates, to anticipate them and try to plan a programme in advance before them. The realism which pervades some of my work and which has been branded pessimistic is nothing but a very square, sharp look, I have depicted scenes of devastation, I have depicted the depression in the minds even of those who are committed to these changes and who are actively engaged in these changes simply because it would be starry-eyed to do otherwise.

Ofeyi's mind reels in confrontation with this initial failure. Total failure can only be conceded however, if one fails to take stock of the events in the rest of the novel, especially at the end.

Although the Cartel's power for death and destruction appears immense, there still exist pockets of resistance which prove its ultimate vulnerability and sets a limit to its power. At Irelu and its environs, the agents of the Cartel-manipulated party, Jeku, paid with their lives for the excesses of their leaders. The engineer, Nnodi, was able to deal death in return to some of his baiters. Both at Shage and with the engineer, and presumably in many other locations, some elements of Cross-River origin have sufficient humanity in them to attempt to forestall their own leaders' plans by sending out warnings to the intended victims of atrocity. At the Tabernacle of Hope, where a number of aliens take refuge, their lives were saved through the intervention of Aliyu, himself a Cross-River man, who acted as a guard. The prospects at the end of the novel seem even better. At Temoko, Ofeyi attempts once again to 'stir up a dangerous awareness' in Suberu, a representative of the oppressed, exploited, misguided masses: 'But for faithful dogs like you the Amuris of this world could not trample down humanity with such insolence. You snap at the heels of those who would confront them and afterwards you bury their bones in the back garden' (p. 316). This lesson appears to have penetrated Suberu's consciousness, for, when Ofeyi escapes with Iriyise from Temoko, Suberu abandons his own post, 'bolt[s] the gate behind and walk[s] steadfastly ahead'. In addition, the Dentist and Dr Chalil had 'harnessed the prevailing chaos' to effect the release of both Iriyise and Ofeyi. And so, the main idea lives for another renewed effort with the experiment.

Therefore, all is not entirely lost. As the men of Aiyero march back to their home base, Cross-River is already astir with the seeds of the new idea. Men like Suberu, Aliyu, other simple common men, even in the ranks of the military, are beginning to feel uneasy with the old dispensation. 'Eventually,' Soyinka has said,[13]

> it is not to the intelligentsia that we must look for salvation in the society. One responsibility which the genuine ones in this group can assume is the real political education of the masses ... about their own potential in society.

Ofeyi and the Dentist and men like Spyhole and Daccheus (even if inadvertently) live up to this responsibility. At least Suberu has been won over and, once he knows his strength in society, the revolution can be left in his hands and those of his colleagues. It is not the simple complacent operation which Ofeyi had planned and expected to have easy passage that will automatically revolutionize the nation. It would be like 'expecting a one-dimensional statement' which the reader wants from the writer and which Soyinka considers as 'looking for a cheap injection of optimism in their nervous system'.[14] Therefore, far from the conclusion arrived at by the reviewer in the Times Literary Supplement, who writes of its 'narrower margin of hope', Season of Anomy ends on an optimistic note.

Thus we see clearly that Soyinka's two novels are united through their common theme of the role of the intellectual in the possible reconstruction in a society that is afflicted with excessive socio-economic and political malaise. Whereas in The Interpreters the passivity of the intellectual results in paralysis and a stultification of the creative genius, his combativeness in Season of Anomy takes up the challenge of revolution and reform. Even though the road is painful, bloody and uncertain, it is offered as the only sane course for the future in the given circumstances.

NOTES

1. Page references are to Soyinka, W., The Interpreters, London, Heinemann, London, 1970; Season of Anomy, London, Rex Collings, 1973.
2. 'Dragon slayer', Times Literary Supplement, 14 December 1973, p. 1529.
3. Moore, Gerald, Wole Soyinka, London, Evans, 1971, p. 3.
4. Agetua, John, When the Man Died, The Midwest Newspapers Corporation, Benin City, 1975, p. 42.
5. Jones, Eldred D., 'The essential Soyinka', Introduction to Nigerian Literature, ed. B. King, Lagos, Evans, 1971, p. 114.
6. Alli, Billiamin A., 'Acculturative forces: Nigeria in transition', Journal of Black Studies, vol. 4, no. 4, June 1974, p. 384.
7. Ravenscroft, A., 'African literature V: novels of disillusion', Journal of Commonwealth Literature, no. 6, January 1969, p. 125.
8. Larson, Charles R., The Emergence of African Fiction, London, Indiana University Press, 1971, p. 246.
9. Provizer, Norman W., 'The other face of protest: the prisoner and the politician in contemporary Africa', Journal of African Studies, vol. 2, no. 3, Fall 1975, p. 393.
10. Ofuatey-Kodjoe, W., 'Education and social change in Africa: some proposals', Journal of African Studies, vol. 3, no. 2, Summer 1976, p. 230.
11. For an elaboration of this myth see Izevbaye, D., 'Soyinka's Black Orpheus', Neo-African Literature and Culture, ed. Bernth Lindfors and Ulla Schild, Wiesborden, Heymann, 1976, pp. 147–58.
12. Agetua, op. cit., p. 39.
13. ibid.
14. ibid.

The Inward Journey of the Palm-wine Drinkard

John Coates

J oseph Campbell's comments on the value of myth in eas-
ing man's problem in accepting life form a useful introduction to this, not the least important, aspect of Amos
Tutuola's book. Campbell points out that 'it is the business of
mythology proper, and of the fairy tale, to reveal the specific dangers and techniques of the dark interior journey'.[1] The journey may
on the surface appear to be through an external world, but 'fundamentally it is into depths where obscure resistances are overcome,
and long long, forgotten powers are revivified'.[2] The most important result is to free the hero who undertakes the journey from the
limitations of time and space.

Campbell's emphasis on the inwardness of the journey and its
therapeutic function should awaken the reader to an aspect of
Tutuola's symbolism. It is an aspect easily demonstrated because
easily identified with universal human experiences and probably
readily accepted because free both from the jargon of psychology
and from its tendentious assumptions.

The palm-wine drinkard in the first phase of his life enjoyed an
existence untroubled by demands or stresses. In those days everything was cheap and when his father discovered that the only work
he could do was drink, 'he engaged an expert palm-wine tapster for
me; he had no other work more than to tap palm-wine every day'.[3] It
is a suggestion of a kind of pre-moral, almost pre-conscious state,
characterized by self-indulgence, ease and the absence of imperatives of every kind, and perhaps corresponding to childhood before
one's earliest memories or at least before one's earliest sense of
contradiction or mystery. The death of the drinkard's father,
closely followed by the finding of his tapster dead beneath a tree,

brings this idyllic dream-state to an abrupt end. He tries to prolong it, touchingly refusing to admit the new reality, but without the constant supply of palm-wine his friends no longer visit him. He is left, that is, with the need to find conscious, and mutual, kinship with others.

Like countless versions of the 'Hero and the Quest' from *Gilgamesh* onwards, the palm-wine drinkard is obviously concerned with man's need to accept the fact of death but it is concerned with much more than that. Each stage of the journey corresponds to specific psychological tensions and problems involved in self-definition or development towards stability and wisdom. In addition to this personal significance, there is its universal ontological application. It is at once the story of a man's development to what must, apologetically, be called maturity, intended to ease the journey by a *rite de passage*, and also a mythical account of the origin of man's estate as it now is, intended to aid understanding and acceptance.

Readers will be struck by the degree to which the world of *The Palm-wine Drinkard* is the world of *illo tempore*, the paradisiac state as defined by Mircea Eliade whose 'marks are immortality, spontaneity, freedom; the possibility of ascension into Heaven and *easily meeting* the gods; friendship with the animals and knowledge of their language',[4] freedoms man has lost as a result of a mutation of his own condition 'as well as a cosmic schism'. The palm-wine drinkard's early title, 'Father of gods' who could do everything in this world, recalls these paradisial freedoms. He is a ju-ju man able to exercise magical powers, to transform himself into various shapes, capable, as his earliest adventures show, of a resourceful trickery.

These early ruses, the finding of what the old man had ordered from the blacksmith, the discovery of the way to Death's House, the outwitting of Death himself, have a quality of cocky self-confidence about them. The palm-wine drinkard, at the inception of his quest, has a bumptiousness due to his meeting no problem which cannot be solved by a cheap trick. Death, at this stage, has no moral or spiritual problems. He is simply a rather foolish, easily outwitted old man. Possibly in personal terms this early jokester or 'wide-boy' corresponds to a quick-witted adolescent skating over the surface of life. He cannot be hurt by death because, as yet, he does not believe he can die. There is all the difference between this early meeting with the old man Death and the melancholy wisdom of the Deads' Town at the end of the quest. In ontological terms the return of the drinkard with the old man Death caught in a net, as his taskmaster had bidden him, provides a mythically satisfying explanation for Death's origin in the world. Like Eurystheus with Hercules, the taskmaster trembles before what he has ordered to be brought and 'I threw down Death before his door and at the same time that I threw him down the net cut into pieces and Death found his way out'.[5] Death appeared in the world through a moment of petulant carelessness; an incident which well displays the drinkard's moral development at this stage.

The incident of the rescue of the young lady from the 'curious creature' or 'complete gentleman', the next ordeal, marks an important point in the growth to wisdom. The drinkard is told by a headman that he knows the way to the Deads' Town, where the drinkard hopes to recover his tapster. He will not tell the drinkard the way unless he rescues his daughter from the curious creature. This is a different ordeal from the early pranks and the drinkard is about to refuse 'but when I remembered my name I was ashamed to refuse'.[6] Recovering the lost woman involves quick-wittedness, certainly, but it also involves psychological acuteness. She had refused many men of her father's choice and one day in the market had followed the 'complete gentleman', a superbly handsome man of an almost intimidating perfection. The spectacle of this 'curious creature' brings the drinkard to his first real check: 'I cried for a few moments because I thought within myself why was not I created with beauty as this gentlemen.'[7] Two insights emerge from this check to his self-esteem. He realizes that inner nature is more important than outward appearance. Every single one of the gentleman's perfections has been rented and must be returned. In fact, in his true shape, he is only a skull; a suggestion, possibly, of the difference between innate qualities and assumed personal or social manners. A more important step forward is the drinkard's acceptance of the fact that he cannot blame the lady for falling captive to the 'curious creature'; anyone would have done so. The prankster has gained a dimension of tolerance and sympathy for others' mistakes.

The recovery of the woman involves elements of the detective and of the adventure story. The 'investigator', as the palm-wine drinkard is for the moment called, has to discover where the woman has been taken. Her captivity in the 'skull's family's house' seated on a bull-frog, suggests, among much else, an imprisoning and degrading relationship. Of course, the symbols are not counters. A parallel interpretation may be constructed which partly expresses the truths contained in the allegory, but the allegory is not merely a translation of a moralizing argument into abstract terms.

It is, perhaps, significant that the rescue should have two stages. The first is purely physical; her flight in the form of a kitten with the palm-wine drinkard in the form of a bird. It suggests the earlier ruses. The second stage, however, adds a psychological to the detective and adventure elements. 'There remain greater tasks ahead' since the drinkard must sever the cowrie tied around the lady's neck, which prevents her from talking or eating and by its terrible noise does not allow anybody else to rest or sleep. The physical imprisonment of the lady by her treacherous lover is somehow less significant than what is hinted at here: some kind of residual emotional hold or dominance. The investigator must return into the darkness, discover the secret, symbolized by the magic leaves, and dispel its power. At first he is daunted by the magnitude of the task but thinks of his title 'Father of gods' and is shamed into making the effort. It is successful and 'this was how I got a wife'.[8]

What follows the marriage is a handling of easily recognized, almost universal tensions. The father will not reveal the secret of the way to the Deads' Town because he does not 'like to part with his daughter'. The resulting three and a half years of waiting corresponds, perhaps, to the necessary stabilizing of early marriage and, interestingly, the new wife seems to accept her husband's idiosyncrasy; she helps him carry his palm-wine from the farm to the town.

The birth of their son, more than tensions with her father, proves the real strain. In the monstrous figure of the child, with his insatiable appetite and exorbitant demands, Tutuola suggests an infant's rages: 'He was smashing everything on the ground to pieces, even he smashed all the domestic animals to death,'[9] and greed: 'He asked for food and they gave him the food and he ate it; after, he entered the kitchen and ate all the food he met there as well.'[10] In a sense the child repeats, in more emphatic form, the unthinking egotism of his father 'before the fall'. The fantasy has a psychological truth to human impulse which scarcely needs comment. It brings to the surface and dispels through dream and humour unspoken and perhaps unspeakable desires; the hatred of the intrusive child, born monstrously and pitilessly destructive of others' rights and identities. The drinkard and his wife attempt to escape and finally enact the ultimately unmentionable fantasy, to burn down the house with the child in it. This attempt to escape is

ineffective. The child and his demands cannot be evaded: 'I saw
that the middle of the ashes rose up suddenly and at the same time
there appeared a half-bodied baby, he was talking with a lower
voice like a telephone.'[11] The pressure grows worse now. In fact, the
child could eat everything in the world without being satisfied.
The problem cannot be evaded. It must be accepted and trans-
cended, as it is through the clearly allegorical 'Drum, Song and
Dance'. These 'three good creatures' who 'take away our trouble'
offer no rational answer to the intrusion of the child into the
parents' lives. The outrage is subsumed into another rhythm:
'When "Dance" started to dance the half-bodied baby started too,
my wife, myself, and spirits were dancing with "Dance" and
nobody who heard or saw these three fellows would not follow
wherever they were going.'[12] It affords an excellent example of the
power of myth to change the perception of the world, to provide a
means by which man can be freed from its exigencies; an instance
which fully supports Campbell's generalization: 'The objective
world remains what it was, but, with a shift of emphasis within the
subject, is beheld as though transformed.'[13] The acceptance of the
child is immediately followed by one of Tutuola's endearingly
specific details. Husband and wife build a canoe and, charging 3d
for adults and half-fare for children, ply a ferry across the river for a
month earning £56 11s 9d. Mundane life can now be handled with
substantial success.

The *Palm-wine Drinkard*'s function as an outstanding instance
of 'wisdom literature' is evident not so much from incidental
details or moralizing allegorical episodes as it is built into the very
rhythm of the book. Interludes of peace or content in Wraith Island
or with the Faithful Mother in the White Tree are set against places
of torment such as Unreturnable Heaven's Town or ordeals such as
the encounter with the Spirit of Prey. The suggestion of an ebb and
flow of happiness and misery, inseparable from the journey of life,
is inescapable. More important, the context of these incidents often
supplies a moral inference. The torments have two features: they
are of the nature of purgatorial ordeals, (Unreturnable Heaven's
Town follows the theft of the cola-nut) and they tend to suggest the
limited value of human wit and ingenuity. The drinkard drives
away the sword-beaked birds with his ju-ju powder but their dis-
appearance is a signal for the far more horrifying 'spirit of prey'.
Here no devices will serve, nor any of the smartness the drinkard
has shown in his early dealings with Death or the Old Man. If the
Spirit closes his eyes then 'no more, we had perished there. But God

is so good he did not remember to close his eyes by that time'.[14] The narrative accepts with an easy grace the existence of events absolutely beyond human control.

Ingenuity has little part to play in the drinkard's eventual escape from 'Unreturnable Heaven's Town'. Tutuola is careful to connect the continuous specifically detailed physical cruelties practised here with the complete irrationality of the town's inhabitants. They do not wash themselves, but wash their domestic animals; cut the animal's 'finger-nails' but leave their own uncut for one hundred years. The cruelties are not dramatic or colourful but curiously automatic although ingenious. They are a way of life, the logical extension of the 'unknown creatures" way of doing everything 'incorrectly'. The perception that even the most horrible cruelties can become quite mundane and run-of-the-mill is part of the educative process of the drinkard's journey. The tortures must be borne, escape being mainly an affair of luck. The fortunate intervention of the eagle which helps to rescue them is partly attributed to the fact that the drinkard tamed such a bird before. The significance of the intervention lies rather in the contrast between an ordinary 'bird of prey', representative of nature's 'cruelty', and the willed irrationality of the town. 'Unreturnable Heaven's Town' is 'against nature'.

However, even here, a cheerful resignation is the right response since the pattern of events is only partly shaped by human will. The eagle could not have helped but for a lucky rainstorm at 3 p.m. which prevents the inhabitants from 'paying the last visit' at 5 p.m. to the prisoners they have buried up to their necks. Even then it cannot help to dig them out as quickly as it might wish because the holes are so deep. The drinkard and his wife only succeed in hiding in the bush on condition that they remain silent while the bush is 'smashed' with them in it. The possibilities for manipulation and evasion of circumstances are much more limited now than at the start of the tale. Stoicism and humour rather than trickery are the resource now and the condition on which life has to be lived.

The new attitude is exemplified in the travellers' 'selling their death' at the entrance to the White Tree for £70 18s 6d. They have, as it were, given it out of their charge and 'cannot die' now in the sense that the worst has been accepted. 'Loaning their fear', for an interest of £3 10s 0d, is a human touch. It is returned to them when they leave. The implication seems to be that only a limited dedication can be achieved and they will continue to be afraid from time to time.

The underlying moral stance of Amos Tutuola's version of the journey to death's kingdom is very marked; sane, balanced between passivity in the face of events and the folly of being wise in one's own conceits; yielding to the laws of life. These attitudes can be seen in the insistence on the rights of the 'tiny creature' and the earth spirit to their due respect in the farming interlude; in the fact that the Faithful Mother may not shelter the pilgrims in her earthly paradise for more than a year and a day; in the folly of the trickster who attempts to make the drinkard and his wife the scapegoats for his crime in the episode of the dead prince in the bag. Throughout all these incidents and elsewhere there is a remarkable consistency. The drinkard must learn to live with other creatures, however diverse; to expect no final refuge before death; to understand the difference between wisdom and cleverness. The ruse of the dead prince in the bag forcibly recalls his own early pranks but the outcome shows the hollowness of these.

The Palm-wine Drinkard, then, may be viewed both in Campbell's sense as a therapeutic and in Eliade's sense, as an ontological myth. It instils right perceptions and attitudes and simultaneously explains how the world came to be as it is. By the time he has reached the Deads' Town the drinkard's moral education has proceeded to the point at which he is ready to accept that his palm-wine tapster cannot now return to minister to him. The ways of the dead are different from our own and although limited communication may be possible there is too radical a division between 'alives' and 'deads' for a shared life. Tapster and drinkard talk and share palm-wine for a while, but must part since the tapster cannot come home and, significantly, the drinkard's wife wishes to be going. Life is to the living.

Conforming to Campbell's 'Hero and Quest' formula the drinkard has made his way to death's kingdom and now returns bearing gifts. The final episode, that of the magic egg, with its analogies with the goose who laid golden eggs, places us firmly in the world we know. The smashing of the egg by men's foolish greed is followed by a famine in which a messenger must be sent to heaven to carry a sacrifice of fowls and cola-nuts: 'The sacrifice meant that land surrendered, that he was junior to Heaven.'[15] The scheme of things that men must now live in has been laid down. Easy communication with spirits, Eliade's hall-mark of the paradisiac state, and hitherto the characteristic of the world of The Palm-wine Drinkard, ceases. When the slave who carries the message to heaven returns nobody will let him into his house for fear he will carry him to heaven too. Fear has cut off the natural from the supernatural. By now, however, the palm-wine drinkard has acquired the wisdom needed to transcend the limitations of the fallen world.

NOTES

1. Joseph Campbell, *The Hero with a Thousand Faces*, 1949; repr. Ohio, The World Publishing Company, Cleveland, 1967, p. 29.
2. ibid.
3. Amos Tutuola, *The Palm-wine Drinkard and his dead Palm-wine Tapster in the Deads' Town*, Faber, London, 1952, p. 7.
4. Mircea Eliade, *Myths, Dreams and Mysteries*, trans. from 1st edn by Philip Mairet, 1957; repr. London, Fontana Library, 1972, p. 58.
5. Amos Tutuola, op. cit., p. 15.
6. ibid., p. 17.
7. ibid., p. 25.
8. ibid., p. 31.
9. ibid., p. 33.
10. ibid., p. 32.
11. ibid., p. 35.
12. ibid., p. 38.
13. Joseph Campbell, op. cit., p. 28.
14. Amos Tutuola, op. cit., p. 54.
15. ibid., p. 125.

Myth and Ritual in *Arrow of God*

Bu-Buakei Jabbi

Wole Soyinka's discussion of *Arrow of God* in his recent book of criticism seems to be misconceived, especially as he claims that this novel gives him 'a genuine feeling of being cheated' through its 'dogged secularization of the profoundly mystical'.[1] The burden of his comments is that moments of man's communion with the supernatural or divine, sterling opportunities for mystical experience, are systematically stifled in Achebe's narrative.[2] But neither a heightened mysticism nor direct exploration of the process of communication between priest and deity or man and the supernatural, significant as they are as valid interests of literary creativity, would seem to be a *sine qua non* even of literature with manifest religious overtones. And although it has been said that 'strong poets make history by misreading one another, so as to clear imaginative space for themselves', such a licence of 'poetic misprision' functions more as a principle of creativity than of criticism.[3] Soyinka's strictures on *Arrow of God* would thus seem to follow an imputed trajectory, an unconscious projection perhaps of his own would-be treatment of such materials, a temptation not implausible in practical criticism by literary artists. It may, however, seek to shift a work's native centre of gravity into line with some other dispositional preference, blaming it for not being what it does not set out to become.

A more surprising oversight in his account of this novel, however, is that he largely ignores its myth and ritual elements as a significant interpretative frame. For mythology and ritual are among the three dominant terms of reference in Soyinka's book. A closer attention to such elements in Achebe's novel would certainly have elicited a sounder assessment from this prolific writer and perceptive critic.

Almost certainly referring to these myth-ritual elements on his part, G. D. Killam continues to consider much of the background of this novel as detrimental to its essential literary meaning or quality:

> A cursory reading of the above suggests that much of the background is there for its own sake, that it has come to dominate the book and has in a sense become the subject of the book. There is much in the novel which has little direct relation to the story the novel has to tell.[4]

This verbatim repeat of a ten-year opinion betrays how such ostensibly 'cursory' readings may sometimes settle into seemingly well-considered final assessments. At least Achebe's fastidiously revised second edition of his novel might have warranted a reconsideration of such earlier unfavourable views in respect of elements he has chosen to retain against the tide of known critical reception. Indeed, although it is founded on the scapegoat theme, *Arrow of God* deserves far more than continuing to be the unwarranted victim of a literary taste too impatient with all would-be anthropology.

More recently, Charles E. Nnolim has attempted to trace various elements of background in this novel to sources Achebe might have utilized in writing it, especially for the myth-ritual dimension we are concerned with here.[5] But in his essay, an unfortunate ineptness in source attribution couples with a basic interpretative myopia to seriously mar what is otherwise an impregnable array of evidence for the historical authenticity of Achebe's background materials. Even his own account of the geography of Achebe's home town in relation to Umuchu, a plausible source of the elements of myth and ritual in the novel, is enough to discredit Nnolim's absolute certainly that Achebe must have had before him the pamphlet entitled *The History of Umuchu* as he wrote his novel. He has obviously grossly overstated his case. And he thereby falls foul of a crucial precaution in source analysis as outlined by his own adopted scholarly mentor, R. D. Altick. For, according to Altick:

> One commonsense question should accompany all attempts to establish the direct indebtedness of one author to another on the grounds of verbal similarities: might not the resemblances be attributable to the fact that both Author A and Author B were nourished by the same culture?[6]

And it should be noted in particular that the crucial *ritual recitation* of the myth of Ulu's First Coming in Achebe's narrative (VII, pp. 70–1), on which we propose here to set some premium of interpretative relevance, has no counterpart at all in Nnolim's extracts from the supposedly exclusive 'source' of this novel. And yet, as recitative, it is central both to the traditional ritual in which it occurs and to the novel itself. In fact, Nnolim remains generally oblivious of either the philosophic import of such elements of myth or ritual within the traditional cultural setting itself or their applied relevance in Achebe's work.

Unlike the above critics, Kofi Awoonor sees the purification ceremony of the Pumpkin Festival in *Arrow of God* as the fulcrum of the narrative.[7] In view of such differences of critical response, a reconsideration of this novel's entire complex of myth and ritual would seem in place. How relevant are the elements of myth and ritual to the meaning and significance of Achebe's novel? Are they mere dead wood perhaps? Or can they be shown beyond reasonable doubt to be indispensable for a sound reading of *Arrow of God*?

Myth and ritual complexes within living cultures tend, in their own right, to be intrinsic systems of ideas and general world-views, of modes of perception and sensibility. A more or less cohesive set of propositions about reality and life, about man's place in the world and in time, may often be deduced from them, though always as an act of interpretation. As Achebe puts it, they are created by man 'to explain the problems and mysteries of life and death – his attempt to make sense of the bewildering complexity of existence'.[8]

Now, depending on the manner and extent of depicting such elements in a work of literature, they may enter into varying modes and degrees of interplay with it in respect of the structuring or evocation of meaning and significance. Unfortunately, however, African literature criticism has not seldom tended to be impatient or oblivious when confronted with sheer cultural phenomena. It was to temper down such impatience that Eldred Jones suggested the test of suitability for any literary *donnée* to be 'the degree of integration it achieves with the writer's chosen theme'.[9] But a critic's perception of this 'integration' would obviously depend in part on his quality of response to conceivable extraliterary experiences and cultural meanings.

An overall multiple functionalism may be stipulated in the artistic symbiosis of certain elements within a work of literature, one in which each of them may be potentially open to a whole range of uses and applications. But the provision of a credibly realistic physical world for general verisimilitude is perhaps the commonest function of any set of background materials in a story. Beyond that, however, there are sometimes at least two other modes of subtler interaction into which they may enter even in a realistic novel. They may, for example, serve a dramatic, structuring or other aesthetic purpose in varying narrative contexts. Certain minor myths and rituals in *Arrow of God* tend to function at this additional aesthetic level in places. For instance, they sometimes afford enabling dramatic occasions for enacting crucial tendencies of character or personality and for anticipating subsequent action or event, whereby they may also help shape tone and response in advance. The most significant example of this is probably the adumbrative mutuality of fate and hubristic affinity of temperament between Ezeulu and one of his sons, the rash and unpredictable Obika. The public incidents during the Akwu Nro festival in Umuachala, especially Obika's brazen attack on the dreaded medicine-man Otakekpeli, are a memorable dramatic occasion for enacting this process in relation to Ezeulu's own later confrontation with the whole of Umuaro (XVII, pp. 196–201). Other elements of myth and ritual also help to sustain two trails of predictive imagery (that is, of death and lunacy), which attach to Obika and Ezeulu respectively from the start of the story until they are literally realized at the very end. In these ways, Obika's general characterization may be seen in part as serving to keep in objective view certain tendencies of temper which lie precariously dormant in Ezeulu until they are unleashed in the second half of the story. So that this characterization of father and son as mutual paratypes not only foreshadows the novel's concluding tragic encounter, but also begins long beforehand to induce a readerly attitude of ironic regard towards that impolitic vendetta by which Ezeulu precipitates it. These modes of integration do not necessarily derive from the mythic or ritual essence as such; but are, instead, contingent aesthetic effects purely incidental to the specific narrative movement.

Another mode of applied usage may be defined as thematic. This tends to obtain mainly with the dominant myths and rites of Umuaro, whose intrinsic cultural meanings are potential interpretative bases for a viable assessment of *Arrow of God*. In these publicly oriented rituals, it is the Chief Priest or Eze-Ulu himself who officiates either as principal celebrant or as sole vicarious participant.[10] Each marking a specific calendrical stage or phase of seasonal progress, their observances are always re-enactments of crucial functions of the central priesthood of Ulu in respect of public destiny in Umuaro. The welfare and interest of the total community is the guiding *raison d'être* of each of them. The rite of welcoming the new moon, performed once a month at every new moon, is the basic unit in this central ceremonial cycle (I, pp. 1–7). The second major ritual is the festival of the Pumpkin Leaves, which is both a purification ceremony and a pre-planting supplication festival (VI–VII). It is the most elaborate and complex of them all. The new yam feast, which proclaims the fiat of harvest and also marks the turning of the old year into the new, is the calamitously abortive festival Ezeulu refuses to call at the end of the story (XVIII, pp. 201–16).

The first two of these rites, which are the only dominant ones fully dramatized in the novel, are suffused through and through with the general import of the Umuaro myth of origin, with the priesthood of Ulu firmly implanted at its very heart (II, pp. 14–15). It is in these fusions of myth and ritual that we may find some of the novel's most promising seeds of meaning and significance. The myth of Ulu's First Coming, for instance, is ritually enacted and recited by the Eze-Ulu during every Pumpkin festival (VII, pp. 68–71). And it is generally a ready mine of rhetoric frequently invoked by either Ezeulu or the people as well in connection with various significant encounters and experiences throughout the narrative. In this way, the philosophic import of its entire myth-ritual complex is recurrently elicited and enacted as a major interpretative perspective in the novel. The priesthood of Ulu and its vestments of myth and ritual are thus a veritable organic nucleus in *Arrow of God*. For, beyond some of the pragmatic functions of these dominant rites, the moments of interfused ritual and mythic expression are symbolic enactments of that priesthood as a pivot of the people's outlook on their own insertion within history and the cosmic scheme.

Meanwhile, we may briefly outline one crucial dramatic application on the secondary strain of myth centring upon the Idemili cult and its totem of the sacred python (IV, pp. 40–54). Moses Unachukwu's spirited formulation of this myth in the haven of the Christian converts generates a conflict from which the young impressionable Oduche – the son Ezeulu has turned over to the learning of the white man – derives his urge to kill a sacred python. The abomination consequently committed in Ezeulu's compound unleashes a major dilemma for the Chief Priest, threatens open conflict with the priest of the python cult and with the clan, and also sorely tries Ezeulu's own genuine conviction in the wisdom of his dealings with Oduche. The dilemma thereby hatches a major theme of the novel, that of innovation and change. For Ezeulu's steadfastness in his proposed disposal of Oduche in the face of such widespread misgivings and irritating dilemmas is the novel's chief means of enacting both his personal predisposition towards change and new ideas and the quality of his insight into the Ulu priesthood as a traditional fountainhead of cultural renewal.

In reverting now to a fuller explication of the central rites and myth, the welcoming of the new moon in Umuaro would be a convenient starting place. The overt priestly responsibility here is 'to look for signs of the new moon', always starting to search the sky 'three days before its time because he must not take a risk' (I, p. 1). And when he sees it, he announces its appearance to a prepared and joyfully welcoming Umuaro, and proceeds to mark his calendar count by eating one of the twelve yams kept in the sacred shrine for the purpose. But these pragmatic functions are also the basis of a philosophic purpose. For the ritual also seems, in effect, to ensure the people's joint or collective experiencing of the passage of time and the flow of history, the Eze-Ulu being spiritual guardian and initial vicarious bearer of their communal consciousness. It seems he must have prior engagement with major new eventualities, whether biocosmic or historical, so as to mollify them if necessary before sanctioning his people's encounter with them. Hence, after spotting the new moon, he beats out his *ogene* to proclaim to Umuaro the sacred fiat of acceptance and welcome, and then goes on to perform a sacrifice in the hope perhaps of determining its posture *vis-à-vis* his people's general welfare. The new moon would thus be a ritual and cosmic symbol of all emerging manifestations, all new eventualities and virtualities of transitional phases, whether they are merely recurrent or truly unprecedented. As ritual guardian of calendar transitions, the Eze-Ulu of Umuaro is also therefore an institution for detecting all such emanations and possibilities in the womb of time. He always keeps ahead of his people so as to establish prior rapport with the new eventuality, plumb its fundamental realities or possibilities in advance, and thereby facilitate his people's ultimate accommodation to it. He is thus a diviner and harbinger *par excellence*. Insight and prescience are basic characteristic faculties of his vocation, and mantic vision is its prime historic purpose. This interpretation of the new moon rite, as will soon be shown, is continuous with the import of the Umuaro myth of origin.

The basic pattern of concern among the people on each

appearance of the new moon, indeed, at every major transitional juncture in their ongoing traverse of history, seems to be enacted by Ezeulu's two wives. (I, p. 2):

> 'Moon,' said the senior wife, Matefi, 'may your face meeting mine bring good fortune.'
> 'Where is it?' asked Ugoye, the younger wife. 'I don't see it. Or am I blind? ... Oho, I see it. Moon, may your face meeting mine bring good fortune. But how is it sitting? I don't like its posture.'
> 'Why?' asked Matefi.
> 'I think it sits awkwardly – like an evil moon.'
> 'No,' said Matefi. 'A bad moon does not leave anyone in doubt. Like the one under which Okuata died. Its legs were up in the air.'

The implications and inherent possibilities of the new phenomenon for the people's individual or collective welfare is their constant concern.

A major aesthetic feature of the novel issues directly from this rite of the new moon. For as the story unwinds, references to Ezeulu's monthly peering at the sky in search of the moon gradually settle into a running imagery of sight, insight and prescience, an imagery which underpins both Ezeulu's apprehension of his responsibilities and the quality of his continuing commitment to the ultimate demands and implications of being an Eze-Ulu. As he himself tells his lay friend Akuebue, an Eze-Ulu is ideally or vocationally endowed with unusual prescience and clairvoyance (XII, p. 132):

> 'I can see things where other men are blind. That is why I am Known and at the same time I am Unknowable ... I can see tomorrow; that is why I can tell Umuaro: *Come out from this because there is death there or do this because there is profit in it.*'

Thus a continual issue in many a major encounter is how far this rhetoric is translated into concrete reality, or the extent to which this ideal of priestly vocation is realized in the exertions of the living incumbent. Sight and vision thus become a pervasive thread of imagery in the narrative, informing its main themes and touching off some of its most dramatic encounters.

Even that ominously daring temptation to speculative wilfulness which Ezeulu betrays quite early in the story is a manifestation of this imagery (I, 3–4):

> Whenever Ezeulu considered the immensity of his power over the year and the crops and, therefore, over the people he wondered if it was real.

It was true he named the day for the feast of the Pumpkin Leaves and for the New Yam feast; but he did not choose it. He was merely a watchman ... No! The Chief Priest of Ulu was more than that, must be more than that. If he should refuse to name the day there would be no festival – no planting and no reaping. But could he refuse? No Chief Priest had ever refused. So it could not be done. He would not dare ...

His mind never content with shallow satisfactions crept again to the brinks of knowing. What kind of power was it if it would never be used? Better to say that it was not there, that it was no more than the power in the anus of the proud dog who sought to put out a furnace with his puny fart ...

Ezeulu's meditative habit of intellectual curiosity, true as it is to his vocation of insight and foresight, certainly tends to overreach itself here. For he is misconstruing a delegated constitutional prescript for an invitation to megalomaniac self-exertion, at least as a potential temptation to himself. So, early in the story, we thus begin to sense presages of trouble. Indeed, as he himself later warns Obika with one of those proverbs which turn out to be so ironically adumbrative of his own fate, 'the death that will kill a man begins as an appetite' (VIII, p. 89). For, as we see in the end, it is precisely Ezeulu's refusal to name the day for one of these public festivals, however motivated by intervening circumstances, that ultimately precipitates his own ruin and threatens the very survival of Umuaro and its central priesthood.

The part of the Pumpkin festival following the mythic recitative is the purification rite proper (VII, pp. 72–3). It involves the ritual hazing of the Eze-Ulu as 'thousands and thousands' of Umuaro women symbolically hurl upon his person the evils and misfortunes of their households in the form of bunches of pumpkin leaves which each woman has brought to the ceremony for the purpose. The Chief Priest thus serves as ritual carrier of the community's sins and misfortunes for burial in the shrine of Ulu. Scapegoatism and vicarious responsibility are thus enacted as a pre-eminent institutional condition of the Ulu priesthood. The main literary relevance of the rite, apart of course from the sheer drama of it, accordingly seems to spring from its being the most heightened evocation of the scapegoat psychology in the novel. For this dimension is later on intermittently invoked as a valid perspective for our apprehension of experience and the attribution of liability at crucial points in the rest of the story. So, for instance, in his fateful incarceration by the white man, it turns out after all that Ezeulu merely fell innocent victim to a conspiracy between a bungling arrogance of power and history's freakish aptitude for wavering

(XIII–XV). But also, that in wreaking his vengeance for this upon Umuaro by artificially inflicting a famine on them, he was obviously making a scapegoat of his people for what could after all be seen as an accident of history. Indeed, Ezeulu seems caught in a cycle of scapegoatism in more senses than one. Incumbent of a priesthood founded upon vicariousness, he is predictably exposed sometimes to undue molestation and undeserved victimization, not to mention the yearly exertion of ritual hazing; but that priesthood also gives him perhaps too free a hand to inflict unspeakable suffering on too wide a scale by mere act of will. He is endued with the scapegoat psychology as much by force of habit as of destiny. And perhaps the greatest irony of the whole story is that its most dire consequences seem to flow directly from the very cultural provisions made by the people for their own welfare.

It is during the initial perambulatory rite of the same Pumpkin festival that the Chief Priest publicly enacts the myth of Ulu's First Coming, following it up with a full recitation of it (VII, pp. 68–71). The intrinsic meanings of such periodic rituals which incorporate recitative enactments of cosmogonic myths have been the subject of some active debate among historians of religions.[11] The basic philosophy at the heart of the Umuaro myth of origin as recited here by the Eze-Ulu is the general presumption of the ideal pliancy of experience and malleability of history. The recitative would seem to encapsulate the people's habitual mode of response to the more challenging eventualities of their ongoing experience of history, attitudes now crystallized in their general conception of the Ulu priesthood. The mythic form condenses that outlook, authenticating and sanctioning it as it were with the imprint of immemoriality. But both its internal structure and the outer ritual pattern enveloping the recitative, an insistent recurrence in either case, seem to affirm the myth as a proven mode of perception and response to which the people may perennially resort during historic contingencies and pressures or challenges of transition, whether these are historically or cosmically generated and whether they spring from a purely intracultural or partly external interplay of forces. History is thus depicted as ideally tolerable: it can be made sense of and put to man's use instead of being escaped or denied. Man can humanize time; he can sometimes tame the seeming intractability of all new experiences for integration into the relevant culture system. And with tact, patience and insight, even the inscrutable powers of event may be anticipated. The Ulu priesthood is Umuaro's institutional means of seeking to embody such a world-view and to solicit its transition into reality in every phase of their onward journey through time and history. Its enveloping mythology and rituals are symbolic enactments or embodiments of that philosophy and their continual aspiration to realize it in their historical experience.

At the founding of the Umuaro polity and its central deity of Ulu, so goes the myth of origin, the first Eze-Ulu had agreed to assume the immense task of spiritual leadership only after considerable reluctance. Having accepted it, however, he presumably at once enacted a symbolic journey through time, during which the basic Igbo units of time or of their four-day week (Eke, Oye, Afo, Nkwo) separately constitute themselves into major successive challenges or threats of 'evil' to all Umuaro. It is apparently this journey that the Eze-Ulu acts out at the Pumpkin festival even before he recites its accompanying myth (VII, p. 70). At any rate, the myth personifies each day into a symbol of some formidable force of happenstance or history, heralded by a set of disconcerting phenomena and emanations which seem in turn to symbolize the virtualities and challenges in transitional phases of existence and history. The Nkwo emanation of an old woman 'dancing strange steps' on a hill is probably suggestive of such a symbolism of transition and change. In the people's encounter with each of them, it is their Eze-Ulu who first has to meet the new challenge or 'obstacle', discern the basic circumstantial imperatives of its attendant realities, and then find an appropriate way to conciliate or 'remove that evil'. In that way he defuses the situation, as it were, and so clears the way for his retinue of adherents to go past on their continuing journey. As in the case of welcoming the new moon, which is remarkably continuous in import with this myth, it is partly through sacrifice and supplication that the Eze-Ulu effects his feat of mollifying the hitherto unforeseen. Among the more important aspects of his vocation highlighted in the recitative may be mentioned his responsibility of anticipative vision or insight, the stipulative compact of the people's supportive fellowship with him at every crucial juncture of transition, together with his own balancing obligation of a clear-minded perception of realistic solutions at such junctures.

An extract from the recitative itself, with some of its pointers to aspects of the Ulu priesthood emphasized, may give a clearer idea of its basic pattern and symbolic structure:

As day broke on Nkwo and *the sun carried its sacrifice* I carried my Alusi and, with all the people behind me, set out on that journey. A man

sang with the flute on my right and another replied on my left. *From behind the heavy tread of all the people gave me strength.* And then all of a sudden something spread itself across my face. On one side it was raining, on the other it was dry. *I looked again and saw* that it was Eke.
I said to him: 'Is it you Eke?'
He replied: 'It is I, Eke, the one that makes a strong man bite the earth with his teeth.'
I took a hen's egg and gave him. He took it and ate and gave way to me. We went on past streams and forests . . .
. . . and then I saw that my head was too heavy for me. *I looked steadily and saw* that it was Afo.
I said: 'Is it you Afo?'
He said: 'It is I, Afo, the great river that cannot be salted.'
I replied: 'I am Ezeulu, the hunchback more terrible than a leper.'
Afo shrugged and said: 'Pass, your own is worse than mine.'
I passed and the sun came down and beat me and the rain came down and drenched me. Then I met Nkwo. *I looked on his left and saw* an old woman, tired, *dancing strange steps* on the hill. I looked to the right and saw a horse and saw a ram. I slew the horse and with the ram I cleaned my matchet, and so *removed that evil.* (VII, p. 71; my italics)

We see recurring here a basic pattern of prior priestly detection of strange or disconcerting phenomena, followed by a sense of confrontation and subsequent propitiation of the opposing force through sacrifice. And yet, as Afo's immunity to it would suggest, sacrifice is not an absolute panacea, just as not every challenge of existence may be readily amenable to man's humanizing quest. But, again as Afo's empathetic understanding and compassion would show, certain challenges of experience tend sometimes to be easier to assimilate. When, however, a major force of history is too refractory and its prime-moving personnel not half as understanding as Afo here, a people up against its inevitability can hardly hope for options other than the tragic.

The recitative's midrib motif of a journey intermittently held up by some adamant 'obstacle' or 'evil' is itself a timeless symbol of man's perpetual traverse of time and his inescapable encounters with unfolding forces of event. One such force in the mythical past of Umuaro had been the raiding soldiers of Abam, whose threat to their survival had apparently led to the establishment of the Ulu priesthood itself as 'the central unity of the six villages' in their newly founded confederation (II, pp. 14–15; XVI, p. 187). These raids have got settled within the Umuaro memory and sensibility as a symbol for all intractable forces of experience and history. The European presence with which they are now confronted in the narrative is merely another such force, the latest 'obstacle' or 'evil' in their collective march of history. Ezeulu's invocations of the myth of Ulu in connection with various encounters and experiences in the story suggest that he perceives this new confrontation with the white man in accordance with the underlying philosophy and historic destiny of the Ulu priesthood as outlined above. And Achebe's own occasional glossing of Ezeulu's mental operations during his people's engagement with the advent of Europe would seem to invite a similar interpretative framework. 'He [Ezeulu] said, "This thing is coming ... Let us absorb this thing that is coming; let's arrest it before it ruins or breaks us".'[12]

Implicit in Ezeulu's concern here and in his general preceptual admonition to his people is the priestly responsibility in respect of innovation and cultural renewal, an aspect of the Umuaro sensibility which is only minimally enacted in the refined symbolism of the recitative. There is adequate evidence for it, however, in the awareness and exertions of both Ezeulu and the people themselves. For Achebe sustains in this third novel a renewed emphasis on the endogenous inducement of change as a traditional culture function. In the earlier novel *Things Fall Apart*, indigenous motivations to change are either merely inchoative at the level of the individual conscience or otherwise diffusely spread in the community's capacity for accommodation. That is, culture change is neither institutionalized into a specific culture functionary nor politicized into a self-conscious personal vocation of some significance. Only the novel's ironic symbolism and the people's wider tolerance seem to carry this crucial theme of the necessity and appreciation of change among the people of Umuofia. In *Arrow of God*, on the contrary, the emphasis in this regard has now shifted considerably. For cultural renewal is not only implanted now into the central character as a positive dispositional consciousness; this is the main point of Ezeulu's strenuous explanations of his reasons for his dealings with his son Oduche and for his general attitude to the new dispensation of the white man (XII, pp. 129–34). But beyond that it is also depicted as a time-hallowed function of the central priesthood of Ulu, as Ezeulu's references to a few historical instances of selective elimination of cultural traits by two previous Eze-Ulus should clarify (pp. 132–3). And since that priesthood is the nerve centre of the people's consciousness of history, an evolutionary principle of endogenous change is thereby incorporated into their general philosophy of history. The periodic reactivation of this principle, as is considered requisite in varying historic circumstances, thus emerges as a key responsibility of the Chief

Priest of Ulu. So, of course, it is true that 'there was scope for change in traditional society', as Obiechina says. But it is certainly incorrect for him to read *Arrow of God* as affirming that such scope for change 'had to be in areas outside those made sacrosanct by the religious and ritual order'.[13] Surely, neither the founding of a central deity in Umuaro, nor the disestablishing of another in Aninta (as Nwaka never tires of pointing out), nor even other cultural shifts proudly cited by Ezeulu or solicitously commended to him by the elders, would be seen as merely marginally sacrosanct by the people concerned. It is the same principle of innovativeness that the elders appeal to when they seek to persuade Ezeulu to avert the famine threatened by his delay of the harvest at the end of the story; they wind up their delegation aptly and emphatically with 'numerous examples of customs that had been altered in the past when they began to work hardship on the people' (XVIII, pp. 205—9).

Major dramatic conflict and action in this novel are consistently informed by two related basic concerns. The first, which is essentially philosophic, relates to the general quality of Ezeulu's personal apprehension of the highest purposes of the Ulu priesthood. And the second, ultimately of a more dramatic and political upshot, concerns the depth and consistency of his practical adherence to the fundamental principles and circumstantial dictates of an Eze-Ulu's historic destiny. The more significant encounters of the narrative tend to revolve around these vital questions; hence the invocation of the rhetoric and mythology enveloping this central priesthood in reference to most of them.

For instance, Ezeulu's disagreement with his people in their war with Okperi seeks justification from their myth of origin (II, pp. 14—29). And his accommodative dalliance with the white man's new dispensation, especially as reflected in his dealings with Oduche, fraught as it is with irritating dilemmas like the boy's violation of the totemic python prohibitions, ultimately invokes the same creation myth as its primary motivation and justification (XII, pp. 133—4). Even the old priest's summoning and imprisonment by the white man at a most neatly inopportune time of the Umuaro ritual calendar is reinterpreted in the end as conceivably compatible with his priestly destiny as enacted in myth and ritual (XII—XVI, esp. pp. 188—9). And in his retaliatory decision to suspend his people's inalienable right to a reasonable harvest, the implications in terms of his priestly obligations and the import of the Ulu myth seem to be the relevant terms of reference (XVIII–XIX). In all these encounters, which trace the entire backbone of dramatic interest in this novel, the people or Ezeulu himself repeatedly seek to refer motivation, action, reaction or response back to the proper conception of their central priesthood and its enabling mythology, in the light of which each conflict may then be reinterpreted or sought to be resolved. This is how Ezeulu's perception and performance of the basic conditions of his vocation are also systematically elicited and tested. And in the process the relevance of the central myth and ritual complex to the novel's meaning and significance is still further revealed.

Ezeulu dispels all doubt about his philosophic perception of his responsibilities when he explains to Akuebue his reasons for turning Oduche over to the new ways of the white man's dispensation. After citing historical innovations effected by the two Eze-Ulus immediately preceding him, he plunges into the hieratic idiom of their myth of origin to justify his dealings with the boy and, by implication, his trying accommodativeness towards the white man in general:

> Shall I tell you why I sent my son [to a strange religion]? Then listen. A disease that has never been seen before cannot be cured with everyday herbs ... And our fathers have told us that it may even happen to an unfortunate generation that they are pushed beyond the end of things, and their back is broken and hung over a fire. When this happens they may sacrifice their own blood. This is what our sages meant when they said that a man who has nowhere else to put his hand for support puts it on his own knee. *That was why our ancestors when they were pushed beyond the end of things by the warriors of Abam sacrificed not a stranger but one of themselves and made the great medicine which they called Ulu.* (XII, pp. 133–4; my italics)

Ezeulu is rendering here an interpretation of the Ulu myth and also reapplying its essential import at the same time to the disconcerting historic circumstances prevailing in Umuaro since the coming of the white man. According to him, a people do sometimes come up against unprecedented but inescapable challenges of existence or history, fraught with discomfiture and dilemmas, during which only acts of extraordinary courage or imaginative daring are likely to ensure their survival and the possible assimilation of the new force. He obviously considers the advent of Europe as one such juncture in the history of Umuaro, one when they are practically 'pushed beyond the end of things'. He also seems to be suggesting that his dealings with Oduche, together of course with his accommodating inclinations towards the white man's literacy, are new imperative applications of the fundamental principles enshrined in the original founding of Ulu, especially the priestly obligations of vision, advanced engagement with new forces, and of eclectic innovativeness in requisite circumstances. And although personal motivations are always part of such strategies, Ezeulu's manoeuvres would accordingly be a sort of general precept to his people in the circumstances. His personal predisposition towards change is unquestioned.

His adherence to the dictates and imperatives of his historic calling, however, is neither altogether consistent nor always in his people's collective interest. For in his last five years of sanity Umuaro is plagued at least twice by that classic dilemma of political life, the stalemate of divergence between general popular consensus and the personal leadership will or conscience. This happens, respectively, during the land dispute and war with Okperi (II, pp. 14–29) and later on again during the famine caused by his own artificial delay of one year's harvest (XVIII–XIX). The dilemma in each case is either merely aggravated or actually set in motion by the intrusion of the white man. But while the Chief Priest's conscience is apparently untainted and even vindicated perhaps in the earlier disagreement, it is certainly soured and impaired by the time of his refusal to call the public harvest.

His unprovoked and ill-timed imprisonment by the white man is the main factor that helps taint Ezeulu's conscience. For it exposes a deep-seated irascibility and vengefulness that the Chief Priest has hitherto barely managed to suppress. Henceforth they increasingly get the better of the old priest, befuddle his clarity of perception, and upset his balance of public judgement. From now on he is practically blinded to the circumstantial implications and requisite imperatives of his priestly vocation. Meanwhile, however, his rejection of the offer of chieftaincy which leads to extension of his detention incidentally earns him some invaluable vindications. For he is thereby practically acquitted of the crude secular megalomania his critics in Umuaro had always suspected from his natural haughtiness of character or from their own sheer malice. It is also barely a couple of weeks afterwards that his captors are instructed from headquarters against any further appointments of new Warrant Chiefs. This surprise vindication by a caprice of history, though unknown to either Ezeulu or his people, gives edge to a growing feeling 'that he had been used very badly' indeed (XV, pp. 176–78). The imprisonment shows Ezeulu in fact as a true

victim of history, a non-ritualized enactment yet again of his voca-
tional fate as scapegoat. And his rejection of the chieftaincy is
perhaps the finest moment of his entire career. By the time of his
release from detention, however, he has already started on his
heedless plunge into vengeful betrayal of that sacred trust of public
destiny with which his priesthood is charged.

His new state of mind as he returns home is an ominous mixture
of an irascible persecution mania and a vengeful sado-masochism.
While some of these traits spring naturally from his native character, however, a few others are all too probable psychological consequences of a long career of active ritualistic scapegoatism and
rhetoric of vicariousness. These latter would include his newly
heightened sense of self-persecution and his gloating indulgence
of suffering as a means of maximizing grievances in order to further
justify ultimate revenge (XIV, p. 165; XV, p. 178; XVI, pp. 182–4).
For Ezeulu had long been concerned about the internal dissensions
in Umuaro as a potential threat to the entire Ulu institution as the
centre of the people's unity. The elders' lapse of presence of mind,
as revealed in their failure to appreciate the ominousness of the
white man's importunate summoning of the Eze-Ulu just a couple
of days before a new moon is due to be announced by him, only
aggravates his earlier misgivings by contributing to his imprisonment (XIII, pp. 140–8). He therefore returns home now indignant
and bent on teaching Umuaro a severely punitive lesson. Fed fat for
months on a meditative ritualizing of the suffering self, however,
his ultimate retaliation turns out to be out of all proportion to the
original provocations.

It is at this crux of affairs that the balance of blame and liability
becomes an especially insistent issue in this novel. But this question can be fully answered only in relation to a relatively total
conception of the priesthood of Ulu and a wide enough appreciation of Ezeulu's personal exertions in respect of it throughout the
narrative. The withheld harvest, though undoubtedly inexcusable,
need not be the sole point of reference. And, in any case, one must
be mindful of his vicarious role as an institutional scapegoat in his
people's confrontations with history and how that may be realized
sometimes outside the realm of mere ceremony or ritual. Northrop
Frye has set out a basic outline of liability in tragic fiction centred
upon such a 'a typical or random victim':

We may call this typical victim the *pharmakos* or scapegoat ... The
pharmakos is neither innocent nor guilty. He is innocent in the sense

that what happens to him is far greater than anything he has done
provokes, like the mountaineer whose shout brings down an avalanche.
He is guilty in the sense that he is a member of a guilty society, or living
in a world where such injustices are an inescapable part of existence.
The two facts do not come together; they remain ironically apart.[14]

The basic point here is the delicacy of moral balance, while the
respective sets of determinant 'facts' would be manifested in varying degrees in different cases.

Meanwhile, the general famine unleashed on Umuaro by Ezeulu
later on intensifies; and it deepens a growing popular hostility
against him and his household. So when the myth of origin recurs
for the last time in the narrative, the contextual emphasis now falls
clearly on the discrepancy between the original purposes of the
priesthood and this unfortunate abdication coming really so late in
the life of an Eze-Ulu who has hitherto shown such understanding
insight into its workings and conditions:

> Because no one came near enough to him to see his anguish – and if they
> had seen it they would not have understood – they imagined that he sat
> in his hut gloating over the distress of Umuaro. But although *he would
> not for any reason now see the present trend reversed* he carried more
> punishment and more suffering than all his fellows. What troubled him
> most – *and he alone seemed to be aware of it at present* – was *that the
> punishment was not for now alone but for all time.* It would afflict
> Umuaro like an *ogulu-aro* disease which counts a year and returns to its
> victim. Beneath all anger in his mind lay a deeper compassion for
> Umuaro, the clan which *long, long ago when lizards were in ones and
> twos chose his ancestor to carry their deity and go before them chal-
> lenging every obstacle and confronting every danger on their behalf.*
> (XIX, 219; my italics)

Ezeulu's compassion for Umuaro in its plight may be touching and
sincere. But he is too fully knowledgeable about the purposes of the
Ulu priesthood and the dire consequences of its betrayal or violation for his wilful rejection or balking of positive action to be
redeemed by a mere depth of sincere compassion. For, to recall his
own specious reasoning in his earlier temptation to speculative
wilfulness (I, pp. 3–4), what kind of compassion was it if it would
never reverse a self-induced general distress which it has the
power, means and duty to remove? Better to say that it was no less
than the final realization of that tendency to wilful self-exertion
which had earlier on been manifested merely at the level of medita-
tiveness. For Ezeulu seems clearly aware here, though not daunted
by the expected consequences, of the cosmic enormity involved in

thus seeking to perpetually dislocate his people's sense of time and the entire biocosmic rhythm of their life. The real human agony is, of course, patently the fate of all to endure. It is clear now to elders and populace alike that the Chief Priest has deserted relevant dictates and implications of his office in the prevailing circumstances, that he has betrayed the sacred charge of public trust. For he lets slip at last, after nearly twenty years of presumably diligent priesthood, that requisite sense of public responsibility and moral insight which should always go with all such immensity of power held on trust. The consequences for priest, people and priesthood are swift and far-reaching.

Arrow of God is thus an insightful study of power, leadership and their joint interplay with history and community. And it is informed by a rudimentary philosophy of history that is thoroughly and authentically African, a philosophy which determines the terms of the people's perception and integration of the vicissitudes and challenges they encounter in their general experience of history. The pivot of that philosophy is their central priesthood of Ulu. So that the intrinsic meanings of the enabling mythology and ritual cycle surrounding that priesthood afford a crucial guide in interpreting the novel and assessing its significance. The would-be anthropology of *Arrow of God* encapsulates the thematic core of the novel and is the very humus of its rhetoric.

NOTES

1. W. Soyinka, *Myth, Literature and the African World*, Cambridge, Cambridge University Press, 1976, pp. 91–2. See also my review of it in *Lore and Languages*, Sheffield, July 1977, pp. 50–1.
2. Chinua Achebe, *Arrow of God*, London, Heinemann, 1964, rev. edn 1974. The second edition is the one cited here, all references being to chapter and page numbers.
3. Harold Bloom, *The Anxiety of Influence*, London, Oxford University Press, 1973, p. 5.
4. G. D. Killam, *The Writings of Chinua Achebe*, London, Heinemann, 1977, p. 61.
5. C. E. Nnolim, 'A source for *Arrow of God*', *Research in African Literatures*, 8, 1977, pp. 1–26.
6. Richard D. Altick, *The Art of Literary Research*, New York, Norton, 1975, p. 95.

7. K. Awoonor, 'Tradition and continuity in African literature', in Karen L. Morell (ed.), *In Person: Achebe, Awoonor, and Soyinka*, Seattle, African Studies Program, University of Washington, 1975, p. 143.

8. C. Achebe, *Morning Yet on Creation Day*, London, Heinemann, 1975, p. 35.

9. E. D. Jones, 'Nationalism and the writer,' in J. Press (ed.), *Commonwealth Literature*, London, Heinemann, 1965, p. 156.

10. This analysis finds it necessary to stress the distinction between the office and the person of the novel's all-important priesthood of Ulu. Accordingly, the hyphenated form 'Eze-Ulu' and its English equivalent 'the Chief Priest' are used here to refer to the office or vocation of that priesthood, while 'Ezeulu' refers to the person of the present incumbent.

11. See in particular Mircea Eliade, *The Myth of the Eternal Return*, 1949, trans. W. R. Trask, New York, Bollingen Series, Pantheon, 1954, esp. pp. 51–92; and Samuel G. F. Brandon, *History, Time and Deity*, Manchester University Press, 1965, esp. pp. 1–30, 65–73. Our interpretation here is an implicit confutation of Eliade and is more in accord with Brandon.

12. C. Achebe, in *Palaver*, ed. B. Lindfors *et al.*, Austin, Texas, University of Texas, 1972, p. 9.

13. Emmanuel Obiechina, *Culture, Tradition and Society in the West African Novel*, Cambridge, Cambridge University Press, 1975, p. 228.

14. N. Frye, *Anatomy of Criticism*, Princeton, NJ, Princeton University Press, pp. 41–2.

Sunset at Dawn: A Biafran on the Nigerian Civil War

Alex C. Johnson

A disinterested assessment of recent history is always a diffi-cult undertaking, especially when the people involved are still alive and all the facts may not be available. This is clearly a problem for the historian but it is no less a problem for the creative writer or the critic whose concerns are specifically artistic. This is because the proximity of the experience, the deep passions engendered by events and the personal involvement of the individual do have a direct bearing on the artistic creation. It would not be unusual therefore for literary works based on such recent history to be partisan, strident or recriminatory and hence fail as art. But if the writer were to avoid these dangers and, while being true to his experience, give his material a critical perspective and literary form, he would have asserted the triumph of his art over his baser instincts.

For those who lived through it, the Nigeria/Biafra War[1] was a signally horrific and traumatic experience. The shock waves were felt throughout the Nigerian Federation and Nigerian writers were among the casualties, the most notable fatality being Christopher Okigbo.[2]

As with all significant human experience, it was inevitable that much literary activity would follow it, especially with the concen-tration of writers in Nigeria and their personal involvement in the war. The creative output has taken many forms: verse, *Christmas in Biafra* by Chinua Achebe and *Casualties* by J. P. Clark; reminis-cences, *Sunset in Biafra* by Elechi Amadi and *The Man Died* by Wole Soyinka; novels, *Survive the Peace* by Cyprian Ekwensi, *Sunset at Dawn* by Chukwuemeka Ike, *Forty-eight Guns for the General* by Eddie Iroh, *Behind the Rising Sun* by S. O. Mezu, *The*

Last Duty by Isidore Okpewho; and short stories, *Girls at War* by Chinua Achebe.[3] Each of these texts presents a fair account of different aspects of the war with varying points of view and degrees of literary competence.

Amadi's subtitle, *A Civil War Diary*, indicates that the emphasis is on an individual's experience of actual people and events, but it has an overtly pro-Federal stance. He therefore consistently discredits the Biafran position so that every description, interpretation and evaluation of incidents and events is coloured by this attitude. Even where towards the end the whole thrust of events in his narrative could only justify the secessionists' claims about the treatment of civilians by Federal troops, the diarist shies away from this interpretation. Perhaps this is understandable in view of the unjustified imprisonment and harassment he suffered at the hands of the secessionists, and the agony and indignity of detention which many like him experienced. However, he does make some concessions to the Biafran position in some of the generalizations he makes about the tribe and the herd instinct as well as the individual acts of humanity shown to him in the rebel areas. Nevertheless, a picture of what events during the war looked like from one side emerges in this work and gives historical actuality to it.

In *Behind the Rising Sun*, Mezu explores yet another aspect of the war by showing the hazardous manoeuvrings in the arms black market by the Europe-based Biafran diplomats as they attempt to secure desperately needed supplies for their blockaded republic. The scope of the novel is widened when the writer brings some of those diplomats to West Africa on a near-epic but futile diplomatic offensive and ultimately into Biafra itself. Mezu is critical of these diplomats for they are seen to be inept and too ostentatious in their life-style considering the urgency of the situation. There is too much jockeying for power and rivalry among them when they ought to be aware of the urgent fact that the lives of whole units and civilians depend on the supplies they can secure. They are further exposed when they fall for bizarre deals and exhibit gross incaution and inexperience.

They may, however, be partly excused for their failures for the writer shows that the European arms black market is a veritable minefield where unscrupulous, shady con-men operate. But in spite of this, the reader is still critical of them, for as the deals became more involved and too extravagant, they should have paused to consider the situation or check the credentials of some of the people they were doing business with as one of them did at one point. The more one reads this section of the novel the more astonishing and unreal some of the schemes become, for a complex web of deception emerges whose intricate convolutions are so glaring that one wonders how history might have been changed if the large sums which were lost had been more productively used.

The ineffective foray into West Africa is given too much space and the triviality of some of the incidents makes the reader lose sight of the main design. But this section of the book does bring out the hazardous night flights by gun-running and relief-carrying planes through the Federal gauntlet and the vagaries of the weather. The courage of the fliers and the frustrations of the organizers are much in evidence.

Mezu's treatment of recent history is quite objective for a 'Biafran' as he does not spare the establishment but rather exposes the irresponsibility of the military and civilian authorities, their misleading reassurances to the civilians when they knew that military situations were hopeless, their insensitivity to the feelings of the masses, the way they let down the refugees by failing to evacuate food stores, as at Owerri, and many more. There are serious inadequacies in the conception and realization of experience which diminish the success of this novel but on the whole it does present a balanced account of recent events.

Ekwensi's thriller goes to the end of the war to give an insight into the situation at the time of the Biafran surrender but it does so in an altogether anecdotal and badly organized manner typical of his writing. The material is there which could have been presented in a disciplined way so that a more engaging and consistent account of the surrender and its aftermath would have emerged. But the reporter's sweeping viewpoint and desire for sensationalism skims over, among other things, the Biafran soldiers shedding their uniforms to join in the mass panic, others fighting on unaware of the surrender, the 'attack' women and their lucrative trade across fighting lines, the relief and rehabilitation efforts and the armed robbers trying to survive the peace through violence. From the confused presentation some impression of the situation at the time could be extracted but there are too many extravagant postures and implausible events and the felt reality of human experience takes second place to the reporter's instincts. The historical events have therefore not been refined into art though the actuality is there and can be discerned.

Much more consummate artistry is in evidence in *The Last Duty* which is more obviously fiction than the other novels. The violence of war is minimal and peripheral to the plot though rebel guerilla attacks and air-raids take place; but the war situation forms a pervasive and inescapable background to the events and these would never have occurred had there been no war. This is quite appropriate as the story is set, not in Biafra, but in liberated Federal territory not too far from the front line.

While exploring a number of themes, the writer describes certain events and states of affairs which existed during the Civil War: how the rhythm of life in the community was disrupted; the stress imposed on individuals on an emotional and psychological level; the vindictive manipulating of the military authorities for selfish and wicked motives; the distasteful settling of old scores by exploiting the opportunities presented by the changed situation; the military tribunals investigating the detained; the vigorous efforts by the military authorities to protect all, even members of the rebel tribe; the assertion of personal integrity and self-respect in the face of overwhelming odds. Through a sensitive exploration and development of these events and his themes, Okpewho succeeds in giving the reader the feel of life in a war situation. The writer lays bare each individual's soul, motives and character reinforcing each by the use of appropriate language and the first-person narrative. Thus the characters emerge as every bit human and we share in their passions, needs and every human instinct that they show.

Sunset at Dawn contains the impressions of a writer who experiences the war from inside Biafra. What may be called the 'plot' consists of a chronological account of events during the war in military, political and human terms with dates and important stages in the struggle. This gives a historical overview and adds actuality to the events. The writer follows each by examining and exploring specific situations and incidents and through these shows how the lives of the people were affected. This gives substance to the content and, together with the main forward development of the story, enables the writer to present the war in profoundly human terms.

The emphasis in this novel is on the human experience of these recent historical events. The characters so carefully handled in these contexts, whose lives we witness as they go through the war and are changed by it, can be classified into two main groups. There is an urban, business, intellectual and professional class and an essentially rural, traditional community of ordinary people. Professor Ezenwa, Dr Amilo Kanu, his wife Fatima, Duke Bassey a wealthy businessman, civil servants Akwaelumo and Onukaegbe, belong to the first group; and Chief Ofo, 'Chief' Ukadike, Mazi Kanu Onwubiko and the other Obodo villagers represent the second group.

Ike distinguishes these two groups of people very effectively in terms of their social and educational class, their concerns, preoccupations and life-style during the war, their language and conception of the enemy. For example, for the urban group, the enemy is the vandals or Nigerians but for the Obodo villagers it is the Hausas. This unique differentiation is revealing as it brings out the deep-rooted tribal animosities which informed the war and injects further historical actuality into the novel. When the villagers decided to fight, their strong feelings about this enemy, about what they thought they could endure from him and when they had to stop running away from him are clearly brought out in terms which underline the tribal dimensions of this conflict.

The westernized urban group are shown as part of the secessionist establishment and, historically, it constituted its main support. They hold the various war directorates, dominate the military, pursue war research and are seen to be near the centres of power, for they can reach H.E. himself or those nearest him. These people therefore enjoy the privileges which that position gives them and are in an ideal position to cushion themselves against the more violent shocks of the war. As military reverses multiply, they help mislead the people with one implausible explanation after another or promote unjustified optimism whilst quietly taking steps to protect and secure their families. At times they appear to wander around rather purposelessly indulging in drink and sex as the malaise and stress of a hopeless war threaten to overtake them. But as the war becomes more difficult and takes a toll of their lives and property, they too show the impotence of their situation and share in the common anxiety.

The main focus of attention in this group are Dr Kanu, Fatima and Duke Bassey. Kanu is one of those who considered their interests very carefully before embracing Biafra but when he does so, it is with total involvement and commitment. As Director of Mobilization he applies himself with dedication and a sense of purpose. It is this conviction and sense of mission which lead him to take up arms and ultimately die during an air-raid, while convalescing. In Fatima, a Hausa married to an Ibo, Ike successfully underlines a specific truth about the war – that even though there was an overtly tribalistic dimension to it, people from both sides of the tribal divide were caught up on the wrong side. Fatima loses her elder son in a mortar attack on Enugu and is forced to take refuge in a typical Ibo village where she does relief work among the children. She experiences the horror and carnage of the air-raids and sees the misery of the refugees. The horrible actuality about her and the tension it causes shatter her nerves until she almost suffers a mental breakdown and has to be sent out of the country to Libreville. Through personal suffering and exposure to the suffering of others like her kinswoman Halima, she develops and changes. By the time she returns home, to witness her husband's funeral, she has become a thoroughly committed if not fanatical Biafran who almost rejects her Nigerian parents. Professor Ezenwa is not fully developed but is given enough substance to be seen as a representative of the committed intellectual who is both cautious and critical. His growing awareness of the failures and mistakes of the leadership makes him so disenchanted and cynical that, by the end, the others doubt whether he still believes in Biafra.

It is largely through the characters in the first group that the writer reveals the evolving military situation and the hopes and fears on the political and diplomatic fronts since discussion of peace conferences, international recognition, criticism of the establishment could more consistently become topics for conversation among them, especially as they are all part of this establishment. Ezenwa is made to voice disquiet about the wisdom of striking into the mid-west and through Akwaelumo and other civil servants we hear the real concern about the military losses. It took the shrill attack of his wife and the incredulous wonder of his superiors to shock Akwaelumo into evacuating his family from the threatened Enugu. At the end, it is through him that the inevitability of the Biafran collapse is presented.

The second group of characters, the villagers at Obodo, are ordinary people who do not have the advantages of some in the urban areas. For these the war means the enforced removal from their homes, wanderings from village to village and eventual placement in refugee camps. There is relative normality among them at the start even though the war has already produced some changes. For example, the conventions and conduct of village affairs, styles of speech and address, and social relations and expectations still remain but the strange Civil Defence Committee and similar innovations also exert their influence. It is the war which gives the boastful but cowardly liar Ukadike the chance to climb socially and attempt to usurp the authority of Chief Ofo.

Though there are these two specific groups of people they are not isolated from each other but rather they are linked through family relationship, mutual interdependence and above all by the struggle to survive a common experience. Dr Kanu's father lives in the village and his wife takes refuge there. Through these groups of characters, Ike impresses the scope of the war on the reader, underlining the fact that it was not confined to a segment of the nation but brought misery to and touched the lives of all.

The developing uncertainty and fluctuating mood, expectations and morale among these people as the military situation deteriorates or improves which constitute the plot is initially conveyed by the use of a sun and weather image. For example, secession and the hopes it brought are put in this way:

> The Biafra Sun shone brightly from 30 May until the outbreak of war on 6 July. Its presence as an emblem on a soldier's uniform instilled in him a sense of national identity and pride ...
> The Sun's dazzling rays dispelled the clouds of insecurity and hopelessness which had eclipsed the lives of Eastern Nigerians, particularly the Igbo, for over a year.[4]

But with serious reverses on the different fronts, 'the yellow-on-black Biafra Sun lost its dazzle and much of its authenticity'. Then with a consolidation of their resources and the thrust into the mid-west:

> The week before, the sun had been driven into hiding, abdicating its exalted throne for ominous clouds which had enveloped the earth in daylight darkness and unleashed torrential downpours on a saturated earth. The August break enabled the sun to assert its supremacy once again over the powers of darkness, and the sun responded by showering down its rays lavishly.
> The Biafra Sun burst free from near ignominy and shone radiantly from its position of supremacy, triumphant as a cockerel descending heroically from the back of a hen it has conquered.[5]

However, when the euphoria of the mid-west adventure has subsided and they have been chased out, there is a similar shift in the imagery;

> September 1967.
> The fine weather had come to an end. Heavy rains again took over, driving the sun from the sky, even at noon. The Biafra Sun found itself similarly chased off the sky. August had been its month of glory.[6]

This changing situation is closely tied to character development and the exploration of specific events to maintain the human terms of the war. The anxiety and uncertainty surrounding Enugu under threat from Federal forces occupies all in the town for they are directly affected, especially those who have had to evacuate other towns before. We therefore see the desperate but rather foolhardy preparations for a matchet attack to defend the city which Dr Kanu is planning. During these preparations, there is a mortar attack which sends everyone diving for cover and kills Dr Kanu's son. When the town falls, Dr Kanu and Akwaelumo are understandably demoralized and the former becomes very bitter at the failure of the Biafran leadership to exploit the town's natural defences. The loss of Enugu is followed by other losses – Onitsha, the Rivers Area, Port Harcourt, Owerri, Obodo and Umuahia. There is a perceptible chronology in all this showing the war moving to its inevitable end and Biafran territory shrinking.

The human consequences of this deteriorating military situation can be seen in the person of Duke Bassey the wealthy owner of a chain of supermarkets who is typical to the extent that he represents the kind of loss suffered by individual business-owners as the war continued to go against the Biafrans. He suffers a series of losses at Enugu, Onitsha, Port Harcourt and in the Rivers Area. In this last area, it is not only his business but his house, and we presume with it his family, that is destroyed and he almost loses his own life in a mad but belated and futile dash to save them. The psychological effect of all this is that he is reduced to near-insanity and ends up seeing visions, burning candles and joining prayer-groups. This same technique of showing the effects of important milestones in the war on people is in evidence in the attitudes or concern expressed at the roles of Russia, Britain, the USA and the OAU in the conflict, the peace initiatives and international recognition of Biafra. As the fate of Port Harcourt hangs in the balance, the suggestion of peace talks provokes angry outbursts from Professor Ezenwa.

Even in the rural setting, the same pattern of making the fortunes and preoccupations of the people reflect the changing situation is in evidence. The threat to Enugu is alarming to the Obodo villagers because of their proximity to that town. They discuss this with the same anxieties as the town-dwellers but with a more profound feeling of injustice, of having been pursued into their own homes by a common enemy and with an equally common determination to defend the village to the last man, though with an essentially pathetic underestimation of what it means to take on a modern army. There is an awareness and preparedness in the face of this threat and the people are on edge, hence the panic when someone thoughtlessly fires the shots to celebrate the Tanzanian recognition of Biafra. As things get worse the human consequences of the war become more serious. War comes to the village in its full horror as an air-raid is launched against it and the writer presents this in the image of a circle of death which takes in among others the colourful village lecher Prophet James, his church and congregation. The feeling of increasing insecurity after this raid creates mass suspicions and the tendency to find scapegoats especially among the refugees. The tension is such that the usually conciliatory village assembly called to consider the imminent threat to Obodo would have ended in uproarious and frustrating disorder had the Federal mortar attack not broken it up. This ground attack is the signal for the mad race from Obodo to the next village Obia, for as one villager puts it:

> The time to run is when the Nigerians bring their ferrets. Then the sound changes, and you'll hear the Nigerian guns sound as if they are shouting kwapu kwapu unu d-u-u-um! When that sounds, even the lizard runs without further warning.[7]

Thus in an evacuation typical of hundreds more like it, the people are forced to give up the dignity of simple village life for the miseries of a refugee camp. The writer shows what evacuation meant in cultural and human terms with its pathos and even with its snatches of comedy, for displacement profoundly overturned those values which make the people what they are:

> To abandon the town was an even greater abomination. It was tantamount to utter betrayal of all the ancestors of the town, to run, leaving their mortal remains behind to be desecrated by the enemy. It was tantamount to leaving the ancestral homes to grow wild, as if the ancestors had died without male issue. Who would pour libations to the dead and offer them cola every morning? Who would attend to the gods of Obodo?
>
> The sun knew it was an abomination which would provoke the ire of the ancestors, and so refused to show its face. The wind knew it, and so sought an alibi by migrating to other towns, leaving Obodo without the mildest breeze.
>
> Chief Ofo knew it. He also knew that tradition forebade him from sleeping outside his palace for even one night; no Odo of Obodo had ever done so, far back as the human memory could go. He dared not carry the ofo of Obodo to another town, neither could he abandon it at

Obodo without renouncing his title to it. He therefore had no choice but to stay with his ofo in his palace.[8]

It is because Mazi Kanu Onwubika and Chief Ofo did not want to go against this natural order of things that they refused to leave the village.

Besides all these reverses and the fall in morale which they brought, Ike also shows the intermittent surge of optimism with each success or improvement in the military and political situation. Real or anticipated, these affected the character and mood of the people. There is much unjustified hope in the face of Federal pressure, mass optimism due to a belief in their own abilities, misplaced expectations of political developments among the Yoruba favourable to Biafra, the euphoria surrounding the Tanzanian and other diplomatic recognition, the victory at Abagana and the recapture of Owerri.

This rhythm of development, rising and falling morale as the situation unfolds, is continued until even Umuahia is conceded to Federal forces and, as everything crumbles around the Biafrans, Akwaelumo is used to show the desperate and untenable position that had been reached. He reflects on the fact that Biafra is exhausted; that starvation if not guns would force them to capitulate; that their future would be bleak in a forcible reunited Nigeria; that there can only be a forlorn hope of a confederation; that there is a real possibility of a massacre following a military collapse. When the total collapse comes, Ike employs the sun image once again. He even extends it to achieve a many-faceted effect and so communicate something of the local and public response to the departure of H.E. from Biafra at the collapse:

> January 14 1970.
>   Total eclipse over Biafra ... No sign of the Biafra Sun. Not even at noon. Hibernating, like a migratory bird? Gone with the soul of Biafra? Or just disappeared ...[9]

Ike's handling of the war is from the point of view of the insider who must have shared some of the feelings of his characters. His presentation of character and situation is critical and indicates some of the frustration felt at the inexcusable failures of the leadership. There is irony and satire in his treatment of some of these. For example, some of the songs that are intended to be inspiring and morale-boosting turn out to be ironic and rabble-rousing in view of the developing situation and the points in the story at which they occur. Dr Kanu and Professor Ezenwa are invariably criticizing the failures and inadequacies of the leadership. There is a distinct impression that the writer speaks through his characters like the old man who came to plead for an end to the war if people like him had to be conscripted. The conduct of those who reassure the people and hold out hope of resistance but quietly evacuate their own is held up for criticism. Poor leadership in the military and cowardly acts in the face of the enemy are also ridiculed. Though this aspect of the war is given much prominence, the other side comes out as well. Biafran prowess, resilience and achievements in improvisation, weapons production, oil refining and in the military and organizational field are also portrayed, and enable one to see how they were able to sustain thirty months of uneven war.

There are some weaknesses in the total artistic conception, especially in the way some of the historical facts are incorporated into the texture of the novel. When this is badly done, we get less of art and more of documentation and an intrusive heavy-handedness of the historian is unmistakable. Reports of Biafran success in the military and technical fields or their shortage of manpower can be viewed in this light. Halima's harrowing account of how she lost her husband during the 1966 massacres in the north may be necessary to motivate Fatima's development but it seems odd since she could not have been ignorant of such events. The air-raids too are shown as they affected Fatima, but when the writer proceeds to outline the casualties and the gruesome death they meet, the story is held up as he drives home the horrors of these raids on non-military targets.

Nevertheless, the novel does not suffer seriously from these undigested historical details but rather shows controlled artistry and a measured presentation of recent history. The writer's complex attitude and mature response to his experience secures the success of this novel.

NOTES

1. Fought between 6 July 1967 and 14 January 1970.
2. The well-known poet killed fighting on the Nsukka front.
3. Chinua Achebe, *Christmas in Biafra and other Poems*, New York, Doubleday/Anchor, 1973. Almost the same collection available as

Beware Soul Brother, Enugu, Nwankwo-Ifejika and London, Heinemann, 1972.

Chinua Achebe, *Girls At War*, London, Heinemann, 1972.

Elechi Amadi, *Sunset in Biafra*, London, Heinemann, 1973.

J. P. Clark, *Casualties*, London, Longman, 1970.

Cyprian Ekwensi, *Survive the Peace*, London, Heinemann, 1976.

Chukwuemeka Ike, *Sunset at Dawn*, London, Fontana/Collins, 1976.

Eddie Iroh, *Forty-eight Guns for the General*, London, Heinemann, 1977.

S. O. Mezu, *Behind the Rising Sun*, London, Heinemann, 1972.

Isidore Okpewho, *The Last Duty*, London, Longman, 1976.

Wole Soyinka, *The Man Died*, London, Rex Collings, 1972.

4. Ike, op. cit., p. 16.
5. ibid., p. 18.
6. ibid., p. 26.
7. ibid., p. 194.
8. ibid., pp. 204–5.
9. ibid., p. 246.

Glissant's Prophetic Vision of the Past

Juris Silenieks

Historical consciousness, the existential 'being-in-history', as P. H. Simon puts it, is likely to permeate the sensibilities of contemporary writers. What the writer today means by history, Simon continues, 'is not, of course, a reconstitution, even if it were complete, of the past, it is the human becoming, in its total reach, past, present, and future, integrally bound as the very essence of the human adventure and sometimes the entire cosmic adventure'.[1] This existential notion of the import of history is likely to be amplified with those writers whose commitments, with the emergence of new geo-political realities, are directed toward the tasks of nation-building, emancipation and accession to national consciousness. David S. Gordon epitomizes the significance of historical awareness in these terms: 'History as the collective memory of a people of its past experience, its heroes, its great deeds, is a basis for its sense of identity, a reservoir upon which it can draw to give itself meaning, and a destiny, as well as to endow its young with a collective pride and dedication to the tribe, the state, the nation, or the religion.'[2] For many writers of the Caribbean region, historical identity is one of their principal preoccupations proceeding directly from the complexities of their situation.

The Caribbean region is sometimes referred to as an archipelago adrift in search of its identity. In a way, the metaphor is appropriate. It characterizes not only the region's geo-physical and geo-political situation, but also its socio-cultural relations with the other continents. The geographical proximity to the Americas, especially the United States, is sometimes felt as a menacing presence, poised for attack, sometimes as a counterforce promising liberation from the strangulating cultural and economic paternalism of the Old Continent. The Caribbean ties with Africa are complex. For some, following negritude's rediscovery of Africa, the continent looms as a repository of nostalgic intimations of a lost past, as a 'metaphor for black beauty and vanished dignity'.[3] Others look to Africa as an instructive actuality, a paradigm of social co-operation, collectivism that can counter the imposition of European concepts of individuality, freewill, private property, and so on, upon the originally non-occidental, heterogeneous cultures of the Caribbean.

The trauma of the past is ever-present, reaching back to the genocide of the warring Indian tribes by the first European conquerors, the arrival of the African slaves, their brutalization, their violent uprisings and equally vindictive punitive counter-measures, the colonial exploitation that, persisting in the present, has brought about vehement strikes and fostered endemic unemployment and degradation of those who must accept social dole. The policies of cultural assimilation have encouraged the young and the gifted to shed their ethnic traits in exchange for education and job security. M. Jean Benoist concludes his study of the Caribbean region: 'To sum it up, . . . the original Caribbean societies and cultures, which have incurred both the good luck and the misfortune of having a past so murky that their future must be invented, first must know themselves more thoroughly.'[4]

In a way, a vicious circle is implied: in order to know oneself, one must know one's past. But, as Césaire laments: 'I look into my mute past',[5] the past is not immediately accessible. Fragments of old legends, chants and dances still echo the distant times of African freedom. Tales of defiant rebel slaves and brave maroons evoke the misery and the glory of the days of Caribbean slavery. Folklore, however, represents, as Glissant put it, the 'collective unconscious', and to raise the past to a higher level of conscious apprehension, the poet and the historian must co-operate in the effort. The white historians, with but few exceptions, have either distorted accounts of the past, or, even worse, deliberately neglected the history of the black race as essentially unworthy of the historian's interest. Particularly rankling are Hegel's notorious notions of African history. Hegel considered Africa as 'the land of childhood, which, lying beyond the day of self-conscious history, is enveloped in the dark mantle of Night'.[6] He dismissed Africa as essentially a-historic, 'for it has no historical part of the World; it has no movement or development to exhibit' (p. 157). The black race has been excluded from universal history. Now it is a question of 'historical reinsertion', involving not only correction of factual inaccuracies and rectification of white bias, but also re-creation of the past concurrent with the vision of the future, 'a prophetic vision of the past'.[7] Such is the attempt of Edouard Glissant whose life and work are dedicated to the elaboration of a viable concept of *Antillanité* from the inherited cultural *métissage* that is to be viewed not as a curse but as a unique potentiality for shaping a distinct regional destiny.

Edouard Glissant, a Martiniquan writer, educator, and civic activist, has written novels, plays, poetry and essays. His work, at times intellectually hermetic and complex, frequently remains inaccessible to instant analysis and does not evince the characteristics of a committed writer. For Glissant, writing as an act of individual engagement can be of dubious value. Literary creation, generally, is admission of the imperfection of intention realized: 'the writer is always the phantom of the writer he wants to be'.[8] It is through the projection of the individual consciousness into collectivity, through the dialectic relation of 'the I of the other' and 'the other of the US', of the actual and the potential, that the writer's intention can be actualized: 'the consciousness of the nation is thus the consciousness of the relation' (*IP*, p. 207).

The function of the black writer is to commit himself to 'the decisive act, which, in the domain of literature, means to build a nation' (*IP*, p. 185). Nation-building exacts a vision that can 'perceive of the consciousness, the one and only operative, of our being' (*IP*, p. 192). It is also predicated on the recovery of the past. Glissant insists that 'for those whose allotted share of history is only darkness and despair, recovery of the near or distant past is imperative. To renew acquaintance with one's history is to relish fully the present' (*MT*, pp. 7–8). A conscious collectivity is bound together by the apprehension of a common past. Thus, 'collective memory is our urgency: lack and need. Not the "historical" detail (not that alone), but the innermost is to resurge: the diastasis from the womb of Africa, the bifid man, the reshaped brain, the violent useless hand. An absurd manifestness – where poverty and exploitation are wedded to something ineffably ridiculous – and where, noticeable to us alone, a drama without apparent import is being enacted which it is incumbent upon us to transform soon into a fecund Tragedy' (*IP*, p. 187).

Descriptive history, claiming objective criteria, seeking to reproduce *wie es eigentlich gewesen* according to Ranke's aspiration or from Jacob Burchardt's 'Armedian point outside events', is impossible here. The historian must be seconded by the poet, since the task is not only to record and to interpret events, but to re-create the past in a new image, to invest it with a new meaning.

In his epic poem *Les Indes*, Glissant recalls the discovery of the New World, replete with brutality, rapaciousness and idealism of the white adventurer, merchant and priest, who raped the land, massacred the Indians and enslaved the blacks. But the poem concludes with the hope that from this period of violence and mystique of white aggressiveness will emerge a new universal consciousness of humanity. Glissant comments, 'this history is not mine' (*IP*, p. 40), since the white individualist and adventurer reduced the black to a passive spectator of his own victimization. The black 'suffers a history I did not make and yet could not ignore' (*IP*, p. 28). Thus, for the black, 'history suffered' must become 'history to be made' (*IP*, p. 62), with the full realization of one's freedom from imposed and accepted ideologies and moralities: 'I can negate this History, if I am free to do it (if I am free to make it)' (*IP*, p. 215). A new meaning is to be given to the passage of the chained black from Africa to the New World to replenish the void that came with the genocide of the Indians. The violent separation from Africa must serve as a kind of sacrificial consecration of a future communality. In the preface to Kateb Yacine's theatre, Glissant writes: 'Today more than ever, we cannot conceive of our lives or our art, independently of the tremendous efforts of those men who from various races and cultures seek to come together and to know each other. Today the circle is closed, we are all in the same place: it is the entire earth. From this arises the Tragedy of our times, which is that of Man facing the nations, that of the personal destiny confronted with a collective destiny.'[9]

Consciousness of historical time becomes one of the major preoccupations of Glissant's novels. Glissant's first novel, *La Lézarde*, is set in Martinique during those hopeful postwar days when Martiniquans for the first time were allowed to elect their true representatives to go to the metropolis. The narrative focal point is the assassination of a turncoat, who epitomizes the success of French colonial policies, by a group of young conspirators to forestall his competing in the upcoming elections with the candidate of the progressive group. Much of the novel's action derives from the characters' consciousness of the past, 'juxtaposing the banality of the present and the splendor of remembrance'.[10] In its physical features, the island, like the world itself, offers universal contrasts between the mountain and the plain, the land and the sea, the lush rainforest and the arid salt plain, the fertile field and the volcanic landscape, reminders of past disasters and proof of invincible regeneration, scarred and verdant, the immobile presence of the ocean and the unceasing flow of the Lézarde River. Martiniquan space has an immediate, interfacial relation with the past. The ocean is the repository of indelible, haunting visions of the crossing from Africa in the dark hulls of the slave ships and the severance of ties with the ancestral land. 'He who discovers the sea has suddenly the taste of black bread in his mouth' (L, p. 143). 'He who discovers the sea has this gravity ... this gravity was born from regret, not from confidence' (L, p. 145). When Thäel, one of the young conspirators, and his fiancée Valérie embrace on the beach, 'here where time patiently lies in wait for you' (L, p. 144), they sense significations of their racial destiny present in the physical environment. 'They lived a thousand years in this place since the first gesture of love to the implacable act of justice ... They felt the taste of fruit from the maroon's forest. They returned together to the present' (L, pp. 206–7). Before leaving, 'they listened to a faint murmur', the whisper from the sea: 'The sea of the Caribs ... They have been massacred ... May the sea at least keep their memory ... May it also keep ours' (L, p. 207).

On his death-bed, Papa Longoué, the wise medicine-man, a direct descendant of the original maroons, the last link with Africa, once more recalls the Middle Passage: 'there was a smell of rotten sea, faint rolling tormented his body' (L, p. 187). Isolated on his mountain slope, immobilized in the present, Papa Longoué lives in a preteritive state of consciousness of the turbulent past.

Papa Longoué becomes the antagonist in Glissant's second novel, *Le Quatrième Siècle*. As suggested by the title, black history in the Antilles enters its fourth century. But the subjective experience of time, the four temporal modal categories of present, past, future and conditional are to fuse into one consciousness of Martiniquan time. The subordination of chronology to the apprehension of the experience of time forms the novel's central dialectic confrontation between Papa Longoué and Mathieu, the young intellectual.

Mathieu visits Papa Longoué urging the old man to pursue his account of the past, from the crossing of the Atlantic to the present. The central motif of the narrative is the correlative destinies, disparate and fatally joined by hatred and mutual attraction, of two families, whose progenitors, Béluse and Longoué, upon arrival in the New World, fought a prodigious battle. Once on land, Longoué escapes to the hills where he leads the proud and precarious existence of a maroon. Béluse is sold to a plantation. The paths of their descendants, on the one side the savage mountain maroon, 'those who refused', and on the other side, the assimilable slave of the plain, 'those who accepted', constantly cross, resulting in vendetta murders and intermarriages. Papa Longoué, who lives alone high up on the mountainside in his solitary hut where he practises the magic arts of the past, is the last member of the maroon lineage. Mathieu, a Béluse descendant, the young intellectual, senses a kind of shallowness and weightlessness of his being in the presence of the old man. 'We try to use the light of the past, but we feel too fragile under the weight, and to fill our presence, we are too hollow in the absence, in this oblivion.'[11] Mathieu must find answer to the burning question: 'What is the past? What is left us of the past?' (QS, p. 15). Papa Longoué insists that 'we must not follow the facts logically, but guess, anticipate what has happened' (QS, pp. 57–8). Mathieu, on the other hand, wants dates and motives. The voodoo sage and the educated young man symbiotically complement each other. 'We want to know by ourselves, you who know and yet would understand nothing, if I talked to you aloud, and I who know nothing and yet I can already understand you ... yes, we want to uncover from the inside, restart from the moment when everything was not dark' (QS, p. 58). Papa Longoué cautions Mathieu: 'The past is not in what you know for sure' (QS, p. 146). If, however, Mathieu's quest for historical consciousness must go beyond mere acquisition and ordering of historical data, Papa Longoué's self-incarceration in the past is a gratuitous exercise of the will to refuse. The Antillean must recognize the irreversibility of history and the futility of the nostalgia for Africa. 'The infinite country over there beyond the waters was no longer this place of marvels ... but ... that part which, negated, in its turn, negated the new land, its peopling, its work' (QS, p. 287). Papa Longoué has reached an impasse, since he cannot 'attach ... the past to the future' (QS, p. 19). But the past can derive meaning only from its relation to the future and the potential. The past is not the immobilized, con-gealed existential *being-in-oneself*, but rather its opposite, 'this absence, this oblivion', whence, through a 'prophetic vision', will arise 'the dizziness of memory' (QS, p. 30).

The present, however, in this dialectic reciprocity between the past and the future, the actual and the potential, remains uncertain. The present 'is a yellowed leaf on the stem of the past growing on the far side where neither hand nor look can reach it. The present falls on the other side, it is dying endlessly. It dies' (QS, p. 224).

The agony of the present predominates Glissant's third novel, *Malemort*, where wry humour and poignant sense of helplessness admix. *Malemort* is a polymorphic work of a variety of narrative techniques with changing perspectives, contrasting stylistic devices, modulating rhythms and alliterative sound interplays, peculiar creole speech patterns, and so on.

Malemort has no chronologically sequential plot-line as the narrative focus scans back and forth between 1788 and 1974. Personages from *La Lézarde* and *Le Quatrième Siècle* reappear, sometimes unretouched, but most frequently with an added dimension as representatives of types formed and difformed by some historical-cultural determinants. These present-day Martiniquans, jobless, eking out a welfare subsistence, wander aimlessly like unwanted exiles in their own land.

They are contrasted with the primaeval maroon, the *négateur*, the archetype of the *enraciné* in banishment, who, nurtured by the land, lives in concordance with the forces of nature. This race of proud and uncompromising naysayers started with the newly enslaved black who escaped the very first night after his arrival in the New World. Hunted down, persecuted, banished and executed, they have always risen from the dust and death to continue the defiant non-acceptance of the colonizer's ideology and morality. These legendary figures are projected in a myth-like vision to apotheosize their eternal violent death, their pitiful and glorious destiny as 'fallen-risen'. The maroon is consubstantial with the totality of Martiniquan time and space. He emerges from the earth that has witnessed his suffering and soaked up his blood and sweat and, slain by the oppressor, returns to it, partaking of the Martiniquan spatio-temporal contiguity. Martinique is thus this 'uncertain land where the yesteryears disappear into the earth, but whence tomorrow never rises'.[12]

Judging from *Malemort*, one would be tempted to conclude that today's geo-political realities have dispersed Glissant's original poetic 'prophetic vision of the past'. In the glossary appendix of *Malemort*, while offering explanations of certain local creole terms to the outside readers, Glissant admits that the indigenous reader is yet to be born. From the *Realpolitiker*'s point of view, there may be something quixotic in his attempt to inspire in his people a vision of the future through a past sublimated. On the other hand, the historical sensibility that subtends his work accords resonances of high intensity and originality.

NOTES

1. Pierre Henri Simon, *L'Esprit et l'histoire*, Paris, Colin, 1954, pp. 14–15; my translation.
2. David C. Gordon, *Self-Determination and History in the Third World*, Princeton, Princeton University Press, 1971, p. 3.
3. Beverly Ormerod, 'Beyond negritude: some aspects of the work of Edouard Glissant', *Contemporary Literature*, vol. XV, no. 3, Summer 1974, p. 362.
4. Jean Benoist, *L'Archipel inachevé*, Montréal, Les Presses de l'Université de Montréal, 1972, p. 343; my translation.
5. Aimé Césaire, *Cadastre*, Paris, Seuil, 1961, p. 90; my translation.
6. G. W. F. Hegel, *The Philosophy of History*, tr. J. Sibree, New York, Collier, 1902, p. 148.
7. Edouard Glissant, *Monsieur Toussaint*, Paris, Seuil, 1961, p. 7. Henceforth identified as *MT* (all translations mine).
8. Edouard Glissant, *L'Intention poétique*, Paris, Seuil, 1969, p. 36. Henceforth identified as *IP* (all translations mine).
9. Kateb Yacine, *Théâtre*, Paris, Seuil, 1959, pp. 10–11; my translation.
10. Edouard Glissant, *La Lézarde*, Paris, Seuil, 1958, p. 72. Henceforth identified as *L* (all translations mine).
11. Edouard Glissant, *Le Quatrième Siècle*, Paris, Seuil, 1964, p. 58. Henceforth identified as *QS* (all translations mine).
12. Edouard Glissant, *Malemort*, Paris, Seuil, 1975, p. 190; my translation.

African Oral Tradition – Criticism as a Performance: A Ritual

Solomon O. Iyasere

> Well a tale is not a tale
> Without a word or two on how it fares:
> My ears are opened to the ground
> For what errors you may find.
> It is simple and plain
> That one hand cannot wash a story clean
> It needs the help of the other.[1]

L iterary criticism as a self-contained, individualized, intellectual endeavour is not an activity common to the African past. It is not that the traditional African had no refined aesthetic or critical sensibilities, or that he lacked 'constructive imagination' as Mary Kingsley[2] would have us believe, or that the critical evaluation of a creative work is a new phenomenon in Africa. Rather, the traditional African form of literary criticism, a highly developed art, differed in form and mode from literary criticism as it is practised in the western world at the present time. In traditional Africa, criticism was not a dogged, impersonal, dispassionate and autonomous intellectual activity, but a creative performance, a ritual. Each literary piece was presented orally, involving the entire community in the creative process. So, too, with the criticism.

More so in traditional African communities, where story-telling was an advanced and complex art form. The evaluation of an artistic performance was given unqualified emphasis, for no story-telling session was complete without a form of evaluation. Thus, every recital was followed by an analysis and appraisal by the audience, particularly by the elders, who were themselves skilled in the arts of story-telling and rhetoric. This integration of criticism with performance was ever the practice not only among the Binis, but also the Akans, the Luos, the Limbas, the Yorubas and the Tivs.

In keeping with traditional emphasis on creativity in all artisitic endeavours, the critical evaluation was considered a creative act, an artistic performance. No matter how insightful or imaginative a critic might be, if he lacked the art of theatrical rendition, verbal dexterity and, specifically, the mastery of the rhetorical techniques of delivery, he would hardly find an audience, for it is like dancing with irregular steps. As the Yorubas would say:

> Dancing with irregular steps you are heading for the marsh,
> Dancing with irregular steps you are heading for the marsh,
> If you dance with irregular steps, you will never be a good dancer.[3]

The same was true for the honey-tongued critic who lacked depth of perception and the art of artistic composition. In many regions, the 'creative talent and the critical faculty coexisted in the same person'. And often, as among the Akans and the Yaos, the reputable literary critics were also the distinguished poets and story-tellers of the community.

The atmosphere in which these activities took place was usually lively and informal (the after-dinner type of affair with the elders sipping palm-wine and occasionally blowing a cloud of smoke into the air from their huge elongated pipes) so that the critical evaluation was rendered in 'leisurely, or unstructured form'. Ruth Finnegan's study of the Limba arts revealed that, in a creative performance, members of the audience did not listen silently nor wait for the chief performer's invitation to join in. Instead, the audience would break into the performance with their additions, questions and criticisms.[4] This practice was common in the expected case of story-telling and in the more formal situations as that of the complex Ijala chants. The performance by one Ijala artist would be carefully listened to by the other experts present; if another expert thought the performer had made a mistake, he would cut in with words such as:

> I beg to differ, that is not correct.
> You have deviated from the path of accuracy ...
> Ire was not Ogun's hometown.
> Ogun only called there to drink palm-wine ...[5]

Thus interrupted, the performer might then try to defend himself by pleading his own knowledge or suggesting that others respect his rendition:

Let not the civet-cat trespass on the cane rat's track,
Let the cane rat avoid trespassing on the civet-cat's path.
Let each animal follow the smooth stretch of its own road.[6]

Such criticism of the chief performer's factual distortion of events was not uncommon since the plot and skeletal outline of most tales and chants were known to the various members of the village community.

This critical evaluation was not limited to factual contents alone. The formal elements, though often buried under the web of eclectic meanderings, were likewise stressed. Significantly, the chief performer's skill in weaving into an artistic whole the several episodes of a well-known tale or poem might come under serious scrutiny. *If a critic found flaws in the chief performer's rendition, in either the factual content or the technique of composition, he would not only point them out, but also retell the story from his own point of view, giving it his personal stamp. His re-creation of the same story would then form the basis of his criticism.* This form of creative criticism, or para-criticism, often became a kind of chain narration, a frequent occurrence at story-telling performances among the Edos.

I once attended a story-telling performance in Benin City, where 'The murder of Adesua' was being presented. After the story was performed by one artist, another was quick to point out the flaws of the first rendition, by re-creating the tragic story, giving it the following opening:

Please be patient, open your ears and listen,
Stay awake wide-eyed to the end.
I have the same tale to tell,
A tale I know full well,
Not a plain tale as those
That have reached your ears,
But a tangy tale of double sorrow
Full of fits and fever
Of fate that fell –
O how a noble creature was plucked unripe
By force and fraud

Ogwegu, O You Fathers of Tales
Wordless I stand before you naked
Give me the Living words to re-create
Those woeful lines
Which themselves lament as the chart
These dark events.
Ewawa, You Mother of Design

> Stay with me till the end
> Edion A Son You Guardian of Sleep
> Give us some room
> Stay away for a while.

He closed his presentation thus:

> Here is where my story ends –
> Forgive me for what defects there may be
> In this tale of woe:
> Not for the old knots here and there
> Brought by old tangles in the broken yarn,
> But for those rifts brought by my own runs.

> Well, a tale is not a tale,
> Without a word or two on how it fares:
> My ears are wide open to the ground
> For what errors you may find.
> For one hand cannot wash itself clean
> It needs the help of the other.

The critical, at times ritualistic, retelling and reliving of the same tale by second and subsequent artist-critics went on for the rest of the evening. At the end the chief performer told a different story in which he satirized the critics – the other performers.

On yet another occasion, I attended a story-telling session at which the same tale, 'The murder of Adesua', was again presented by the same semi-professional artist-critics but before a different audience. The type of audience present, in this case, mostly old and middle-aged women, affected the rendition itself, the critical comments and the re-creation that followed the initial recital. When the entire performance had ended, I asked the chief performer the reason for these adaptations and inconsistencies. He chuckled and replied, 'Can't you see, there are too many old women here tonight. My friend, a good story teller should make his story reflect the situation.'

The Edos, as in several traditional African communities, regarded criticism as a creative performance, and every performance was a unique and complete literary event. Every literary production existed only as embodied in the performance, continuously created anew. Under such circumstances, consistency in critical evaluation was impossible: with each retelling, the story was adapted to the situation, the prevailing taste and the mood of the audience; the criticism had to change with the tale. Thus, a respectable critic in the African folk tradition was one who was not only insightful in his commentary, but also skilfully creative in his presentation. He had to be both creative artist and entertainer as his ability to please and delight his audience was vital to his performance. John S. Mbiti summarizes the situation well:

> Story-telling is another form of entertainment which draws everyone in. Stories contain singing, drama, sadness, joy, surprise, and suspense; they interest and intrigue the listener, and a good story-teller will even sandwich jokes between parts of a story. Since the telling of a story is enlivened by actions, the audience is entertained not only by the narrative, but also by the facial expressions, the 'gimmicks', the singing, and the dramatic performance of the story-teller as he tells the story, imitating amazement, old age, or sorrow, as the case may be. Although they serve other purposes, stories are told chiefly as a form of entertainment after the day's work.[7]

Significantly, a form of literary criticism that emerged in traditional African societies is as follows:

(1) informal critical comments from the audience;
(2) the retelling of the *same story from a different point of view*;
(3) meta-criticism, the criticism of critics (through the employment of satirical stories).

Thus, the role of the critic in the African oral tradition was a complex one. He was not a literary technician in search of ossified precision and foreign patterns and designs, but a spontaneous entertainer, a historian and a wordmaster – in short, an artist. Criticism was not divorced from the creative process but an essential part of and adjunct to it. Creativity and criticism enjoyed a symbiotic relationship. Critical evaluation and the composition of a work of art were regarded as facets of the same process and, in most cases, aspects of the same moment. This interrelationship formed the literary climate that fostered the production and growth of such traditional works as *The Mwindo Epic*, *Sundiata an Epic of Mali*, and the *Yoruba Ijala*, and nourished and shaped the creative sensibilities of the legendary poet-critic Amadou Koumba.

All in all, the traditional African considered the critical evaluation of a work of art as a vital human activity, a creative endeavour in which the whole community participated. It is aimed at the maximum expansion of a literary work and not a curtailment of it. Thus, a good critic must possess not only critical insights but, more important and in keeping with the oral form of the tradition, the ability to expand, to illuminate and to make criticism a creative and lively performance.

NOTES

1. Solomon O. Iyasere (trans.) 'The murder of Adesua'. unpublished.
2. Mary Kingsley, *Travels in West Africa, Congo Française, Corisco and Cameroons*, 2nd edn., unabridged, London, Macmillan, 1898, p. 356.
3. Janheinz Jahn, *A History of Neo-African Literature*, London, Faber and Faber 1966, p. 92.
4. Ruth Finnegan, *Oral Literature in Africa*, Oxford, Clarendon Press; 1970, pp. 10–11.
5. ibid., p. 12.
6. ibid.
7. John S. Mbiti, *Akamba Stories*, Oxford, Clarendon Press, 1966, p. 22.

African Adaptations of Greek Tragedies

E. J. Asgill

There are three remarkable adaptations of Greek tragedies
by three African playwrights. Ola Rotimi's adaptation of
Sophocles' *Oedipus Rex*[1] in *The Gods Are Not to Blame*[2]
has proved most popular with African audiences. Efua Sutherland's *Edufa*[3] and Wole Soyinka's *The Bacchae of Euripides*[4] are
adaptations of Euripides' *Alcestis*[5] and *The Bacchae*[6] respectively.
Whilst these preoccupations may reflect to some extent the depth
of classical learning that featured in the syllabuses of colonial
education, there are undoubtedly other more interesting reasons
for this concern with Greek plays: the potentials certainly exist for
an easy cultural transfer from Greece to West Africa especially.

The mythologies of Greek religion and literature have their
referents in African, but most strikingly in Yoruba, culture. The
hierarchical Olympian godheads, with specific attributes and
roles, incessantly involved in the fortunes of men in their human
world, replete with systems of priests, seers, oracles, and so on, are
complemented fully in Yoruba theogonic structures.

Also, the choral element in Greek drama with miming, dancing,
chanting, observing and participating, approximates closely to the
features of a whole theatre which is proving a continuing tendency
in African dramatic tradition. But perhaps most important are the
common springs of dramatic performance. The historical and the
legendary are the literary storehouses of Greek drama the enactment of which constitutes a religious celebration. Not uncom-
monly, African traditional drama takes its resource in festivals
celebrating harvest, initiation or expiation rites and the historical
and legendary origins of a people. In consequence, for both
dramatic traditions, originality does not reside in the story that is
(re)told but in the various points of dramatic emphases from the
'creator's' perception. In these three particulars, both Grecian and
African dramatic traditions enjoy common features.

The plays subjected to adaptation are perhaps among the best of the works of the Greek dramatists but each African playwright it would seem has made his or her own selection for special reasons. Soyinka's play was commissioned by the National Theatre of Great Britain, but undoubtedly the ecstasy of Dionysian harvest rites has found fraternal solace in *Idanre*, the passion poem of Ogun, 'elder brother of Dionysos', as Soyinka himself attests. Rotimi's title *The Gods Are Not To Blame* implies a compelling dissociation from Sophocles' thesis in *Oedipus Rex*, which by implication (according to Rotimi) is that the gods are to blame. One is not certain Sophocles implied this[7], but Rotimi's distinctive presentation bears close analysis.

Sutherland has worked on a Greek theme that is familiar as it is indeed a popular African mystical belief, also, that a man could postpone his own death by the substitution of another's life. This, according to popular belief, is an inclination of the affluent and successful in life to prolong unduly their hegemony. Accordingly, Sutherland has dispersed with the dynastic exigencies which indemnifies Admetus considerably and has replaced this motif appropriately (in an essentially African extended family system where a dynastic recession is too remote) by a selfish greed for continued wealth and longevity entirely for its own sake. Thus, while the bare skeleton of the story remains, the play to a great extent is rewritten.

The innovations in *Edufa* are a logical consequence of this fact of dispensing completely with the Euripidean conflict. In the Greek play, Admetus charges his father for this reason (pp. 459–61):

> Ye let her die, a woman
> Not of our house ...
> Me hadst thou son and heir under thine house
> So that thou wast not, dying, like to leave
> A childless house for stranger folk to spoil.

Pheres, Admetus' father, counters with equal righteous indignation (p. 463):

> no debt of mine to die for thee.
> shamelessly thou hast fought against thy death:
> Cunning device has thou devised to die
> Never, cajoling still wife after wife
> To die for thee!

So, whilst Admetus has dynastic considerations in view, an important trump, given the political values of the times, Pheres has the human justification on his side. In Euripides, this potentially tragic impasse is finally averted by Hercules who rescues Alcestis from the grave. This twist, in fact, seems to assert that whatever reprehension may be put on Admetus has not been truly deserved.

Naturally, with Sutherland's elimination of the dynastic motive of Admetus goes his defence, and his action is readily rendered insincere. Edufa's attempt to substitute someone to die for him becomes a subtle piece of guile which boomerangs. The victim was to be, not his father, Kankam, as he had hoped when he threw 'the question into the air with studied carelessness' (the question was who loved him well enough to die for him), but his beloved wife. He had not calculated on this when he attempted to commit his father to an oath unwittingly, and the play now becomes decidedly tragic with a proper moral focus. Ampoma could no longer forswear effectively, and the ritual remedy to burn the charm in an act of public confession proves too much a sacrifice for Edufa. The Herculean bonanza in *Alcestis* becomes irrelevant and the father–son controversy is consequently clearly painted white and black or right and wrong so that very early in the play Edufa must reflect on his condemnation as due to his 'failure to create a faith'.

Hercules' role is altered into that of Senchi, throwing into contrasting relief the enormity of Edufa's sin. His search for solidity, by which he means wealth and status in his society, is countered by Senchi's freedom of mind (in spite of his bankruptcy), his convincing happiness and his tremendous self-assurance, which Edufa lacks.

The conflict in *Edufa* therefore is not that between father and son which compels the latter to sacrifice his wife, but it becomes internalized in Edufa, torn between intense love for his wife who is condemned to die through his sad miscalculation and his supposedly inviolable esteem in the eyes of his society; between the secret and pathetically futile but desperate ritual efforts to forestall the realization of the oath, and the acceptance of his guilt, the only means by which his life and soul can be ennobled. The titles more cogently appear significant. Whilst Euripides' play is entitled *Alcestis*, and appropriately so, as the wife is the central figure around whom the pathos of the play revolves, Sutherland's title is *Edufa*, and the husband it is who now usurps the central interest in the play which is essentially an issue of moral choices for him.

This shift of conflict has a consequence necessitated in restructuring of characters and their roles. The elaborate mythological details behind Apollo's presence in Admetus' household is dispensed with. Apollo intimidates Admetus with the imminent death threatening him and which could be averted by a replacement. In *Edufa* it is through the normal practice of divination for protection and security that Edufa gets to know of his imminent death. Similarly, the conflict between Death and Hercules is rejected since the happy consequence of the original is now disposed of. Admetus' son does not appear in the adaptation, as his role in *Alcestis* serves only to heighten the pathos of his mother's death which is not, of course, a concern in *Edufa*. The elimination of such characters offers a greater economy and control which concentrates attention on the tragic conflict for Edufa himself.

New characters, however, are created and they in turn reveal new dimensions of the central character, Edufa, and thus heighten his tragedy. Senchi, though still a reveller and thus corresponding to Hercules in *Alcestis*, throws into sharp focus the moral shortcomings of the hero. The former handmaid to Alcestis and another servant are fused into the matronly Seguwa who is ever ready to assist and cover up for Edufa but would prove at last unable to. She in fact would articulate for Ampoma the wretched abuse of her womanhood and accentuate as it were the chasmic awfulness of Edufa's perversity. Abena is found at first collecting dewdrops for the ritual therapy to avert Ampoma's imminent death. She strikes us instantly with her unstinted fidelity to her brother, offered, however, in ignorance to one undeserving of it. Already on the threshold of matrimony, she underscores Ampoma's unquestioned loyalty to Edufa and how grossly he has betrayed it.

Sam, an idiot servant in the house, plays a minor role, bringing back from a mission to a diviner three ritual items which are supposed to save Ampoma. But the ominous owl he claims to own defies the efficacy of the ritual solution. Sam, however, as an idiot, fails to come alive. In the first place he says too much and very knowledgeably at that too, and his language is certainly not that of an idiot. He says (p. 34):

> not the village itself. That is beautiful, floating in the blue air on the mountain tops, with a climb-way in the mountain's belly going zig-zag-zig, like a game.

The authorial stage direction, 'he thoroughly enjoys his description', can only be seen as an apology.

The Chorus of five in *Edufa* functions differently from the Chorus of Euripides. Their first entrance is to perform cleansing rites. Undoubtedly their presence causes tensions to rise in Edufa's house. Their timing and the nature of their visit are quite striking. They become a threat to Edufa's desperate plight to cover up the circumstances of Ampoma's fatal illness. Besides, they flesh out Senchi's raillery which establishes a contrasting mood piece to the gloom in Edufa's mind. Most important, as witnesses to Ampoma's unabashed declaration of her love for her husband and to the ultimate revelation of what has gone wrong in Edufa's house, they become the public testimony of his guilt.

To all intents and purposes, the connection between *Edufa* and *Alcestis*, beyond a bare statement of one dying for another, is quite distant. Sutherland's adaptation is almost a new creation. The fact that the theme is an African one also further reduces her indebtedness to Euripides. But, of course, there are still obvious Euripidean strains; in Kankam the father always chiding; the revelling Senchi; Ampoma, fragile, devoted and passionate to the last; and even in the matronly superintendence of Seguwa. However, the emphasis has shifted from Alcestis to Edufa (wife to husband), Kankam assumes a patriarchal dignity whilst Edufa correspondingly sinks into the abyss of degeneracy as we descend from the elegance of royal polity and exigency to the vulgarity of ruthless materialism and shamelessness. The new characters become silhouetting expressions in this direction.

Further innovations by Sutherland are consistent only with the localization of the play. African symbols are used to underscore the tragic mode. The ant-hill with a screaming figure on top of it in Abena's dream portends Ampoma's death. Instead of the bewailing in *Alcestis*, the efforts to avert her death take on symbolic forms. The three pebbles signifying her three falls, on an inscribed sign of the sun at the entrance to Edufa's room, was the backcloth of her final fall, blotting out in fact the figure of the sun which had promised life and sunshine. The charm which was burnt and buried had apparently put paid to her hopes. The public pledge of Ampoma's waist-beads to Edufa in the presence of the Chorus, though it reflects Admetus' pledge to Alcestis never to be supplanted as wife, in a more symbolic context, constitutes an act of condemnation of Edufa, albeit ironic. To quote (p. 53):

> My husband, you have honoured me by
> your words and by your precious gifts of flowers.
> I wish to honour you in return in language
> equally unashamed.

If Edufa is to wear it 'with honour' it will, like the Mariner's albatross, serve as his conscience of guilt.

Symbols apart, an African world-view is also established. Edufa's praise-names are chanted, Kankam refers to his Ntoro and its taboo therewith. The sacredness of courtesy to strangers is invoked, libations are poured and the Chorus of women are seen in a burial rite of purification. However, this is not a major concern in the play.

Sutherland's adaptation places in proper perspective a familiar ritualistic belief of the possibilities of 'changing heads', as the expression goes in Sierra Leone. It reveals the inordinate lengths to which a morally degenerate mind can go in a vain attempt to translate the bubbles of earthly pleasures into a more lasting indulgence, however tenaciously and desperately retained. That future which is desired but not deserved by Edufa backfires against his love for Ampoma, and the central action of the play is no longer the mere bewailing in *Alcestis* but the tragic pathos of hopeless attempts to reverse an irrevocable doom. The experience for Edufa is a process of inner suffering, moral growth and enlightenment.

Because, unlike Sophocles', Rotimi's presumed audience does not have the advantage of a prior knowledge of the background details on which an appreciation of the play so much depends, he has devised a prologue which supplies his background, not in an isolated prosaic preamble, but as part of the dramatic action. Between a narrator and Odewale, the background story is taken on to the onset of the plague which later proves to be the result of an act of abomination, committed and condoned, albeit unwittingly. Interestingly, the narrator not only tells but comments on a foregoing mimed action and further becomes an individual participating actor communicating with the miming characters.

In the case of Odewale, the narrative techniques alter quite appropriately. As a central figure in the drama his dramatic monologue carries the *tour de force* of a confident personality impressing us forcefully as the person whose lot is the concern of the play. This impact is created through exquisite stylistic repetitions, strong pauses, antithetical balances and well-poised proverbial exhortations.

The narration apart, the prologue is enriched with loaded action and atmosphere, a plenitude of miming characters, dancing and drumming to buttress the narration, and elaborate symbolic sound and stage effects. All these, even though on minor keys, are meaningful aids to communication. The effect of these various devices of communication is to tell the story several times over and simultaneously too, thus adequately compensating for the audience's lack of background knowledge. When the play proper begins, the audience is fully fortified with the necessary details for the drama, and more immediately so.

There are a few major alterations which should prove relevant and interesting for a modern African audience. A war replaces the sphinx in *Oedipus Rex*. Saving a people from the ravages of war and from the loss of patrimony are reasons enough to exalt such a saviour as Odewale to the highest position in the land. It makes sense that the absence of King Adetusa gave the people of Ikolu the daring to attack Kutuje.

Secondly, the quarrel over land rather than over right of passage is a more credible proposition to result in death. Besides, King Adetusa proceeds to destroy Odewale's crops and to insult his tribe. Also the fight is not wholly physical but begins at a ritualistic level. This perhaps ensures the exclusion of the servants of the king in the confrontation and obviates the possibility that one person can defeat another who has supporters.

Aderopo, as son to Ojuola and King Adetusa rather than brother only to Jocasta the Queen, lends greater justification to Odewale's misgivings and accusation of the former as an ambitious usurper. A flashback scene dramatizes the story of the killing of the former king for the benefit of Alaka, an outsider, and not Ojuola. Besides amplifying the action of the play, it makes possible a delayed dramatic climax for Ojuola which later comes upon her quite suddenly.

These specific alterations apart, the stage is crowded with new characters providing greater interaction and scope for inventiveness such as Odewale's rapport with the citizens on herbal remedies against the pestilence. However, unlike Sutherland's new characters who throw into relief the tragic dimensions of the central figure, we fail to recognize any significant dramatic function of a proliferating cast beyond the organ swell of abundant action.

The strength of Rotimi's adaptation seems to reside mainly in the power of production techniques imposed (action, suspense, colour and sound) than with any actual individual treatment of the original theme or thesis. *The Gods Are Not To Blame*, on stage, can be a very powerful performance indeed. In the localization of his play, the very choice of names in a language which is very tonal reflects a certain histrionic quality. Costumes, props and stage movement can have tremendous symbolic effects underscoring as a kind of replay and heightening of the dramatic action. Biting the sword of Ogun, for example, takes the play to heights of emotional tensions when positions become irrevocable. The total cultural world as portrayed subscribes to this abiding dramatic quality in Rotimi. Prostrations as an endorsement of levels in social relationships, the habit of conversation that tends towards elaborate genealogical peregrinations, and the gestic flamboyance of a royal bard, and so on, are ready instances of this tremendous power of Rotimi's stage.

This overwhelming sense of drama is further reflected in Rotimi's humour, his irony and his use of language. There is abundant laughter but far from undermining the tragic mode it ironically heightens the tensions in the play. The laughter is generally not shared by characters who unwittingly provide it. Sophocles' ironic mode is exploited to the full, and in some places Rotimi can be painfully caustic as when Odewale reviles Aderopo: 'Bedsharer! there, let him come and marry his own mother. And not stopping there, let him bear children by her'; or when Ojuola is herself awfully implicated in the tragic outcome: 'A son is a son; a husband is a husband. A woman cannot love both equally.'

African images and idioms are sometimes translated but when too directly done, Rotimi's control of the medium seems lost as in such obscure syntactical constructions as 'how hard to rule is hard'. Like the images and idioms, proverbs evoke an authentic African milieu and lend poetic embellishments to the language. More interestingly they promise dramatic excitements: they are capable of evoking in mental flashback a whole situation of conflict, intrigue and ultimate guidance. One however wonders whether Rotimi had in view this potentiality of the proverb in his dramatic conception. If he were using proverbs advisedly as part of his thematic structure, then perhaps he ought to have been more careful who used which proverb, in which given time and situation. As seems to be the case, the play is overlarded with proverbs but without an overall structural development.

The title implies that Odewale's tragedy is self-imposed and from the outset the need to struggle is a recurrent thematic refrain. Odewale's insistence on struggle seems to call attention to an authorial warning against the possibility of overreaching himself, or attempting to exceed his human limitations and consequently creating a situation for his tragic fall. Therefore, Aderopo's consolatory 'It is the way the gods meant it to happen' is vehemently countered by Odewale's 'No, No! Do not blame the gods ... They knew my weakness, the weakness of a man easily moved to the defence of his tribe.' Incidentally, and strangely too, Rotimi at this point seems to peg the weakness down to a patriotic fanaticism. The tragic potential build-up of the play is more than this: Odewale's rashness betrays each time a crookedness of thought, as for example not insisting on a definite answer from the oracle to his specific question; not being circumspect enough to avoid marrying a woman old enough to be his mother; and not being patient enough for tangible reasons to conclude on Fakunle's collusion with Aderopo against his throne, which rash conclusion finally impelled him, after biting the sword of Ogun on oath, unwaveringly to his self-discovery. The blame on Odewale can be traced specifically to his compulsive drive to struggle beyond his capabilities.

It was within Rotimi's grasp therefore to have recognized the potential of using a proverbial structure, given the abundance of proverbs in the play, to underscore the dramatic conflict. A good number of proverbs warn against exceeding one's limitations and status in life, in as much as a good number also encourage one to press on. The oracle had warned Odewale, 'Just stay where you are', and more forcefully in a proverb, 'the snail may try but it cannot cast off its shell'. Odewale's reaction naturally was to run away, justifying his reaction by a proverbial counter: 'The toad likes water, but not when the water is boiling.' This is a beautiful situation when two proverbs are structurally arranged to underscore the dramatic conflict.

Unfortunately the pattern is not sustained. Rotimi ought to have aimed at proverbs, for Odewale particularly, which endorse action and effort. Only perhaps, towards the end, at his moment of self-revelation, could he have employed proverbs which hint at the limitations of the human spirit. Otherwise, his acknowledgement of his limits any earlier in the play should be clearly seen as ironic. Rotimi would then have been consistent in identifying Odewale's fault – rashness in thought and action. And the final proverbial stoicism would have been in place (p. 72):

> When the wood-insect
> Gathers sticks
> On its own head it
> Carries
> Them.

But even this is bathetically undermined by the dying stage-management: 'They start on their journey, passing through a mass of Kutuje townspeople who kneel or crouch in final deference to the man whose tragedy is also their tragedy.' This constitutes a belated association with Aristotelian catharsis[8] when the antecedents of the plot structure do not prepare us for this. Rotimi's use of proverbs seems finally motivated only by considerations of their impressive oratorical flamboyance and not by any effort to give structural meaning to his work.

It would seem that Rotimi saw instinctively the stage potentials of rendering *Oedipus Rex* in an African context, amplifying and intensifying the action through a myriad of forms other than verbal and introducing only such innovations as would improve its dramatic impact. Otherwise such innovations are peripheral to the original conceptual vision of Sophocles in spite of the new didactic title.

This argument so far, if tenable, would seem to be leading to the conclusion that Rotimi's treatment of Sophocles' *Oedipus Rex* is specifically an Africanization rather than an adaptation. It approximates nearly to Apronti's conclusion that in much African drama words are replaced by action at climatic points.[9] Rotimi's rendition of *Oedipus Rex* is basically a tremendous exploitation of the vigour of traditional African dramatic elements. Efua Sutherland, whilst she achieved a considerable degree of localization in her adaptation, was more interested in the treatment of theme and character. Her innovations and techniques are dictated by this originality of her perception.

Soyinka's adaptation of *The Bacchae* demonstrates a remarkable difference from both Rotimi and Sutherland. His prescribed audience is essentially non-African. The theme of Dionysos' assertion of his god-head and his avenging the slander of his mother remain intact in his treatment. Characters retain their Greek names and the world-view is predominantly Grecian. Soyinka's particular concern, it seems, is to reinvest Euripedes' *Bacchae* with greater dimensions and complexity.

The Bacchae exhibits interesting adaptability to African literary traditional forms. Soyinka's imagination, it seems, recognized too readily in Dionysos' birth, nature and function a kinship with Ogun. He himself has acknowledged his indebtedness to lines taken from the passion poems of Ogun which have been inserted especially in the praise chant of Dionysos. The harvest of grapes ushering the celebration of the Dionysian festival is reminiscent of Soyinka's associations of harvest. Harvest heralding the beginning of a new year readily suggests the need for expiation, an overwhelming thematic conceptualization in Soyinka's dramatic thought as evidenced in some of his plays – *The Strong Breed, Kongi's Harvest, A Dance of the Forests* and *Death and the King's Horsemen.*

We may note the Herdsman's reply to the slave leader's query (p. 237):

Leader: Flogged to Death? In the name of some unspeakable rites?
Herdsman: Someone must cleanse the new year of the rot of the old, or the world will die. Have you ever known famine? Real famine?

The concept of the carrier, the role of Eman in *The Strong Breed*, is repeated by the old slave who was to have been that carrier (p. 293):

> The ways of god are hard to understand
> We know full well that some must die, chosen
> To bear the burden of decay, lest we all die –

But in this case, the real carrier is Pentheus whose death becomes inevitable as Dionysos bursts upon Thebes on a mission of assertion and vengeance. Pentheus' role is ironically suggested by Dionysos himself (p. 306):

> Yes, you alone
> Make sacrifices for your people, you alone.
> The role belongs to a king.

Meanwhile, such being the nature of the expiation as seen in the procession of Eleusis, and with the underlying natures of Pentheus (harsh, cruel, intolerant) and Dionysos (vengeful, benevolent and joyful) in the hands of Soyinka's thought processes, the theme of expiation yields ultimately to a new theme of liberation of a once-migrant people. The triumph of Dionysos over Pentheus now becomes twofold: his vengeance and apotheosis are complete and his adherents find in his worship not only joy and ecstasy but the means of emancipation.

Now such an elaborate thematic concern has necessitated certain technical manipulations. The Bacchantes are specifically the strangers and original converts who have followed Dionysos to Thebes. The Vestals, in the procession of Eleusis, and the slaves, both functioning separately at first within the ambits of the themes of expiation and liberation respectively, render a complete dramatic union on stage with the Bacchantes, as converts all together through their bacchic chants in praise of Dionysos. All three together proceed onwards to function precisely in the capacity of the Chorus as in *The Bacchae*.

Besides the new dimensions to the original theme, Soyinka has created a very colourful drama approximating to African traditional dramatic behaviour of a whole theatre. The Greek choral chants had already suggested it. Two incidents stand out. The first is a dance of possession which climaxes the praise chants of the Bacchantes, and the slave leader, in a state of sheer excitement at the prospect of freedom, is possessed and in that state becomes, as it were, a votary of the god Dionysos. It is against this background of a demonstrated instinctive acceptance of the god in Thebes that Pentheus' resistance to the new god can be seen in its proper perspective. It intimates the potential collision course he has undertaken first in respect of Dionysian worship and more important the incipient rebellion which is part of the liberation theme. The revolt, in fact, not long after, approaches its climax when Pentheus in blind rage calls for the desecration of Tiresias' temple, and proceeds to commit a second abomination by slapping the old slave who ventures to point out the sacrilege.

A second major spectacle is in two parts, the wedding scenes which show the past and future of Dionysos. The first pantomime reveals the freedom gained by Hippoclides, a worshipper of Dionysos, from the constraints of a marriage to a very ugly bride, and that is in spite of her ingratiating wealth. This scene is a replay at a different level of representation of the past relationship between the house of Kadmos and Dionysos. The second scene shows the future of Dionysos, the celebration and the infectious joy of partaking of Dionysos' wine. Both pantomimes function together as an underscoring of the triumphal assertion of Dionysos' rites. This apart, the wedding scenes serve to produce a hypnotic effect on Pentheus and from this point his resistance begins to break down, especially following the drinking of Dionysian wine in that state of hypnotism.

In Euripides' *The Bacchae*, Pentheus succumbs consciously to a disguise because of a vulgar indulgence to spy on the Maenads. Soyinka, on the other hand, has magnified the stature of Pentheus, and the confrontation now no longer is an easy one for Dionysos. His effeminate nature is now replaced by a ruggedness betraying a determination in a god for an undoubtedly tough encounter. Pentheus accordingly rejects the enticement to spy on the Maenads and Dionysos' first attempt at hypnotism is easily shaken off.

Pentheus' defeat came from a curiosity to know more about the god he had rejected and is fighting against. Such a curiosity is in fact already self-defeating. However, Soyinka sufficiently demonstrates that there is indeed the need for a greater striving on the part of a god in this conflict between god and man.

On a similar dramatic note, the prolonged monologues of Pentheus, Tiresias and Cadmos in the first episode in *The Bacchae* are broken down and there is now greater dialogue and verbal action between the three. The result tends towards an improved dramatic realism on stage. To achieve a degree of tightness and speed of movement at the same time, Soyinka has made two notable omissions which are not relevant to his dramatic conception. The first dispenses with the first two futile attempts by the Maenads to capture Pentheus who has already been discovered hiding up in a tree. A more important rejection is the punishments meted out to Cadmos and Hermonia his wife, and to Agave, Pentheus' mother, and her sisters. Instead the play ends on a more positive note. Each orifice in the impaled head of Pentheus is seen to release jets of red wine to which the house of Kadmos drink in solemn communion celebrating the validity of Dionysos. It appears Soyinka would not allow Kadmos and his daughters any further punishments than the loss, and the circumstances of it, of Pentheus. Anything beyond this would be bordering on the melodramatic. In any case, the image of Dionysos as a gentle, jealous boy is more in consonance with this final act than any further pursuit of justice without mercy to the point of vindictiveness.

A slight but interesting addition by Soyinka is, of course, the updating of his work by introducing present-day registers and hackneyed expressions. A close examination of these reveal a touch of sarcasm, and, with few exceptions such as Kadmos' collapsible thrysus, they are directed at the meaningless rantings of present-day political rulers. Such expressions as 'a general call-up', 'state of emergency', 'territorial integrity', 'agent of subversion for some foreign power', 'professional code of conflict', and so on, whilst they may provoke sniggers, are a more serious attempt to associate Pentheus with the faithlessness and ungodliness, the tyranny and arrogance of contemporary world rulers. Pentheus is to be seen both in the capacity of a blasphemer against a god and a cruel intolerant ruler, a notion suggested in *The Bacchae* and which Soyinka has augmented by introducing into his adaptation the phenomenon of slavery and the need for emancipation.

The preoccupation with Greek drama as shown already by three

West African playwrights seems to indicate certain fundamental affinities between the literary behaviour of the Greeks and West Africans. Theogonic conceptions in Greek drama are not unfamiliar in African literary and religious traditions. The choral nature of Greek theatre lends itself easily to African dramatic behaviour replete with dance, movement, drum, music, mime and chant. Finally both cultures seek essentially their literary resources commonly from their religious, historical and legendary storehouses.

Rotimi's primary concern has been simply to give to Sophocles' play a local flavour and to invest it with a greater dramatic verve through abundant action, colourful expressions sometimes, and individually suggestive proverbs. However, his use of proverbs is without any significant structural purpose and his title belies any serious attempt to dissociate the adaptation from Sophocles' point of view.

Edufa is intellectually a more satisfying work because of its originality of treatment. The moral ambivalence in Euripides' *Alcestis* is discarded and the happy outcome of the original is rendered, in the adaptation, irrevocably tragic. The theme alters considerably and the characters figuring in the play are new creations responding superbly to the exigencies of theme and meaning.

In *The Bacchae of Euripides* the theme of vengeance and assertion of Dionysian god-head is extended to include that of expiation and political emancipation. In addition the embellishments of local literary forms are incorporated such as the libations and the dance of possession to achieve a union of two literary cultures. The adaptation becomes loaded in its theme and in its dramatic techniques.

The three African playwrights indeed demonstrate an interesting variability in their adaptations of Greek tragedies. Whilst Rotimi, as it were, has redecorated *Oedipus Rex*, Sutherland has preferred to alter the structural foundations of *Alcestis* considerably and Soyinka has only extended the structure and applied new furnishings.

NOTES

1. Watling, E., *The Theban Plays*, Harmondsworth, Penguin, 1947.
2. Rotimi, O., *The Gods Are Not To Blame*, Oxford, Three Crowns, 1971.
3. Sutherland, E., *Edufa*, London, Longman, 1967.

4. Soyinka, W. *Collected Plays I*, London, Oxford University Press, 1973.
5. Way, A. S., *Euripides IV*, London, Heinemann, 1912.
6. Vellacott, P., *The Bacchae and Other Plays*, Harmondsworth, Penguin, 1954.
7. Kitto, H. O. F., 'The philosophy of Sophocles', in *Greek Tragedy*, London, Methuen, 1966, pp. 145 ff.
8. House, H., *Aristotle's Poetics*, London, Rupert Hart-Davies, 1956.
9. Apronti, E. O., 'Spectacle versus language in African drama', conference on 'The Role of Drama in Education and Cultural Development in Contemporary Africa', Legon, 1975.

The Relevance of African Cosmological Systems to African Literature Today

Mazisi Kunene

Introduction

The implications and assumptions of African cosmological approaches must be examined first before one makes claims for them in literature. Studies of African cosmological concepts have been done mostly by foreigners, and sometimes by Africans who had been deeply influenced by foreign concepts or anthropologists. The result is that few African writers would see any relevance in a system judged frequently as backward, or at best, as of folkloristic interest and quality. To derive maximum intensity for their creative ideas, African writers would rather look to Greek or Judaic mythologies. None that I have read seriously looks into the rich mythological data characterizing many African societies. Only Wole Soyinka has perhaps depicted the Yoruba gods with any degree of seriousness and reverence. Even this imaginative and proliferic writer has tended, however, to use these gods in the role of *deux ex machina*.

Each society is concerned with its destiny within the cosmic arena. Without this perspective, the society can only be stampeded into directions it does not fully comprehend or does not feel ready to follow. There is some truth in the claim that change is possible only through myth, for myth can take many forms. It can reorganize the historical content in terms of modern perspectives. It can create an attractive vision defining in familiar cosmic terms the future possibilities of society. Myth can be used to celebrate the achievements of society, making them fall into an acceptable social order. It is perhaps not necessary to quote how such great writers as Homer, Milton, Tu Fu, Nguyen Du and others used the myth, in one way or another, to create the relevant classics. In the African continent itself, many traditional classics link up the present in cosmological perspectives until all the achievements of the society are made meaningful and current by a deep sense of cosmic continuity. Indeed the greatest of African literature aims primarily at celebrating the life of man and all living things in the cosmos. Hence many epic and heroic poems are invocations in the form of praise and appeal.

The 'modern' African writer has lost for the time being the epic dimension. The reasons for this are many but the primary one is the intensive occupation of the African continent within the last 400 years. This has forced the 'preserver of legends' to write a 'protest literature' and not a literature of long-term national and social goals.

To have a clear picture of how far the African writer has deviated from the enriching cosmological traditions, one must examine some of these cosmological systems and assumptions in greater detail. First and foremost, we must assume an evolution within the African continent of a common, basic world view as described through the cosmic concepts. This assumption is reasonable and can be demonstrated through variation of similar mythologies. It must be made clear that the similarities are not devised to meet a political theory nor to find a social solution to a geographical abstraction. The ecological imperatives of the African continent have made it possible for the African people to develop thought-systems that describe their world in a common language of common symbols. The internal accessibility, size and generally warm climatic conditions of the continent make a common but varied culture a logical reality. In view of these facts, let us examine some of the cosmological assumptions.

The Dual Nature of the Universe

The universe can be described through its physical manifestations; the stars, the moon, the sun. On this level, it is composed of numerous cosmic bodies: some large, some small, some heavy, some light. Common to all these bodies are two special laws (a) continuous growth resulting in an expanding universe, (b) the existence of cosmic boundaries enabling each entity to follow its own direction without interference from others. A cosmic balance regulates all things from the smallest unit to the largest. The interplay among the cosmic bodies and entities aims at enriching each other. This does not mean there are no clashes. But when clashes do occur, they are on such a small scale that the overall balance is maintained. Their cumulative effect is actually to trigger giant cosmic movements resulting in new cycles of growth and change.

The same universe can be seen in mystical terms embracing a variety of cosmic forces some of which can be controlled, some of which can be influenced through specific agents, and some of which can never be controlled or influenced. It is, indeed, desirable that some of these forces cannot be controlled.

The Three Worlds of African Cosmology

The earth is the centre, the *First World* of man. This is demonstrated through the dances that symbolize man's ultimate union with the earth. The earth is man's home, his farm, his responsibility. Man's paradise is on earth. His primary responsibility is to relate to the worlds within and to bequeath his tools after use to the next generation. This world is interlinked with other worlds outside, but because the world, earth, is central to man's existence, worlds outside are valued only in so far as they enrich this world.

The *Second World* comprising the sun, the moon, the pleiades, the evening star, the morning stars (there are three in Zulu: *inkwenkwezi, indonsakusa, ikhwezi*) is elevated as an important source of heroic and legendary epics, showing man's historical triumph over his enemies. Man's enemies include forces that attempt to thwart his purpose. Thus the scale of the legendary heroes is inflated and exaggerated to confront monsters and ogres. In some cases, the legendary characters enlist the assistance of some of the elements. The *Second World* is used symbolically and it describes a relationship with the earth that is functional and aesthetic.

The *Third World* of the stars, and the interplay of distant 'mystical' forces is often described in terms of the gods. The gods are not worshipped in Africa but revered. They are participants in man's life as allies. They themselves may sometimes enlist the services of special men and women to convey their will. Man equally has the right to appeal to them on issues affecting his welfare. It is forbidden, however, to appeal for the destruction of a personal enemy unless it can be demonstrated that the opponent has violated a fundamental ethic. The gods are forces that link man with the unknowable Supreme Creator. This does not mean that man must approach the Creator through them but rather that they are delegated by the Creator with specific creative and divine responsibilities. The gods utilize this potential on behalf of man. Man can appeal to them for their gifts but their power is limited, for man already has a direct relationship with the Creator through the agency of his ancestors. Much of the creative literature dealing with the gods describes the heroic triumphs of the gods as staged through man or through chosen clans and individuals. It comprises appeals and praises accorded to the gods for their gifts and protection. The *Second* and *Third Worlds* are crucial to the meaningful continuation of the *First World* of man. However it should not be supposed that the *First World* is the central world of the universe. It is only the central world of this species of man. It is taken for granted that there are numerous other worlds standing in the same cosmic relationship with our world. These remote worlds are described in the legendary tales and mythologies. Sometimes human species from our planet are depicted as leaping into these legendary worlds beyond our earth. The intention is not to investigate and to conquer but to conciliate our world with these worlds.

The *First World* is the richest in literary expressions, embracing as it does various historical truths and experiences. Within its framework, we see the operation of four earthly worlds with which the world of man coexists. They are the world of water, plants, animals, and inanimate objects, that is, objects without movement. In all these worlds, there exist imagined or real forces which are accredited with personalities to describe man's social drama or the drama of his relationship with these worlds. Much of classical African literature, including tales, fantastical epics and dramas, is based on the personalized events derived from these worlds.

The Myth and the Physical Speculation of the Universe

It is important at this stage to point out the differences between the actual physical descriptions of the universe and the extensive literary material utilizing these descriptions for the purposes of affirming the fundamental social laws. Speculation about the quality, organization, and history of the universe takes second place to what many African philosophers have considered the primary responsibility of man: life on earth. This earth-orientation is a crucial factor in the understanding of African thought-systems. In many cases, out of ignorance, the sky-oriented Europeans have denounced the Africans' lack of interest in cosmic bodies. The American delegation to Africa that brought a piece of the moon with them was bitterly disappointed when Africans in most parts of the continent dismissed it as either a fake or a childish obsession with things that have little relevance to the life of man on earth. Except for military purposes, the whole exercise of moon landing does seem disproportionately costly and wasteful.

The creation of the universe, the cosmos, cannot be directly verified. All statements about the birth of the universe are, therefore, mere speculations. Such speculations can either be serious or merely illustrative of man's role and position in the universe. If they fall under the first category, they require a disciplined few who not only must evolve a fund of information about the behaviour of the cosmic bodies but who must also develop an integrative philosophy, linking cosmic phenomena with the ultimate meaning of life. Fundamentally, speculations about the universe serve as a point of focusing on social behaviour. Hence in order to propagate their social message they are dramatized and interpreted through a large body of mythological and legendary tales. Such mythological tales are seldom extensive, following a common principle governing fantasy in African thought-systems, namely, that nothing purely speculative should be given detailed treatment as though it represented the truth. Consequently mythological tales are short, humorous and educational. If these mythologies lack a logical sequence of events, it is because they are part of a speculative and a fantastical system which allows them to violate normal everyday rules. Because of this they also allow us to probe into hidden phenomena.

The serious part of African cosmic speculation asserts that: (a) the universe came into being in stages, through vibratory movements, willed into existence by the Supreme Creator, (b) there was no participation or involvement of the male–female principle at its birth, (c) the universe was born out of a single event covering an unimaginable number of centuries, (d) the event of the initial birth of the universe is of only partial significance to the everyday life of man.

The Creator who created all life is unknowable. This, in itself, is an act of knowing constituting as it does a recognition of the limitations of the human mind and imagination. The Creator cannot be represented in any art form because the scale and nature of 'his' being is unimaginable to man. Man can only glimpse the mystery and greatness of 'his' being through the manifestations of balance and harmony. The Creator has delegated his powers to his agents who include the gods, the holy men, the visionaries and all the specially gifted people.

Analysis of Zulu and Efik Mythological Tales

Two mythological tales are analysed here to show both the use of literary techniques and the incorporation of the cosmic framework.

Zulu

God having created man decided that man should be immortal, that is, he should never experience death. He sent the chameleon to convey the message. The chameleon was slow and lingered along the way hunting for flies and berries. Meanwhile God changed his mind and decided that man should experience death after all. He then sent the salamander, a speedy creature. On hearing the salamander's death message, mankind rejoiced. When the chameleon arrived with its message of life it was rejected. Man soon realized, however, that death is a painful experience, and ever since he has hated the chameleon for delaying in conveying the message of life.

This creation myth is common in one form or another in various parts of the so-called Bantu-speaking region. The above version is Zulu. We can look at the story either as a simple tale of creation from a people whose ability to conceive creation is limited, as indeed some foreigners have claimed or we can go deeper and attempt to disentangle the meaning of the story and its symbolism. The latter is the only intelligent approach, and it constitutes the greatest challenge for the African scholar today. For he must interpret these symbols in a meaningful and socially relevant idiom. To illustrate the point let us attempt to analyse the various aspects of this story. First and foremost, it must be understood that most creation myths in Africa are composed for children. Secondly, the dual levels of meaning in African literature demand that, though the story is for children, it must, at another level, apply to adults as well. Thus its assumptions should be serious, embracing in different gradations all aspects of human life.

The story operates fundamentally on the principle that since God the Supreme Creator is unknowable, man is free to indulge his imagination in creative exercises about creation. He can explain through illustration the nature of the social order and affirm it through the cosmic order. The unknowability of the Creator and the limited nature of knowledge about the initial creation gives man the freedom to elaborate on the past and present directions of society. Primarily the story focuses on the *whims of life* and its contradictions. The chameleon symbolizes eternal life, or rather the elaborate cosmic cycles in which Being evolves in slow continuous and creative movements. Like the chameleon, it often changes its colours (moods) choosing its own grounds and phases of expression. As symbolized in the chamelon's eyes, life moves in continuous circular movements. It can indulge itself in decay (fertility) as symbolized by the flies, or in the cosmic fruitfulness as symbolized by the berries. The attitude of the Zulus (or the African people in general), their disliking for excessive speed in speech and action, is roundly summarized in the hideous salamander as the symbol of death. Zulus believe that a degree of elaborate and skilful circumlocution indicates a person's good breeding and sophistication. If someone speaks too quickly people often remark: 'This man (or woman) shall be the death of us all.' However, if someone is so slow and uninteresting as to make people impatient, he is also condemned. The emphasis is thus placed on deliberate elocution combined with highly skilled verbal artistry.

The Zulu creation myth, while operating on a simple level, seeks to explain the fundamental laws within the cosmic order. In giving these explanations, two points become obvious: the existence of the short, internal cycle of man, and the elaborate, cosmic creative cycle of life. The agent(s) used in the explanation are not gods or some elevated being, but the salamander-man and the chameleon-man. This indicates the importance of the relationship between man and the animal world. Man learns about the cosmic principles from the animal world.

Efik

The second myth of creation is from the Efik of Nigeria. The supreme god, Abassi, always feared that man would compete with him. He made a pact with his wife, Atai, to see to it that man did not develop such ambitions. At first, the human family ate together with the god's family, and they were all very close to each other. The wife of man, however, decided to till the land and raise crops for her family. Gradually, man found that the food provided by his wife was better, so he began to absent himself from the meals with Abassi and his family. Man's wife also became pregnant and bore him a son and a daughter. In anger, the god scolded Atai, his wife, for failing to keep man in check. Atai, however, assured Abassi that his power would be restored by man's death. She promptly sent death to remove the first man and his wife, causing chaos in the human family.

There are several aspects of this story which have social and philosophical implications. The Efik story, like the Zulu story, does not attempt to explain the sequence of events in the course of creation. It primarily aims at explaining the place of man in the universe and his relationship with the supernatural powers. The Efik story asserts that man's freedom is sacred. To preserve it, man must be prepared to challenge even the gods. Man is not a frightened, subservient being. Through the creative initiative of his wife, he is able to focus on his earth and thus earn his freedom. He obtains better food (life) than the food he ever enjoyed with the gods. At first, the human family is of only secondary importance; the gods take all the initiatives. However its importance gradually grows, until it becomes so powerful that the only way the gods can break its power is through 'murder'. This is scarcely a moral way to assert one's superiority. In fact, even in death, man has demonstrated his superiority and full capacity for fulfilment within his own world. Even his intelligence is shown as originating from experience rather than from the routine power of a god. Both the wife of the god and that of man play important roles in influencing the course of events. They are both calm, creative and wise. The male principle embodied in the man displays power, dogmatism and conservatism. The first phase of Being is without the active operation of the male–female principle. It represents balance rather than the principle of creativity. It is only after the break up of man–god dependence that the active principle of male–female creativity emerges. The son and daughter (male–female principles) of the first man become a family. They are vulnerable, but active and capable of organizing a social unit on their own initiative. The disorder caused by the parents' death will surely be overcome. It may be mentioned that in this story, Abassi is more of a leader over a family of gods than the Creator in the Zulu story.

The Efik story does not deal with theological issues, but rather debates man's role and freedom. The fact that mythological stories change from region to region and from generation to generation attests to their non-sacredness. This must be emphasized since writers like Mircea Eliade have asserted erroneously that: 'We are at last beginning to know and understand the value of the myth, as it has been elaborated in "primitive" and archaic societies – that is, among those groups of mankind where the myth happens to be the very foundation of social life and culture. Now, one fact strikes us immediately in such societies. The myth is thought to express the *absolute truth*, because it narrates a *sacred history*; that is, a transhuman revelation which took place at the dawn of the Great Time, in the holy time of the beginnings *(illo tempore)'.* (*Myths, Dreams and Mysteries*, translated by Philip Maret, London, Collins-Fontana Books, 1968, p. 23.)

The Origin of Man

The idea of the origin of life does not necessarily have the same significance as that concerning the origin of man. In dealing with the origin of man, the myths try to restrict their meaning to realistic speculations. The origin of man in many societies in Africa is associated with the emergence of a human species from water or from the earth. The actual creation of man is seldom detailed.

The forces that were set in motion by the first cosmic event are germs of different potentials which continue creating and re-creating their own species. The creation of species follows the male–female principle. The first event of creation was heralded by a massive explosion which came about as a result of the creative vibrations that set things in motion. These events continue to be reenacted on a smaller scale. The earthquakes, the violent storms, the falling stars, the volcanic eruptions are all replicas of the first fierce movement that released the multiple seed of Being. Man is part of this event, and to ensure that he had a place to live, he first lived in water or in the underworld. By an act of creation and with the help of the Creator and self-will he set out to inhabit the earth. In the Zulu story, man split open a reed, setting out as an ant-like race of man. The reed symbolized the harmony (flute) that was brought about by man's emergence and participation in the affairs of the world. In other stories man is depicted as emerging from the centre of the earth. Man emerges as an adult not a child, often with his wife, but sometimes alone. The first parents soon begin to create a family. From the start, their responsibility was that of supervising all life on earth. The gods, who are agents of the Supreme Creator, have a symbiotic relationship with man. While man needs them to re-enforce his efforts in the exploration of his world, the gods also need him for their harmonious existence. Since creation is their only responsibility, they must be made to feel that they have fulfilled their primary tasks. The endorsement for their actions by man becomes part of their spiritual elevation. Hence the need for praise and endorsement from man. It is man alone as the master of the earth who can effectively circumscribe and define the scope of the actions of the supernatural forces.

Contrary to the common belief held by foreigners, man in Africa is not servile to the forces of nature. Rather, by recognizing their territory in its own terms, that is, as possessing mystical cosmic powers of growth, man is able to generate his own sense of mystery beyond the functionalism of the material dimension. He appeals to the gods only when he needs them and may choose to denounce them when they fail him. The gods are not his masters nor he their puppet. They share the responsibilities of life in his specific directions. Man's relationship with the gods thus demonstrates an independence that is both a responsibility and a statement of self-liberation. In the Fang creation story, man boasts of his hard-won freedom:

> Yeye, o, layeye
> Gods on high, man on earth
> Yeye, o layeye
> Gods are Gods
> Man is man
> Everyone in his house, everyone for himself!
>
> (Ulli Beier, *The Origin of Life and Death:*
> *African Creation Myths*, London, Heinemann, 1966, p. 19.)

African Literature in the Cosmic Context

Because of the oral and public nature of African literature, literature at its best must direct its statement to the cosmic and universal elements. It must aim at being meaningful for all times. Thus is the nature of Zulu heroic poetry. The Zulu poet of the King Dingane era says:

> O, my Lord, generations of man come and go
> But our works will remain
> To make man gaze and weep at the ruins.
>
> (Extract from King Dingane's heroic epic,
> translated by M. Kunene)

Classic African literature takes it as its primary strategy to broaden the base of its characters through mythification and symbolism. Whereas some literatures make the cosmic purpose their goal, African literature begins from the premise that the cosmic setting is the primary basis of all literature. In this sense men and women in society are seen not as individuals who must be inspired to aspire to a wider world but as individuals perpetually interlinked in a cosmic context and cosmic continuity. It is perhaps because of this approach that though many West, North and East African literatures could have confined themselves to a written literary tradition, they also chose to speak and dramatize their literature. Even the Egyptians, despite their early invention of writing preferred a literature that was public, oral and dramatized. It is clear, then, that literature in the African context describes man first and foremost, as a social hero. Not only is he at the centre of things as an individual, he is also a representative of a social order. This may account for the high authority accorded to the fundamental social principles that must guide society if it is to retain its communal (collective) structure. As an individual, man's heroism is viewed as anti-social, for any act carried out for self-glorification is a threat to the solidarity of society. If the hero must comment on his heroic acts, it must be within the context of an ordinary person, not as a superman, who has approximated the social ideal. The narration of an individual's heroic acts must lead to an awareness of the heroism of others, both past and present. Society affirms its approval through acclamation. Misunderstanding the intent of African literature and in particular heroic poetry, foreigners have described its style and content as 'vainglorious self-praise', 'eulogistic' or 'boastful'. What is not understood is that in the African social context, the individual is not so much praising himself as highlighting his *participation in* the social order or community. This is the highest ideal the individual can aspire to. It is in this context that the same literary framework can be used to denounce anti-social acts.

It is clear that in discussing the origin of life and of man in African literature, one is dealing with a serious body of knowledge. Its approach is that philosophy and ethics must use literature as their most efficient vehicle for propagating their social directions. This is not to claim that scientific concepts must be written in a literary form. Indeed African literary categories have tended to exclude any didactic material, preferring, instead, to express such concepts in subtly aesthetic form. The modern African writer, if he is to develop authentic African classics, must not only be steeped in the ancient stories but should also know intimately the principles expressed through them. Above all, he must divest himself of the attitude that there are better models elsewhere than in his own literary world.

The Ancestral World and the Nature of Fantasy

Man's belief in his creative powers leads him to concentrate on the methods and techniques of organizing the earth for his own needs. He sets out to find, without apology, complete fulfilment in his home of the earth. He does not postpone things for some future paradise. The paradise he will experience after death will be the greater for having been enriched by the fullness of his life on earth. If the contribution to society has been rich, he is rewarded first and foremost by his community, and secondly through a full life in paradise. The two cycles of life, namely, earthly existence and life after death are realized through their own separate realities. This means, for instance, that acts committed in earthly life are punished or rewarded directly by society while the fulfilment of life in paradise, in other words in the Ancestral or Spirit world is achieved through a different set of values and responsibilities. This division of life according to separate areas of responsibility means that African literature bears a high degree of realism. The elaborate fantasies about after-life as found in many European literatures are thought of as irrelevant or even childish by many African communities.

In the African paradise live the spirits of the ancestors. Since they are closer to the Supreme Creator than the living, their responsibility is to act as intermediaries who carry the pleas of the living to the Creator. The ancestors live by a different code. Through feasts and contemplative concentration their living progeny are able to translate to them their requests. The assumption is that the ancestors tend to forget. They want to forget the problems of the earth. It is also assumed that they feel they have bequeathed enough to their children to enable them to cope with the various challenges of the earth. Only in extreme circumstances is an appeal to them justified. Because their power is of a different direction and purpose to that of the living, they sometimes over-react, and for that reason the Zulus reverently call them 'The Foolish Ones'.

The land of the spirits is a place of peace and fulfilment. Conceptually, it is at the centre of the earth. This does not mean that the ancestral spirits are confined to the underworld. Their location merely symbolizes the sacred reunion with the earth which is the primary world of man. The ancestral spirits are free to travel to whatever region they desire, and they do often explore worlds once obscure to them while firmly anchored in their original earth-world.

Stories about after-life like those relating to the myth of the origin of life do not claim to be factual. Judging from the limited body of such stories, the African creative artist feels much more secure dealing with things of actual experience than things of pure fantasy, that is, things lacking the quality of reality. This is inherent in the culture and is consistent with the concept of the earth as the major base of all rational speculation. Visions of after-life which claim to come from a contact with the ancestral spirits fall under the category of disembodied fantasy. For that reason they are, according to African belief, suspect, and have little value as literary material. This does not mean that African literary and artistic approach is devoid of fantasy but that fantastical material must have a traceable concrete, social and historical set of events. Consequently, many of the stories that are centred on fantasy are confined to a legendary past. They include legendary tales that deal with some event(s) in the past. This factor has created immense problems for the African writer of novels in English or in French. As he extracts the material from his African world and creates out of it a story of fantasy in the European sense, he changes the approach of the original material. His work is understood and appreciated by the European reader as a disclosure of a different and exciting world. When he tries to achieve the same intensity within his own audience, he only partially succeeds. This is not because his works do not deal with interesting issues, but rather that the mould in which they are put is different. Their new goal is to persuade the audience that the things presented are true. Because of this new approach, a great number of the works by Anglo- and Franco-phone-African writers lose their impact in translations into African languages.

The African story is characterized by a fantasy-tale, or a dramatized report of actual events. Either way, the audience is informed on what to expect. The European story or novel begins from the assumption that it must tell a tale as though it had actually taken place. The characterization is detailed, the plot is elaborated, the scenery is described in vividly photographic terms. The intention is to engage the reader and carry him away into this world of fantasy until he feels events described did take place. In short, the European tale-form, the novel, aims at creating a separate but real world for the reader. The African tale-technique, on the other hand aims primarily at creating a fantasy story out of the events of the past. It is clear that while the European tale-form has concentrated on the novel as its classic tale-form, the African tale-form has elaborated on the legendary tale to create its prose classic. This seems a logical direction since Africa's civilization is largely land based and European culture has been dominated by a centralism that has put an emphasis on areas of population concentration.

No writer, in my view, has succeeded so far in reconciling these two styles. The masterpiece that describes the particularly African urban world has not yet been produced. No doubt there have been some interesting novels but many lack the cosmic scale conception which is so characteristic of the classic African story.

All literatures are based on the intensity of experience, and the high skill of projecting that particular experience. The African world, with its rich artistic traditions, awaits an exploration that is meaningful to its own world. This leads us to the important aspect of how cosmic speculation is affected by the social ideal.

It should by now be clear that the evolution of cosmic concepts depends in part on the overall logic and psychology of a particular people. This in turn depends on the way in which social organization responds to the socio-economic factors. The importance people place on the world beyond the region of the earth depends on how they define their social relations. Generally speaking, it seems that the more fragmented, individualistic, and land-alienated people are, the more they are inclined towards a fantasy that is outside the earth. Their paradise or heaven begins to move farther and farther away from the earth. Equally, the world above assumes a mythical importance far beyond the importance of the earth. The cosmic world becomes a region of possible expansion and spiritual settlement.

This perhaps explains the prevalent excitement about space exploration which simultaneously generates numerous space cults of astro-projection and space fiction. This is not to say that this is the only driving motivation. Nevertheless, it describes a direction of speculation characteristic of the Western culture.

Past civilizations have greatly emphasized the earth as the centre not only of life but of fantasy. The African gods do not live in the sky (though they may at times manifest themselves through the sky world), but on the mountains. They may descend, at times, to occupy earth phenomena like the forests, the ocean, the river, and the wind. Their dwelling place, however, is either the mountains or artificially created mountains or their representations. Among the African people, the earth is seen as a friendly world. Into this world, man creates a womb-like entrance in which his body must be placed and preserved, and the episodes of his life on earth symbolically recounted through tools and artefacts. This is illustrated in the pyramids whose form resembles the mountains of the gods and in which the sacred symbols of continuity and national ethos are enshrined. The mountain-burials of kings, such as those of Swaziland, serve this same purpose. The eastern posture and womb-like position that the dead body is made to assume symbolize a second birth, that is, birth into the spirit world. A well-constructed subterranean grave or cave is also rounded to emphasize the relationship with the earth. Needless to say, in the African continent there are numerous religious ceremonies indicating a variety of cosmic approaches. These arise either out of acculturation or in response to the challenges of the physical and social environment. I believe, for instance, that when King Akhenaton of Egypt advocated a monotheistic system, with himself as the only son of the Great Sun-God, Ra, he was expressing a growing departure among the aristocracy from the powerful African communal ethic into the individualistic, rigid, feudal structure. King Akhenaton was not expressing a belief in one God (which in any case was held by many African peoples) but rather a belief in himself as *the sole depository of power both secular and supernatural.*

Since the meanings of words have different significance in different cultural contexts new concepts defining new cosmic approaches require a specialized vocabulary. The idea that God created man in his own image differs for an African who interprets this to mean that the reference is not to the physical features but to the creative force of Being. The concept of a heaven that is above in the sky fundamentally differs from the concept of a 'heaven' in the earth. Yet to a Zulu heaven simply means the world above (*izulu*), the sky (*isibhakhaka*) means the expanse of the universe, the earth or earths (*umhlaba* or *imhlaba*) mean our earth and, or all other related worlds known or unknown. It is necessary to reconcile these meanings with the concepts of the universe found in various communities and languages. This, however, is complicated by the fact that African cosmic systems tend to integrate scientific speculation with social function. The result is that scientific and mythic directions are often found integrated with each other. The discovery of Sirius by the Bambara was, for instance, made in the course of trying to find the centre of the universe.

Simultaneously with the new interest in space exploration, a new type of Western literature has developed. It is a literature that depicts the inhabitants of these new worlds as hideous-looking, hostile and super-powerful, reminding one of the old concept of a threatening God and a fierce devil. Indeed the space characters are often portrayed as black and scaly like the old devil. A comparison between the African idea of the inhabitants of the outer worlds and the Western concept makes interesting reading. The African space characters in the myths and legends are friendly and peaceful. Sometimes they are depicted as having shining and taller bodies than the earthly species but not supermen.

Without attempting to make final judgements about these two approaches one observes a consistency of attitude to outsiders in the space literature of the two societies. The modern African writer must thus educate himself about all the details of African cosmological beliefs, their meanings and their origins. More than any other factor it is clear that the African writer's success depends on his capacity to understand and interpret the subtleties of African thought systems. He must be steeped in the profound and rich traditions of African tale-forms. For in them is contained the epic-vision necessay for the creation of masterpieces. Only the grasp of the cosmic grandeur of the African thought systems and their meanings can produce the works of artistic excellence that would initiate a great modern African renaissance.

Reviews

Wole Soyinka, *Myth, Literature and the African World*, Cambridge, Cambridge University Press, 1976, 168pp.

K. Muhindi

If the existence of an 'African World' is rarely put to question since the publication of the masterly works of W. E. Abrahams, Kagame, Mbiti, Anton Diop, Tempels, Griaule ... few are those who attempt to express the African world-view without recourse to exogenous reference points.

Here Soyinka thinks the blame lies squarely on Africans who have tended to use, as a yardstick of academic excellence, 'the knowledge and exposition of the reference points of foreign cultures'. In this concise volume, however, he does not appear interested in bandying words with anyone although the polemical intent against 'Negritudinists' and neo-Marxist 'deniers' of African systems of self-apprehension is discernible between the lines. Rather he is motivated by the more positive desire to elicit the African world-view from indigenous history, myths, mores and living works of the imagination.

The alert student of Africa's foremost English-language dramatist will recognize in that finality the transfer to the ground of theoretical analysis of a wager clearly inscribed in Soyinka's drama and poetry: to unveil and transmit in African terms, through adapted conventional media, his perception – which we know to be prodigious in depth and scope – of the replete reality of the African *Weltanschauung*.

In criticism, as in creative writing, Professor Soyinka's principal preoccupation is with drama, and the external structure of this volume bears out the fact. Opening with two cardinal essays on drama entitled respectively 'Morality and aesthetics in the ritual archetype' and 'Drama and the African world-view', it closes with a re-edition of 'The fourth stage'. Between these are sandwiched two essays mainly on the novel but essentially concerned with defining what the author describes as 'the literature of a secular social vision'.

An appraisal of Soyinka's critical methods, however, curiously shows him to be at once more at home and original in examining the novel form than in his study of drama. In the latter, as many critics have duly remarked, his vision suffers from an obnubilation by Nietzsche's *Birth of the Tragedy*. Besides, the wealth of esoteric allusions he uses situates his essays on drama well beyond the purview of the average reader. This is particularly true of the overly compact prose of 'The fourth stage' which has the ring of the tortuous efforts of a self-conscious student writing with a nagging professor breathing down his neck.

When he addresses himself to the novel, however, Soyinka excels. For even as he reflects on that body of contemporary African literature that elects as its main goal to prevent 'the entrenchment of the habitual and the petrification of the imaginative function', he exposes the principal tenets of a critical approach that is both fructuous and fresh.

Criticism for Soyinka is not a backward-looking exercise of dismantling the artistic edifice (e.g. the novel) to highlight the process and prowess of the masonry that has gone into its erection. It is still less an occasion to marvel at the fineness of the constituent materials or to detail their origin. Rather, it is a creative response to a whole. In the respect that the work of art is the way it is and not otherwise by virtue of its being the result of a momentary encounter of a specific subjectivity with the life-process, criticism can only be creative and original if it deploys the critic's individual experience compounded of his own apprehension of the life-process and particular temperament in assessing the impact of a work of art. Evidently, this impact cannot be inferred from a consideration, born of 'man's chronic habit of compartmentalization', of its parts taken singly or in any order other than that in which the artist bequeathed the totality to posterity. And the reason for this is that the parts derive from their new environment a dynamism of signification imperceptible, indeed non-existent, in the parts taken in isolation.

Thus eschewing distraction by the incidental, Soyinka effects a rehabilitation and *rapprochement*, within the cohort of authors with 'a secular social vision', of Sembene Ousmane (*God's Bits of*

Wood) and Camara Laye (The Radiance of a King), hitherto wrongly relegated to the antipodal ghettoes of narrow Marxist propaganda for the former, and of retrogressive fascination with the traditional for the latter. Also elevated to this literary peerage, but more predictably, are Ayi Kwei Armah and Yambo Ouologuem (whose name is mis-spelt 'Oulouguem', consistently).

A unique message distinguishes and links the works of these authors: while striving to be inventive, man must never forget that attachment to innovations ultimately enervates the creative urge and weakens the will constantly to transcend one's realizations.

Paradoxically, as readers of Armah and Ouologuem – and of Soyinka! – will testify, this literature of continual social regeneration is markedly negative in formulation. But this, Soyinka points out, is necessarily so because it embodies the pyrogenic promethean spirit of refusal and challenge, of the constant quest for ever-newer avenues of individual and collective self-accomplishment. And that potentially destructive fire, like the terrifying disaster that is the essential subject-matter of all enduring tragedies, is one that serves 'to decongeal man's imagination'. If these authors appear invariably iconoclastic, therefore, it is only because 'in literature the writer aids the process of desuetude by acting as the termite and by ignoring the old deity . . .' to foster the creation of new ones.

In contrast to this literature endowed with a 'regenerative social goal', Soyinka examines another set against a back-drop of religious ideology. Such is, for instance, the Christian-inspired literature which disregards Christ as a potent agent of social revitalization and instead propagates a demobilizing 'turn-the-other-cheek morality' and of which W. Conton's The African is shown to be an apt paradigm. Such also is the life-negating doctrine of C. H. Kane in The Ambiguous Adventure, a novel largely informed by 'the necrophilic propensity' of his breed of Islam, or the dangerously 'simplistic' and 'reformist' Christian humanism of L. Nkosi's Rhythms of Violence whose 'gratuitous mea culpism enervates the revolutionary will'.

Besides revealing another dimension to Soyinka the dramatist, the poet and the novelist, this major milestone in African literary criticism should above all give an invaluable insight into his own creative method and purpose – through what he says of others.

Poems of Black Africa, edited and with an introduction by Wole Soyinka, New York, Hill & Wang, 1975; London, Heinemann, 1975, 384pp.

Robert Elliot Fox

Wole Soyinka, this anthology's architect, is described by his publishers as 'the most formidable literary force to have emerged in Africa'. To the uninitiated, conscious of post- and neo-colonial Africa only as a vortex of contending political forces and unfamiliar with its creative artists, this assertion may not have much significance; to those with some grasp of the substantial range and vitality of African literature, it is a statement to be taken seriously. Soyinka (if it is not presumptuous to apply a western analogy) is the contemporary African equivalent of a Renaissance man of letters. A poet, playwright and novelist of consummate skill, he has also recounted his experiences as a political prisoner in Nigeria in *The Man Died*, a powerful specimen of autobiography as spiritual indictment and affirmation.

Soyinka claims a fundamental difference of approach from previous anthologies. The nature of this difference becomes clear if we compare *Poems of Black Africa* with an earlier collection of merit, *Modern Poetry From Africa*, edited by Gerald Moore and Ulli Beier (Harmondsworth, Penguin, 1963; rev. edn, 1968). Moore and Beier, according to the usual practice, constructed their book along geographical lines, with sixteen countries represented. This was useful in giving the reader an impression of the relative distribution of poets throughout Africa, but, apart from the fact that anthologies by their very nature are selective rather than inclusive, the impression was a false one: first, because poetry composed in African languages was left out (an omission the editors acknowledged as a regretful necessity); secondly, because the emergence of many new writers, in even the brief five-year period between the book's initial appearance and its second edition, went a long way toward challenging the pre-eminence of a handful of nations in the African literary arena. Moreover, despite an understandable nod to nationalism, the Moore/Beier anthology tended to emphasize uniqueness; the individual voice was paramount. 'In general,' wrote the editors, these poets 'do not seem at all intent upon expressing the collective African soul.'

Soyinka, contrastingly, does not arrange his anthology geographically; instead, it is structured according to theme: 'Ancestors

and Gods', 'Animistic Phases', 'Exile', 'Captivity', and fifteen other
categories. He includes translations of some traditional poetry from
African languages, poetry that has been an influence even on those
poets writing exclusively in English, French or Portuguese:

> Rattler of spears!
> He who is unable to lie down, one side being red with wounds,
> He whose wounds are as numerous as the huts of a large kraal.
> Hornbill that is reluctant to set out,
> Long-tailed leaper like a leopard,
> Redbuck that escapes again and again...
>
> (from the Zulu)

> ...son of Ogun,
> The blacksmith who, as he speaks, lightly strikes his hammer
>   upon his anvil repeatedly.
> Son of He who smashes up an iron implement and forges it
>   afresh into a new form.
> Son of He who dances, as if to the emele drum music, while
> holding the hollow bamboo poles used for blowing air upon the
> coal embers fire in his smithy. He who swells out like a toad
> as he operates the smithy's bellows...
>
> (from the Yoruba)

What emerges is a broader and more balanced view of the spectrum
of African poetry, a view which retains the integrity of the authors'
own uniqueness of vision, while at the same time conveying proof
of a shared sensibility amounting, as Soyinka so aptly puts it, to 'the
experience of Black Africa in the idiom of the poem'. Experience
here is not isolated or idiosyncratic; it is, rather, part of an African
continuum.

The question of one's primal experience is a crucial one, for, as G.
Adali-Mortty (a Ghanaian) declares in the very first poem in this
anthology:

> You may excel
> in knowledge of their tongue,
> and universal ties may bind you close to them;
> but what they say, and how they feel —
> the subtler details of their meaning...
> these are closed to you and me for evermore...
>
> ('Belonging')

The language is, of course, familiar, but the words define a vast
experiential gulf; the perspective remains alien despite a shared
medium. Yet there is an implicit understanding, part of the colonial legacy, which Africans possess regarding Europeans. As is the
case with Afro-Americans and their former masters, this under-

standing, so vital for survival, is unfortunately one-sided. Mazisi Kunene, for example (a South African), addresses himself to the western world with the painful awareness of one who, longing to be embraced, has suffered a brutal violation. 'Once,' he says, 'I believed you had breasts/Over-flowing with milk,' but now, 'I know the hardness of your visions:/You closed the doors/And chose the bridegroom of steel' ('Europe').

Africa's bride, on the other hand, is the earth, and how far from hard are her visions:

> Listen more to things
> Than to words that are said.
> The water's voice sings
> And the flame cries
> And the wind that brings
> The woods to sighs
> Is the breathing of the dead.
> Who have not gone away
> Who are not under the ground
> Who have never died.
>
> (Birago Diop, 'Breath')

The continuous, rather than the linear; spirit as opposed to matter; multiplicity instead of singularity – these are some of the differences in values between the African world-view and that of the West. And while the western construct is metaphorically depictable by reference to Eliot's *Waste Land* and Yeats's 'rough beast' born from disharmony, the African sensibility, though jarred a little from its encounter with an alien epistemology, remains basically unaltered.

Such is Soyinka's awareness. However tall the tree, however many its branches, it cannot live without constant nourishment from its roots. Other anthologies of African poetry have tended to enumerate the branches, which, it is true, are manifold and beautiful. Going further, Soyinka's perceptive design joins root and branch, evoking the whole from an inevitably partial sum of its parts. This is why this anthology is likely to be a standard text for some time to come. Reading it is an experience – a collective ritual – the meaning of which can best be summed up in these lines from one of Soyinka's own poems:

> The quest
> Is all, endless
> Then home-coming
>
> ('Animistic spells')

To which the Ethiopian playwright Tsegaye Gabre-Medhin has
something to add:

> But watch, watch where you walk forgotten stranger
> This is the very depth of your roots: Black . . .
>
> Watch, listen to the calls of the ancestral spirits prodigal son
> To the call of the long awaited soil
> They welcome you home, home . . .
>
> Walk in laughter, walk in rhythm, walk tall
> Walk free, walk naked.
> Let the roots of your motherland caress your body
> Let the naked skin absorb the home-sun and shine ebony.
>
> ('Home-coming son')

These words cut to the heart – warm, vibrant – of the mythopoeic
nature of the African psyche; they are words which, similarly, cast
an illuminating gleam on the cold, barren centre of the (western)
mythotechnic realm.

Steve Chimombo, *The Rainmaker*, Malawian Writers Series 4,
Limbe, Malawi, Popular Publications, undated, 51pp.

Alex C. Johnson

The African writer who takes his subject-matter from oral tradition
and history well known to his audience has to find ways of securing
that audience's attention and making that subject dramatically
arresting. Whatever his intentions, his position is not unlike that of
the Greek dramatists; technique therefore becomes very important
and central to the whole conception.

In his first play, Steve Chimombo has not made any radical
innovation in technique but, significantly, the most successful
feature of the play is the Matsano who perform a choric role like the
chorus in Greek drama. Much like Ola Rotimi, a liberal infusion of
African (Malawian) traditional elements have been used to capti-
vate the audience, add to the dramatic potential and portray an
aspect of Malawian society.

There are three acts in the play and the title of each locates the
place and stage of the action. In Act 1, 'Msinja', drought has struck
the tribe and Kamundi, the python priest, cannot make rain even
though he deploys all his resources. Conflict inevitably ensues
when M'bona, outside the establishment and claiming superior

powers, produces rain, thus challenging Kamundi's power and credibility and building up prestige and following for himself thereby provoking a schism in the cult.

In Act 2, 'The Flight', M'bona's escape from captivity using supernatural powers leads to a long fruitless chase over vast spaces until he voluntarily submits to death thus facilitating the establishment of his new cult at Msange. In Act 3, significantly entitled 'Msange', the final supersession of the old cult is enacted as the python priest lies mad and possessed by the spirit of M'bona and there is societal upheaval and natural disaster because of the denial of the new cult. The play ends with the final rites for M'bona's restless spirit, and a propitiatory ritual with a symbolic dance and mime dramatizing the reconciliation of man, nature and the spirits which is achieved following the ascendancy of the new cult.

Chimombo has worked various themes into the play, but the basic theme is that of growth, change and development and the resistance put up by established conservative but expended forces. However, the treatment is too particular and this basic theme becomes limited in significance though relevant to an evolving and developing African society. The play's significance could have been enhanced if Chimombo had been less a prisoner of his history and oral tradition.

Characterization, too, is limited to the revealing of motives; there is no subtle exploration of character, no developed characterization and only minor significant changes in character. The *dramatis personae* are presented in outline and they only function in the action or reveal aspects of the theme. The two most important *personae* are the characters in conflict – Kamundi, the custodian of the old cult, and M'bona.

It is what they do and stand for which constitutes the central interest in the play. Kamundi is the inflexible conservative who abdicates his responsibility for selfish considerations, clings to his position at all costs and fails to see that M'bona's threatened supersession of him is part of the natural order of things. M'bona personifies the new developments in their society and, because of his powers, is the natural successor of Kamundi. When he submits to death during the chase, it is because he has reached his fulfilment and is ready to initiate his new cult. This is the most significant development of character in the play and it is necessary because of M'bona's thematic role.

As drama, the action in the play could have been enhanced a

great deal if the overt interaction of characters had been reflected much more in the language. Though there is some variation in tempo, the high points in the action are not arresting enough. This is largely because much of the prose remains rather weak and undifferentiated and is not heightened or varied significantly to match the action. An example is the confrontation between M'bona and his pursuers, Chingale and Chinkanga, during the chase when M'bona stops running. This should have been a high point in the play, but the confrontation is not adequately conveyed through the language as the prose rhythm does not enact this central conflict. There is no clear indication that two mortal enemies or irreconcilable forces are in conflict.

More successful dramatic features include the use of an assembly and the common people as part of the setting, giving the play a communal atmosphere and deepening the group feeling and involvement. Song, dance and mime are used and these add a ritualistic element to the play and root it more firmly in the African environment, especially as they are in the vernacular. The chants and ritual incantation will make the play come alive on stage and, where symbolic, add significantly to the theme.

The Matsano – the most important dramatic device – are described as 'attendants to Makewana and spirits of the forefathers'. In their choruses at various points in the play, they link the various parts of the action, give it coherence and continuity, take part in it, comment on it and give the reader an essential overview of the action. Their important thematic and dramatic role in the action make their contribution central to the play.

Apart from this, their verse is a welcome contrast to much of the prose of the other characters. The poetry is expressive and evocative, makes use of rhythm and other poetic devices and the Africanisms add to the traditional texture of the play. The variation in feeling and tempo in their chants matches the action much more than anything in the dialogue of the play.

An irritant which becomes a weakness when the play is read by a wider audience is the predominance of vernacular words and expressions which require continuous use of the glossary. However, this may not necessarily be so to the more restricted national audience at which the series is aimed. These would add to the rhythm, sound and other effects and would undoubtedly go down well on stage with the local audience, but they are an unnecessary hindrance to the non-native reader. This aside, the play is a successful first attempt not only in the national context, in which it is a significant addition to the series, but in the wider African literary context as well.

Okot p'Bitek, *Hare and Hornbill*, African Writers Series, London, Heinemann, 1978, 80pp.

Kadiatu Sesay

Many of the tales in this collection will be familiar to readers outside East Africa and thus raise the question of common sources for tales which, with various local adaptations, are found in different communities in Africa. Most of the stories about Hare – for example, 'Hare and Hornbill' (pp. 1–2) 'Hare and Crocodile' (pp. 18–19), 'Hare and his wife' (pp. 32–5) are found in Sierra Leonean folktales with little variation, except that in Sierra Leone, instead of the cunning Hare, the cunning Mr Spider appears with all the stock characteristics of Hare in Okot p'Bitek's collection.

One of the most common themes which Okot is preoccupied with in this collection is the theme of love within or outside marriage, a theme dealt with in stories of various kinds; sometimes about human beings – 'The strict man and his wife' (p. 78) and 'A man, his friend and his brother' (p. 75) – sometimes about animals – 'Chameleon and Elephant' (p. 5) and 'Awili and her suitors' (p. 11). The importance of marriage, particularly its social and economic significance for a young man within the society, comes out in the expensive and protracted arrangements and tasks suitors have to undertake in wooing. Okot devotes two stories to the difficulties of wooing and some of the implications: 'Chameleon and Elephant' and 'Awili and her suitors'. Incredibly difficult tasks are set for the suitors, which they are only too willing to perform. In 'Awili and her suitors' (p. 11) the obstinate and fastidious girl rejects many suitors and ends up marrying a monster, thus ensuring her own misery, and eventual repentance. (This is the same basic story as Amos Tutola's 'complete gentleman' in *The Palm-wine Drinkard* and in Ama Ata Aidoo's *Anowa*, to name just two variations of the same tale.)

On the whole, marriage seems to be shown to be a man's great wish but the overall picture of the institution is ambivalent and paradoxical. Men perform difficult tasks to win their wives only to be deceived by them after marriage. But at the same time, as in real life, there are some faithful wives – Chameleon's wife in 'Chameleon and Elephant' (p. 5) as well as a few irresponsible and unfaithful husbands – Hare in 'Hare and his mother-in-law' (p. 79).

Stories about various other aspects of family relationship show the author's unstereotyped view. In 'Okeny and his sister' (pp. 65–6), a nagging sister's rage drives her wicked brother from the village because he ate her grasshoppers. In 'Labongo and Kipir' (p. 71), Kipir forces his twin brother, Labongo, to make a hazardous journey in search of Kipir's spear which an elephant has run off with. Labongo, in turn, forces Kipir to kill his baby in order to recover his bead which the baby has swallowed. These are negative relationships in which the love of one man for his brother is absent. But in 'A man, his friend and his brother' (p. 75), the man discovers that his brother is 'not only my brother but also my best friend' (p. 77).

Friendship and co-operation or their absence constitute another common theme which is treated most obviously in the well-known plot about two friends, each willing to sacrifice himself for the other, its negative aspect being shown in the treachery and jealousy of friends in 'Hare and Hornbill', 'The Old Lion and Hare' and 'Hare and Cock'. Related to this is the theme of revenge, introduced in a simple parallelism where a set of ill-deeds is first perpetrated by one character, then equally revenged by the other. Such stories commonly end with the triumph of the one first injured and an implicit or explicit moral. However for Okot, injury does not in all cases necessarily lead to the punishment of the culprit. In many stories about Hare, the cunning rascal comes out scatheless and free. Thus no one moral or point of view is being put forward. Even the very popular and common themes such as marriage and family relationship are not treated from just one point of view; many different insights and comments are brought in at various times.

Most of the stories in the collection are about animals and the most common character is Hare. He is mostly portrayed as gluttonous, selfish, irresponsible and always trying to outwit others. He is frequently a cunning trickster who gets the better of bigger animals like Elephant, Crocodile and Lion, but, who on other occasions is in turn outwitted by small birds and insects like Bat, Cock and Mosquito.

Hyena is presented as deceitful and gluttonous, whilst Leopard is more honest and reliable. Hippopotamus, Buffalo and Elephant represent sheer physical strength and size in contrast to Chameleon who, seemingly frail, shy and slow, is clever and full of perseverance and thus always outwitting bigger animals. The effectiveness of many of these animal stories depends very much on the known characteristics of the animals concerned. Thus the shyness, slowness and apparent caution of Chameleon together with its size make its triumph over Hippo, Buffalo and Elephant all the more striking and funny. The ugliness of the skin of Hyena is the amusing focus in 'Guinea Fowl, Leopard and Hyena' (p. 3).

A number of the animal stories end with a moral or with an explanation of the origin of some characteristic or habit of an animal or its present habitat, while in others, the abstraction being made seems to be not of the animal but of a certain human situation with implicit meaning for human society. But the moralizing at the end of some of these stories does not by any means reduce their entertainment value.

Sometimes there is little individual characterization, the hero being often just described as a man, or some stock image being presented rather than a distinct individual personality. The reason why there is often so little characterization is that folk tales are normally meant to be seen and heard as a performance rather than composed to be read from a written page. The effect given by the actual performance of a story may be different from that given to a reader; for in a performance, characterization is often dramatized. This applies particularly in the case of animals whose way of speaking is portrayed in the tone and expression of the story-teller and their action and mannerisms are imitated. The narrator's capacity to dress up the skeleton theme of his plot with additional details, vivid description, songs, his use of dramatic repetition and characterization – much of it in response to audience reaction – are important ingredients which often do not feature in the written version.

There are of course ways of heightening effect by exploiting and manipulating the potentialities of the language, sentence structure and various dramatic techniques. To achieve some of these effects, Okot often uses various kinds of repetition to bring out some point in the story more dramatically; sometimes a phrase is repeated again and again at various key points in the story. Duplication of single words and the use of parallel phrasing together with antithesis are also used to get the scene or present opposing fortunes or features of the individuals thus introduced; and for emphasis he also uses exaggeration.

In 'Hare and Hornbill' (pp. 1–2) Okot's descriptive detail, his careful choice of descriptive words and his use of antithesis purposefully emphasize the contrasting fortunes of Hare and Hornbill:

> Hornbill danced gracefully, touching the ground lightly and moving his wings up and down to the rhythm of the drums. His neck swayed this way and that way, and his eyes sparkled with love. Hare danced as best as he could but could not follow the rhythm of the dance and sang out of tune. Moreover his big ears looked funny. Beautiful girls fought to dance before Hornbill but none came anywhere near Hare and when he approached the girls they ran away from him. That night Hornbill slept with a very pretty girl,
> Hare slept cold ...

Okot also exploits his ability to exaggerate the ugly and make it stand out as he does so successfully in *Song of Lawino* and his other songs.

> The next night when Hornbill was asleep, resting beside his fourth lover, Hare tiptoed into the house and unhooked the cork. Three days accumulation of diarrhoea spurted out and flooded the entire house. The stench rose like smoke and the dancers fled from the arena and Hornbill woke up ...

In his story 'The Rich and the Poor man' (p. 30), Okot uses exaggeration, parallel phrasing and antithesis for effect.

> Once there was a very rich man in the land. He had plenty of cattle and goats and sheep and he had many wives, and numerous children. His grown-up daughters were married to other great men's sons who paid many heads of cattle for dowry so that his wealth was always increasing ... This man's homestead was huge with plenty of food and drinks and much merriment. In the evening ... you could hear the roar of laughter from the other side of the hill. Theirs was a very happy life.
> On the other side of the river there lived a solitary man who had no cattle or goats or sheep. He had no wife, no children and no friends; people laughed at him because he was unmarried and also because his small hut leaked, and was without a proper door ...

Kole Omotoso, *The Combat*, London, Heinemann, 1972, 88 pp.
Eddie Iroh, *Forty-eight Guns for the General*, London, Heinemann, 1976, 218 pp.
José Luandino Vieira, *The Real Life of Domingos Xavier*, London, Heinemann, 1978, 84 pp. (Translated by Michael Wolfers.)

Kadiatu Sesay
Eddie Iroh's *Forty-eight Guns for the General*, José Luandino Vieira's *The Real Life of Domingos Xavier* and Kole Omotoso's *The Combat* present, in different ways, the devastating effects of war.

Eddie Iroh and Kole Omotoso write about the Nigerian Civil War; while José Luandino Vieira writes about the premonitions of the Angolan War.

In writing about the Nigerian Civil War in *The Combat*, Kole Omotoso explores his theme through the use of allegory. Chuku Debe and Ojo Dada, who refer to each other as 'brother and friend', are to have a combat because Chuku has run over a child with his car and refused to apologize (p. 15):

> 'You must apologize for it or else I am not going to live in the same house with you . . . Or else you must accept my challenge to a single combat'.

These two friends represent the two sides of the Nigerian Civil War – Biafra and Federal Nigeria. The child stands for the ideal unity and independence of the federation and the killing of the child symbolizes the September and October massacres of Igbos in the north which eventually led to the secession of Biafra and, to an extent, the killing of the unity within the federation. The combat itself stands for the Civil War.

Omotoso, among other things, satirizes the selfish attitudes of the foreign countries that supported either side of the war. Ojo's South African sponsors tell him: 'You know of course that, nothing is done for nothing' (p. 20), and ask to get the object of the conflict itself, the child and also Dee Madam, as a reward. Chuku's Russian friends see the combat as a target for an indirect confrontation between Russia and the West (p. 35):

> '. . . this is an occasion which will go down in the history of our two countries as the most important . . . coming-together of the forces committed to the revolution of the proletariat against the enemies of the people . . . the capitalist West headed by the fascist governments of the United States and the United Kingdom . . .'

And while the South African military attaché gives a dummy revolver with live cartridges to Ojo, the Russian military adviser gives Chuku a real pistol with dummy cartridges. Omotoso vividly dramatizes the unwarranted precipitation of a war which could have been prevented. As the preparation for the combat progresses, the child, the original object of the combat, is almost completely forgotten and in its place is a preoccupation with ambiguous principles and trivialities.

The uncontrollable nature of war is reflected in the sad feeling Ojo and Chuku have as the time for the combat draws nearer. They have both gone too far and can find no means of avoiding the consequences of their excesses, and the impending result is disaster.

Kole Omotoso, talking about his book, stressed that Nigeria's celebration of her tenth anniversary of independence at a time when the Civil War was going on in the country is the main point of the allegory. In the book, this is symbolized by the celebration of the dead child's tenth birthday at a time when he is already dead. Omotoso seems to feel that an ideal has been permanently destroyed by the war. The child, the symbol of this ideal, has been killed. But there is hope – albeit a slender one – as the illusive Dee Madam believes that the body still has some life in it.

In his narrative, Omotoso, particularly at the beginning, delves into minute descriptive details about Isaac, the child, and psychologically penetrates the child's mind revealing his pathetic plight and his thought processes in general. By so doing, he focuses the reader's attention on the child as the main symbol in the allegory (p. 10):

> He used the cup to scoop up some sand and went back to the rear-guard of the car. He sat down and leaned against the rear-guard. From somewhere near his skin he produced a piece of rounded iron with a hole in the middle. Patiently, he began to scrub the piece of rounded iron with sand. He put sand in his palms running his palms up and down creating friction which began to clear some of the dirt off the iron. Isaac took a look at it and already there was some figure appearing on the piece of iron. It showed that it was a penny piece made of copper, going back to the period of the West African Currency Board. He did not know that this was no longer legal tender.

Such details engage the maker's sympathies and his sense of loss when the child dies.

The satire seems light-hearted at the beginning but eventually turns into the tragedy of two men whose lives get enmeshed in a war they can no longer control. The use of allegory is generally apt and, to a great extent, successful, although some parts of it do not seem to hang together neatly: Ojo gets friendly with the child, Isaac (his own child), without knowing he is the child Chuku and himself are contesting for. The child has run away from his grandparents but it is not clear who he is staying with. The question is how could Ojo be so friendly and kind to Isaac without knowing anything about his family background or is it that Ojo knew Isaac was his child?

Ojo's reaction after the killing of the child is no less ambiguous (pp. 14, 15):

'You have run over somebody, you must go back and apologize to him.'

'You must apologize for it or else I am not going to live in the same house with you.... Or else you must accept my challenge to single combat.'

Ojo does not examine the body to see if the child is dead or not but immediately starts running after Chuku. And who is Chuku to apologize to? Apparently the child is not living with a relation and Ojo does not seem to know much about his family background. In any case, how can a man be asked to merely apologize after killing a child? And why the combat? I think the problem here is that the author is at pains to give a direct cause for the combat. The killing of the child ties in well with the massacre of Easterners in northern Nigeria which finally led to the secession of Biafra and the Civil War, but the killing of the child does not seem to tally with Ojo's reactions and motivations for the combat. It would, perhaps, have made a lot more sense if Ojo knew the child was his.

Eddie Iroh's *Forty-eight Guns for the General* centres on the activities of the Biafran Army and its forty-eight white mercenaries during the Nigerian Civil War. Whereas many novels about the war concentrate on the devastating effects of the war on the lives of individuals – particularly civilians – Eddie Iroh presents the tragedy as seen through the eyes of the men who fought the war – the Biafran soldiers. In spite of the odds against them, the Biafran soldiers rose enthusiastically to defend their new nation, starving with one lump of meat, whilst the white mercenaries, away from the battlefield, were surrounded by 'refrigerators that were generally filled with food and liquor'. What stands out is the desperation and hopelessness of a nation that entrusts the security and defence of its nationals into the hands, not of its citizens, but of uncommitted foreign mercenaries who not only refuse to fight and get killed, but who, when they do fight, do so against the interest of the very nation that hires them.

Even though Iroh, like others, is writing about issues which touch him emotionally, he nevertheless deals with them objectively, not just by blaming and exposing the villainy of the white mercenaries but also by seriously examining the faults and weakness of the Biafrans, particularly the General. He satirizes the villainy of the white mercenaries by presenting Colonel Rudolf as the archetype of all the evil they stand for. Colonel Rudolf with, 'a face as dead as a wax work', has trappings which symbolize his detachment and independence from the campus of whichever war he is engaged in (p. 39):

> It did not matter what country it was; what uniforms and colours its army wore; what personal weapons its officers were issued with, or what codes and regulations were mandatory, Jacques Rudolf always carried and used his personalised red and green emblem, his automatic pistol, and, somewhat inappropriately for his chosen career, the Légionnaires' standard *Honneur et Fidélité*.

The colour of his uniform, 'green and olive camouflage with the pattern of the skin of a newly ecdysed cobra', symbolizes the slippery, deceptive and dangerous figure he is. He is a great tactician and a manipulator of others, exploiting their weaknesses and folly. We follow the intrigues of his active brain from the beginning, and see what the General and Michel failed to see quickly enough – the ruthless and cunning nature of the man.

Unlike the mercenaries, the rebel soldiers were 'fighting for our lives, for our parents, for our new nation' (p. 69). And Colonel Chumah symbolizes this patriotism. Chumah is fighting not merely for personal fame and honour but to save his people, his family. He epitomizes the dedicated soldier, and is a man of great passion who hates white diplomats and mercenaries. 'I'll defend this city with everything I have or die in the attempt' (p. 13). He has the ability to instil confidence and raise the morale of his troops. When he is released from prison, and discovers that his family has been mutilated, he gets a new urge to fight for his country – this time not merely to defend Biafra from Federal bombardment, but from the evil machinations of the mercenaries whose lethargy and indifference he blames for the death of his family.

Chumah is the only man with enough common sense to read through Rudolf's plans. We understand his wish to avenge the death of his family, and this wish is consistent with his hatred for white mercenaries. It is therefore surprising that in the end Chumah, who always makes the right decision and who is the only man who understands Rudolf's ruthlessness and evil character, should challenge Rudolf to shoot him by turning his back to him.

Iroh does not, however, just criticize the mercenaries but also uses irony to satirize the selfishness and gullibility of the General, together with his love of power. The General's character is presented in the description of State House (p. 24):

> The site of State House was selected by the political premier with a deep love for nature, an eye for scenic beauty and an intuitive concern for personal security. The elegant mansion lay some four miles north east

of the centre of the city, high on the top of the table of grassland facing the ranging arc of hills several miles across. From its South portico the General had in the peaceful past ritually enjoyed the scenic panorama of the sprawling city, at night a vast and twinkling field of little fallen stars. As he stood there, like a black Colossus, all else at his heels below, it had always given him a physical feeling of over-lordship, rekindled his spiritual flame.

In spite of his power, he is a pathetic and cowardly figure who locks himself behind steel doors. His naïve gullibility, bordering on stupidity, makes him swallow everything Rudolf tells him to the detriment of his own soldiers.

In portraying the devastating effect of war, Iroh starts Phase One of the book with a harvest image (p. 7):

> Mangoes, oranges, pawpaws and sour pears — loyal trees all — hung green and drooping with their seasonal burden. The rainy season was beginning reluctantly it seemed that year to give way to the dry.

This opening is a seemingly hopeful one with life-giving fruits, but suddenly the season is to change even before the fruits have ripened, for soon shelling begins and young men, 'green and drooping with their seasonal burden', are killed in an untimely and futile death.

Continuing the portrayal of the devastating effects of war, the author continues with the symbol of dawn which is normally a time of hope when men awake with aspirations for a peaceful and successful day; but here dawn looks like dusk, with none of the hustle and bustle of people: 'only gun smoke still drifted up to the low ceiling of cloud'. The only sign of life left in the city is the sound of a military land-rover which 'tore the deserted streets'.

The book is packed with captivating action. The prose is lucid and the author's extensive knowledge and use of military jargon, not being a soldier himself, is commendable.

Our third book, *The Real Life of Domingos Xavier*, is, unlike the other two, about the Angolan situation preceding the war. It is set in the Angola of 1960 in the midst of the underground politics of the liberation movements. The death of a political prisoner occurs, shortly before the liberation movement's attack in 1961 on the prison in Luanda which marked the beginning of a long armed struggle against the Portuguese colonialists.

So, unlike the preceding two books, which are specifically about war, this one presents the premonitions of the armed struggle in Angola. The author demonstrates the suffering of the Angolans in the life and death of the tractor driver, Domingos Xavier.

Premonitions of the armed struggle for freedom can be seen in the suffering of the Angolans: poor housing and sanitary conditions, low-paid jobs with awkward working hours and, worse still, indiscriminate arrests and detention of Angolans with progressive ideas who were interrogated, tortured and sometimes killed.

The people's determination to resist misery and suppression is brought out in symbolic terms. The author juxtaposes the suffering of Domingos Xavier with the apparent defiance and soothing influence of the forces of nature and the human environment in general. Crude attempts are made by the interrogators to break Domingos Xavier's spirit and make him talk. The cipaios are dehumanizing and, in the face of such inhumanity, Domingos visualizes his people, his environment and the future and it is this visual image that tempers his suffering and supplies him with that sustenance and courage that is necessary to stand the torture inflicted by the agents of the regime without flinching. To the Angolans, 'a brother of the people who carries himself as a man' is one who in the face of suffering refuses to tell the secrets of his people.

Before and after being interrogated and tortured, Domingos Xavier gets various visions of hope, with the moon, the sun and the general environment outside the prison giving him sustenance, inspiration and courage (p. 16):

> ... the moonlight spread its soft shawl over the body sprawled in the cell. The white light penetrated a small opening guarded by a steel mesh and the tractor driver, who could hardly lift his head, glimpsed the cloudless blue sky. It was the blue sky and the moon of his land that watched over him.

And before being taken to another session of interrogation he gets another vision of hope (pp. 16–17):

> The morning sun kissed his swollen face then showed him the great iron-clad door opening before him on this clear morning with the cipaios beating and chasing back the people, whose solidarity he felt through their silence and whom he saw before his sticky, swollen eyes. And in this way he went through the door; he did not feel the blows of the cipaios; he saw only women with their babies wrapped up in their cloths, the snivelling babies with frightened eyes – they came to people his memories.

The author, continuing his use of symbolism, uses the River Kuanza to symbolize the attitudes of the people and the situation in Angola at the time (p. 17):

... Maria going out with other women down the river, where the rapids began, to wash clothes, and the river, the broad Kuanza which had witnessed his birth, upon the plateau just a trickle of water, just a noisy child, but which he knew farther on running broad, calm and powerful towards the sea. But there, where Maria and the women of the people did their washing on the rocks, it was angry, maddened by the hills which closed it in, the granite bends which it had cut centuries ago, roaring with rage in the rapids, breaking up into spray, then tamed, running down to Muxima.

The people in Angola, superficially, seemed powerless in the face of suffering and suppression coupled with arrests and detention; but underneath, like the Kuanza which runs broad and powerful towards the sea, the seeming tameness and calm give way to a mysterious and powerful underground movement: 'maddened by the hills which closed it in roaring with rage in the rapids', and finally breaking into an armed struggle which eventually led to independence. It is this vision of hope symbolized by the waters of the Kuanza, and the 'snivelling babies wrapped up in their cloths', that sustained Domingos Xavier.

The prisoner, beaten and tortured by his own black brothers acting as agents of the colonial regime, was faced with the choice of either betraying his people and returning to his wife and son or being tortured to death. His commitment and determination to stay silent in spite of his suffering is signified by his not only tearing up the note he received in detention from his comrades urging him to stay silent, but by chewing and swallowing it with his breakfast.

The portrayal of the struggle and revolt is signalled in terms of the forces of nature, rain, thunder and lightning (p. 53):

... It was the signal. The rain in huge, fast drops began to fall in sheets and you could not see anything a yard away. All of a sudden the asphalt streets turned into torrential streams ... the waters began to turn red ...

The apparent calm of the people, like that of the clear blue sky before the storm, suddenly broke into a tumultuous battle for liberation. Domingos Xavier's death symbolizes the suffering of the people. His blood, like the red water of the rain (p. 67):

... ran from his mouth, from his nose and from his ears, it soaked the tattered shirt, his body and the floor and splashed the policeman, the walls, everything.

Like a sacrificial animal, he allowed his blood to flow for his people and it is not a futile sacrifice, as his death reawakens his people and creates the beginning of a new phase in the history of the Angolans – the struggle for independence. The preparation for the attack on the regime is symbolized by the dance 'as the expression of the people's vitality and enjoyment of life, which could not be suppressed even with the arrest of sons, brothers and friends' (p. 78).

The English version of this book, being a translation, raises the whole linguistic problem of translation and with it the delicate position of the critic who tries to review the translated version of a work of literature. The ability to achieve as good a translation as may be involves balancing all the components of the work at all levels and constructing a version as near in all respects to the original as is possible. This requires a delicate and sensitive appreciation of language.

The translator's preface for the English version states: 'the original text from which this English translation is made is a rich mixture of literary Portuguese, Brazilian and Angolan slang, and words in *Kimbudu*, one of Angola's principal African languages.' One of the questions the translator has addressed himself to is that of an audience. His aim is to make the book comprehensible to people for whom English is a second language, and his model is fairly standard spoken English. This raises the question of correctness and acceptability, for certain expressions could be perfectly acceptable to users of English in one community but be seen as deviations from standard English.

Some of the dialogue in the book contains expressions which, judged by general standards or by the translator's suggested 'fairly standard spoken English', are erroneous either syntactically or otherwise. For example: Maria, asking a young woman to show her the way to the Administrator's office says: 'To speak to the Administrator, can you tell me?' Surely this is not standard spoken English.

Authors normally set up contexts of situation – the relationships of utterances to the situations or environments in which they are said or could be said and the differences of personal status, social relations and other factors; but some of the dialogue sounds out of context and artificial in the mouth of the character speaking the lines. For instance, Chico goes to the village and sees his girlfriend, Bebiana, who he says is the one he now cares for. Bebiana, being jealous of his relationships with other girls in the village, does not believe him. But, holding hands lovingly, they both arrive at the grandfather's house where Chico, to prove his sincerity and seriousness, proposes to marry Bebiana. Bebiana's reply seems incredible and out of context (pp. 32–3):

> The girl snatched free the hand he was holding and feeling insulted said firmly:
> 'Good heavens! You think you can marry just as you please? Have you asked me? Have you spoken to me? Do you think I am one of those girls you pick up at a dance and then sleep with, is that it? Goodbye.'

The reader's expectations are disappointed, for we know Bebiana and Chico have known each other for some time, the parents know about their relationship and Bebiana loves Chico – hence her jealousy of Carlotta and other girls: but this response seems to be coming from a different Bebiana.

And the grandfather's reply is no less artificial:

> 'It's like this young Chico we reap what we sow, but to reap we have to treat well. You youngsters think a girl is trash, then look out!'

First of all we are not sure whether the second part of the second sentence is a continuation of the metaphor in the first part. If the second *reap* and the word *treat* refer to the same crop in the first part of the sentence, is not the word 'nurture' or 'nurse' more appropriate for the metaphor, e.g.

> We reap what we sow, but to reap a good crop we have to nurture/nurse the seed well

Or is the metaphor extended to the treatment of women in the second half of the sentence, e.g.

> We reap what we sow, but to reap her love, we have to treat a woman well?

Except for such odd examples of dialogue, the translation reads reasonably well, and in spite of the sometimes stilted conversation the book makes interesting reading.

Index